MAKING THE PEACE
IN IRELAND

Making the Peace in Ireland

JEREMY SMITH

An imprint of **Pearson Education**

London • New York • Toronto • Sydney • Tokyo • Singapore • Hong Kong • Cape Town
New Delhi • Madrid • Paris • Amsterdam • Munich • Milan • Stockholm

PEARSON EDUCATION LIMITED

Head Office:
Edinburgh Gate
Harlow CM20 2JE
Tel: +44 (0)1279 623623
Fax: +44 (0)1279 431059

London Office:
128 Long Acre
London WC2E 9AN
Tel: +44 (0)20 7447 2000
Fax: +44 (0)20 7240 5771
Websites: www.history-minds.com
            www.pearsoneduc.com

_____

First published in Great Britain in 2002

ISBN 0 582 43836 5

British Library Cataloguing in Publication Data
A CIP catalogue record for this book can be obtained from the British Library

Library of Congress Cataloging in Publication Data
A CIP catalog record for this book can be obtained from the Library of Congress

10 9 8 7 6 5 4 3 2 1

Typeset by Fakenham Photosetting Limited, Fakenham, Norfolk
Printed and bound in China

The Publishers' policy is to use paper manufactured from sustainable forests.

CONTENTS

PREFACE

The text is designed to bring to a general readership the story of how a political settlement was reached in Northern Ireland in 1998 – a readership who, like me, followed the unfolding events of the peace process during the 1990s with a mixture of hope, confusion and deep incredulity, alongside a more general desire to know more about where developments sprang from and how, in the end, 'peace' was made. In telling this story the account focuses upon those political actors and intermediaries who actually made the peace settlement, to the detriment of other more 'structural' developments that played a part in creating the conditions in which such a settlement might be signed, be they cultural, economic and social. This is not to deny the latter's importance but merely to prioritize the former's greater interest and excitement.

Anyone writing on Northern Irish issues faces a minefield of terminological disputes and differences. What we call something or someone is, after all, a means of saying what it is not, what it is hostile to and what it should be. Northern Ireland is a setting where words and phrases are signifiers of position and indicators of loyalty, and the attempt to offer a reasonably 'balanced' version of events well nigh impossible. So let me offer at the outset a blanket apology if I cause offence on the grounds of labelling and language. The fact that I refer to Northern Ireland and not the Six Counties is not intended as a slur on Nationalist/ Republican views but merely a reflection of existing political realities. Similarly, my reference to Londonderry is not to deny the legitimate and widespread use of Derry but simply to locate my language in current political realities whereby the city resides within the UK.

Several people have shown me great kindness and help in the production of this book. Several readers for Pearson made many excellent suggestions on earlier versions of this text. More especially, David Bloomfield and Peter Taylor cast their expert eyes over the manuscript, saving me from innumerable 'howlers', for which I thank them: those that remain are mine and mine alone. The Department of History at Chester College provided an ideal environment to complete the text, and in particular my Head of Department, Graeme White, has shown enormous understanding for the pressures of teaching and writing. I'd also like to use this opportunity to thank my school history teachers, Peter Mills, Ian Shaw and Peter Carr, who fired my interest in history in the first place. Heather McCallum has shown immeasurable forbearance and tolerance in the face of my endless excuses, delays and IT ineptitude, while Bree Ellis and others at Pearson have been extremely efficient and not a little patient. To Pud, for all her love and support which over the past year I have taken such merciless advantage of.

Finally, I dedicate this book to my son, Fred, who knows nothing of the type of hell that Northern Ireland is now, hopefully, emerging from, and I trust never will.

CHRONOLOGY

1798 Rebellion.

1801 Act of Union.

1829 Catholic emancipation.

1845 Start of the great Irish famine.

1848 Attempted rising by Young Irelanders.

1851 Formation of the IRB.

1879 Beginning of Irish land war.

1886 Gladstone introduces the first Home Rule Bill.

1891 Death of Charles Stewart Parnell.

1893 Gladstone introduces the second Home Rule Bill.

1912 Carson and Sir James Craig begin preparations for resisting Home Rule. April: Asquith introduces the third Home Rule Bill. Sept: Ulstermen and women sign the Solemn League and Covenant.

1913 UVF formed. Sept–Dec: attempts to find a compromise solution based upon some type of partition for Ireland.

1914 April: Larne gun-running episode. Aug: the political struggle over Home Rule suspended for the duration of the war.

1916 April: the Easter Rising in Dublin. July: the Somme Offensive sees thousands of UVF men killed.

1917 Irish Convention convenes but fails to make progress.

1918 General election sees 73 Sinn Fein MPs elected to Westminster. Having abstained, those who are not in prison or hiding establish the Dáil Eireann.

1919 Emergence of the Irish Republican Army (IRA). Beginning of the Anglo-Irish war.

1920 The Government of Ireland Act (Partition Act) creates two Home Rule Parliaments in Ireland by partitioning the 32 counties into a 6-county north and a 26-county south. For Unionists the creation of a Northern Ireland, though not their preferred option, at least saved them from a united Ireland. Sinn Fein enters the elections and sweeps the south but ignores the Home Rule Parliament and establishes a second Dáil instead. The Act also institutes a Council of Ireland which British leaders hope in time will form the basis of a united Ireland. Oct: formation of the Ulster Special Constabulary.

1921   May: elections to the northern Parliament return a Unionist majority. July: truce between the British and Sinn Fein. Oct–Dec: negotiations in London end in the signing of the Treaty whereby the 26 counties of the south become an Irish Free State within the British Empire. A Boundary Commission was to be established to reconsider the territorial divide between the north and south. Dec: Emergency Powers Act introduced by the Northern Ireland Cabinet.

1922   Start of the Irish civil war. Introduction of the Special Powers Act and the Methods of Voting and Redistribution of Seats Act for local elections.

1924   Boundary Commission finally meets under Mr Justice Feetham.

1925   Boundary Commission report results in no change to the line of partition. Powers of the Council of Ireland given to the northern and southern Parliaments respectively.

1929   Methods of Voting and Redistribution of Seats Act for Westminster elections.

1932   De Valera becomes Taoiseach at the head of a Fianna Fáil government.

1937   The Irish Constitution Act dismantles much of the Irish Free State and gives the Catholic Church a 'special' position within the state. Ireland becomes Eire.

1938   Britain returns the Treaty ports and signs a trade treaty with the Irish government.

1939   Eire declares its neutrality in the war.

1945   Anti-Partition League established.

1948   Former-IRA Chief of Staff Sean MacBride becomes Minister of External Affairs in Costello's coalition government. Ireland declares itself a republic and leaves the Commonwealth.

1949   The Ireland Act guarantees the constitutional position of Northern Ireland. Change can occur only with the consent of the Northern Ireland Parliament.

1951   A 25-year-old Ian Paisley founds the Free Presbyterian Church.

1955   Westminster election sees Republicans win two seats.

1956   IRA launches its Border Campaign, Operation Harvest.

1959   Sean Lemass replaces De Valera as Taoiseach.

1963   Terence O'Neill replaces Viscount Brookeborough as Prime Minister of Northern Ireland.

1964   Formation of the Campaign for Social Justice in Dungannon. Sept: Divis Street riots in Belfast. Harold Wilson becomes Prime Minister of GB.

1965   Formation of the Campaign for Democracy in Ulster. Sean Lemass visits Stormont.

1966   Fiftieth anniversary of the Easter Rising generates tension amongst Unionists and sees a rejuvenated UVF shoot dead two Catholics. Jack Lynch becomes Taoiseach.

1967   Formation of NICRA.

1968   Caledon sit-in led by Austin Currie. Oct: a civil rights march in Londonderry results in violence and bloodshed.

1969   Jan: violence breaks out on a civil rights march at Burntollet Bridge. April: O'Neill resigns and is replaced by Chichester-Clark. Aug: Battle of the Bogside results in the deployment of British troops onto the streets of Londonderry and Belfast. Oct: Hunt Report on police reforms provokes Unionist violence.

1970   Jan: IRA splits into Official and Provisional wings. June: new Tory government under Heath with Northern Ireland the remit of Maudling, the Home Secretary. July: Falls Road curfew. Aug: SDLP formed.

1971   Feb: first British soldier killed. March: Chichester-Clark resigns and is replaced by Brian Faulkner. Aug: internment introduced. Sept: formation of the UDA. Oct: Paisley launches the DUP.

1972   Jan: Bloody Sunday sees 13 men shot dead by paratroopers. Feb: sees the creation of Ulster Vanguard by William Craig. March: the Northern Ireland (Temporary Provisions) Act suspends Stormont and imposes direct rule from Westminster, imposed with William Whitelaw as the first Secretary of State. June: two-week IRA cease-fire during which Whitelaw meets an IRA delegation. July: Bloody Friday sees 11 killed by 22 IRA bombs in Belfast. Sept: Darlington conference. Oct: government green paper on *The Future of Northern Ireland*.

1973   March: border poll. White paper published on *Northern Ireland: Constitutional Proposals*. June: elections to the NI Assembly sees a large pro-White Paper majority elected (though this is composed of a slight minority of Unionists). Oct: inter-party talks result a month later in agreement on a power-sharing executive. Dec: Francis Pym replaces Whitelaw as Secretary of State for NI. Sunningdale conference opens; agreement to various All-Ireland institutions.

1974   Jan: Power-sharing executive takes office. Faulkner defeated in a UUC vote and resigns the leadership of the UU Party. Feb: general election sees 11 of 12 Westminster seats go to the anti-Sunningdale candidates, the UUUC. Wilson replaces Heath as Prime Minister and Merlin Rees becomes Secretary of State for NI. May: Ulster Workers Council strike to destroy the Sunningdale Agreement succeeds when Faulkner finally resigns as Chief Executive, so collapses the agreement and the power-sharing executive. July: Rees launches Constitutional Convention. Sept: Faulkner launches the UPNI.

1975   Feb: IRA cease-fire and period of truce begins. May: elections to the new Constitutional Convention with the UUUC winning a majority. Oct: the report of the convention advocates majority rule which Rees rejects. Nov: abolition of special category status and helps bring the truce to an end.

1976   March: convention wound up. Sept: Roy Mason replaces Rees as Secretary of State for NI. Beginnings of prison protest. James Callaghan replaces Wilson as Prime Minister.

1977   May: attempted loyalist strike collapses.

1979   March: Airey Neave killed. May: Thatcher replaces Callaghan as Prime Minister, with Humphrey Aitken made Secretary of State for NI. Aug: Mountbatten killed and Warrenpoint massacre. Nov: John Hume replaces Gerry Fitt as leader of the SDLP. Dec: Charles Haughey becomes Taoiseach.

1980   Jan: constitutional conference. March: Thatcher–Haughey talks lead to beginning of an Anglo-Irish Process. Oct: beginning of the first hunger strike which ends in Dec.

1981   March: a second hunger strike begins. April: Bobby Sands wins the Fermanagh–South Tyrone by-election. May: Sands dies (a further nine men will die); two hunger strikers elected to the Dáil. Aug: hunger striker Owen Carron wins the

Fermanagh-South Tyrone by-election. Sept: James Prior replaces Aitkens as Secretary of State for NI. Nov: Anglo-Irish Inter-Governmental Council created.

1982   April: Prior launches his 'rolling devolution' initiative. Oct: elections to new NI Assembly under the Prior plan but when it meets for the first time no Nationalists attend. Nov: Garret FitzGerald becomes Taoiseach.

1983   May: New Ireland Forum. June: general election sees Adams win West Belfast. Sept: Adams becomes President of Sinn Fein. Dec: Harrods bomb.

1984   May: New Ireland Forum publishes its report which is rejected by Unionists and the British government. Sept: Douglas Hurd replaces Prior as Secretary of State for NI. Oct: Brighton bombing.

1985   Sept: Tom King replaces Hurd as Secretary of State for NI. Nov: Anglo-Irish Agreement creates a permanent Inter-Governmental Conference but sparks huge Unionist resistance.

1986   March: Unionist day of action. May: the NI Assembly set up under Prior is dissolved. Nov: Sinn Fein votes to drop its stand of abstention from taking up seats in the Dáil. Ulster resistance is established to undermine the AIA.

1987   May: Loughgall operation. March: Haughey replaces FitzGerald as Taoiseach. Sept: Unionists begin talks with King. Nov: Eskund is seized by French authorities. Remembrance Day bombing in Enniskillen.

1988   Jan: first meeting of Hume–Adams (they will last until Sept). March: three IRA volunteers are shot in Gibraltar. At their funeral Michael Stone kills three people.

1989   July: Peter Brooke replaces King as Secretary of State for NI. Nov: Brooke declares the IRA will not be militarily defeated and that a British government would be flexible and imaginative in its response to a cessation of violence by Republicans.

1990   Jan: launch of the Brooke initiative. March: the McGimpsey judgement. Nov: Brooke declares Britain has 'no selfish strategic or economic interest in the union with NI'. John Major replaces Thatcher as Prime Minister.

1991   Jan: IRA mortar bombs Downing St. March: Brooke publishes his plans for multi-party talks which begin in April and finish in July.

1992   Jan: Brooke commits his faux pas on the evening of the Teebane bombing. Haughey resigns and is succeeded by Albert Reynolds. April: Baltic exchange bomb. Major wins the general election at which Adams loses his West Belfast seat. Sir Patrick Mayhew replaces Brooke as Secretary of State for NI and immediately begins multi-party talks (they will last until Nov). Dec: Mayhew's Coleraine speech.

1993   March: Warrington bomb. April: Hume–Adams talks begin (they issue a joint statement in June and reach an agreement in Sept before submitting their report to London and Dublin). Bishopsgate bomb. July: Ulster Unionists save Major's government on the Maastricht vote. Oct: Shankill bomb followed by the Greysteel massacre. Nov: news leaks of the secret contacts between government officials and Sinn Fein. Dec: Major and Reynolds deliver the Downing Street Declaration.

1994   Jan: Adams is granted a US visa. June: Loughinisland massacre. Aug: IRA announces a complete cessation of its campaign. Sept: Reynolds, Hume and Adams publicly shake hands in Dublin. Oct: the Combined Loyalist Military Command announces its cease-fire. Dec: first official contact between the government and Sinn Fein. John Bruton replaces Albert Reynolds as Taoiseach.

1995   Feb: *Frameworks for the Future* document issued by both London and Dublin. March: Mayhew issues his Washington Three criteria for Sinn Fein's entry into talks which calls for the need for some decommissioning to be seen to begin (Mayhew will meet Adams in May in Washington). Molyneaux is re-elected after a leadership contest but is weakened by the process. July: first of several Drumcree stand-offs. Aug: Molyneaux resigns as leader of the Ulster Unionist Party and is replaced by David Trimble. Nov: joint Anglo-Irish communiqué launches the twin-track approach to try to sort out the problem of decommissioning and multi-party talks. An international body under Senator George Mitchell is established to consider the issue. President Clinton visits Northern Ireland.

1996   Jan: Mitchell Commission Report recommends parallel talks and decommissioning which Major side-steps in favour of elections in the province to an NI Forum from which party delegations for the talks will be derived (London and Dublin agree talks to start in June). Feb: IRA cease-fire ends with the bombing of Canary Wharf. May: elections to the NI Forum. June: multi-party talks are opened under the chairmanship of Mitchell (Sinn Fein is not part of them given the collapse of the IRA cease-fire). July: Drumcree II prompts the temporary walk-out by the UUP and the DUP.

1997   Jan: DUP tries to have the UDP and the PUP removed from the talks. Recommendation by Independent Review of Parades and Marches that a parades commission be established (by March such a commission is already up and running). March: the talks adjourn with an election looming. May: general election sees Tony Blair replace John Major as Prime Minister, with Mo Mowlam the new Secretary of State for NI (Sinn Fein wins two seats at the GE). June: talks resume. In the Republic Bertie Ahern replaces John Bruton as Taoiseach. July: IRA announces a second cessation. Aug: the Independent Commission on Decommissioning is set up under John de Chastelain. Sept: Sinn Fein signs up to the Mitchell principles and enters the talks. The DUP leaves, yet the UUP stays. Dec: Billy Wright, leader of the LVF, is shot inside the Maze.

1998   Jan: Mowlam visits loyalist prisoners to calm their fears. UDP temporarily excluded from the talks. Feb: Sinn Fein temporarily excluded from the talks. March: Poyntzpass killing by the LVF of a Catholic and a Protestant. April: Good Friday Agreement signed at Stormont facilitating the creation of a new NI Assembly, a power-sharing executive and various All-Irish institutions as well as a British–Irish Council. Trimble gets the backing of the UUC. May: a referendum in the north wins a 71 per cent pro-agreement vote. A referendum in the south on amending clauses 2 and 3 wins 94 per cent approval. June: elections to the new NI Assembly. July: NI Assembly meets and appoints Trimble and Seamus Mallon as First Minister and Deputy First Minister designates. Aug: Omagh bomb kills 29 people as a result of which the Real IRA announces a cease-fire. Dec: Hume and Trimble receive the Nobel prize for peace.

1999   Feb: NI Assembly confirms new government departments and cross-border bodies. March: London and Dublin sign treaties on new arrangements in the Good Friday Agreement (north–south body, British–Irish Council). July: with problems continuing over decommissioning and the UUP fixed to its 'no guns, no government' stance, the UUP boycotts Stormont and Mallon resigns as Deputy First Minister. Mitchell begins a review process of the GFA. Sept: publication of the Patten Report provokes Unionist anger. Oct: Peter Mandelson replaces Mo Mowlam as Secretary of State for NI. Nov: Mitchell review recommends parallel government and decommissioning. The UUC allows Trimble to now enter an executive with Sinn Fein, though he has to post-date a resignation letter to become operative if the IRA still refuses to decommission. Both Trimble and Mallon now take up their designated positions at the head of a power-sharing executive. Dec: devolution restored. The IRA appoints an interlocutor to the decommissioning body.

2000   Jan: de Chastelain delays publication of his report on IRA decommissioning. Feb: Trimble says he intends to resign. The day before Mandelson suspends the devolutionary institutions and reverts to direct rule. March: Trimble narrowly survives a leadership challenge from the Reverend Martin Smyth. May: the IRA declares it will 'completely and verifiably put IRA weapons beyond use'. Two international monitors are appointed to inspect IRA dumps. The UUC approves Trimble re-entering the executive on this basis. Devolution is restored. June: the first IRA dumps are inspected by the international observers. Dec: the decommissioning body gives a bleak report on the state of IRA decommissioning.

2001   May: Trimble again threatens resignation (to become operative in July) unless progress is made on decommissioning. Aug: negotiations to try to delay his resignation and move the IRA towards decommissioning. IRA men arrested in Columbia where they were training FARC guerrillas creates adverse publicity in the USA. Sept: the terrorist attack on the World Trade Center sees the USA launch a 'war on terrorism'. Against this run of events, delay in decommissioning will only count against Sinn Fein's political interests. The IRA gives up a 'substantial' amount of ammunition and weaponry. The NI executive resumes.

MAPS

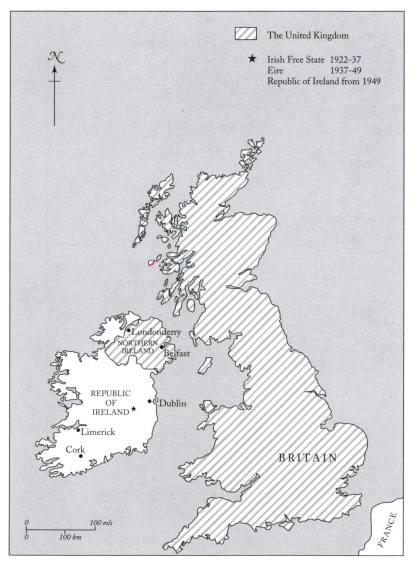

The United Kingdom

★ Irish Free State 1922-37
Eire   1937-49
Republic of Ireland from 1949

N

Londonderry
NORTHERN
IRELAND   Belfast

REPUBLIC
OF
IRELAND ★ Dublin

Limerick

Cork

BRITAIN

FRANCE

0   100 mls
0   100 km

Map 1   The British Isles

Map 2   Ireland

Map 3   Northern Ireland

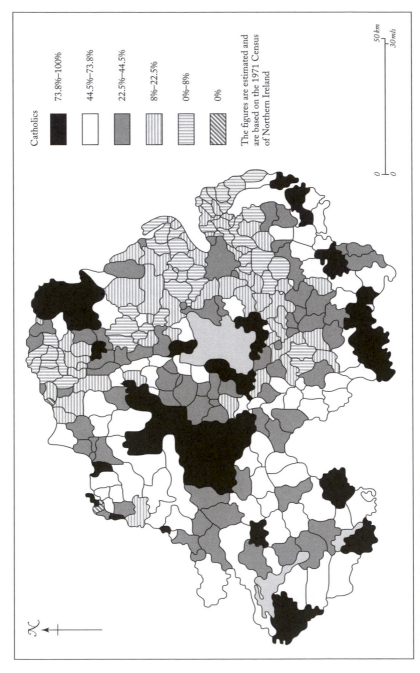

Catholics

73.8%–100%

44.5%–73.8%

22.5%–44.5%

8%–22.5%

0%–8%

0%

The figures are estimated and
are based on the 1971 Census
of Northern Ireland

50 km

30 mls

Map 4   Sectarian Population Distribution

1

NORTHERN IRELAND AND THE PROSPECTS FOR PEACE

'The Irish don't know what they want and won't be happy till they get it.'[1]

British Army officer, 1975

'Many talk about a solution to Ulster's political problem but few are prepared to say what the problem is. The reason is simple. The problem is that there is no solution – at least no solution recognizable in those more fortunate parts of the Anglo-American world that are governed with consensus.'[2]

R. Rose, 1976

'Hell just froze over. There's going to be peace in Ireland.'[3]

White House aide, 1998

AN INTRACTABLE PROBLEM?

FOR MANY YEARS IT WAS ASSUMED THAT THE CONFLICT in Northern Ireland was something beyond solution. However hard politicians (and academics) planned, debated, manoeuvred, compromised, rethought and innovated, the problem remained intractable. Northern Ireland had a conflict that was simply too complex to untangle, a struggle that somehow ignored the normal laws of conflict resolution. The Berlin Wall could fall, Nelson Mandela walk to freedom in South Africa and even Israel and Palestine reach peace agreements in 1993 and 1995 (though these have not survived), but Northern Ireland remained 'troubled'. While other regions turned corners, Northern Ireland could only tread the same path. As other politicians talked peace, hers continued to bellow and roar. And as guns fell silent elsewhere, hers continued to kill. Just two months after Israel and Palestine signed the historic Oslo accord in 1993, an IRA bomb demolished a fish shop in Belfast, killing ten people. Seven days later the UFF replied by machine-gunning dead seven people in the Rising Sun bar in Greysteel. The six counties had given their own particular response to peace elsewhere.

The intractability of the Northern Irish problem was thought the product of a rather unique type of conflict, a battle rooted in seventeenth-century prejudices rather than grounded in the economic or political realities of the late twentieth century. An antediluvian, almost 'Sicilian' blood feud that by its very nature rendered it too remote for 'modern', Western democratic politicians to understand, let alone resolve. For them the region was 'a place apart, somewhere not quite in the modern world', a peculiarity in an otherwise peaceful Western Europe.[4] 'With blithe lightness of mind', Michael Ignatieff has written, 'we assumed that the world was moving irrevocably beyond Nationalism, beyond tribalism, beyond the provincial confines of the identities inscribed in our passports, towards a global market culture which was to be our new home'.[5] A world, we might add, where Northern Ireland stuck out like a sore thumb! Yet the end of the Cold War by the early 1990s brought with it a flowering of ancient 'tribal' disputes, forgotten hatreds, cultural intolerance and ethnic quarrels. Across Europe and the wider world it appeared that the 'repressed had returned',[6] which in turn altered perspectives on the Northern Ireland 'Troubles'. As violent bloodshed revisited the Balkans, Rwanda, Indonesia and Chechnya, and with the continued deadlock over the Israeli–Palestinian question, the notion of an insoluble conflict in Northern Ireland appeared both less anomalous and more plausible. In a world of seemingly 'primitive' and irresolvable ethno-national antagonisms, the unmovable 'Troubles' looked less extraordinary. This wider perspective also diminished a lingering English prejudice that the conflict was somehow uniquely 'Irish' (whether Nationalist or Unionist), a problem rooted in the cultural peculiarities of a 'naturally' quarrelsome people. In other words, Northern Ireland now stood amongst and not apart from developments in the world, and her 'Troubles' had been a premonition of what was to come rather than a residue of what had gone; a window on the future rather than a bolt from the past!

> 66 Understanding the source of the conflict and to what it is related did not make finding a solution any easier 99

Understanding the source of the conflict and to what it is related did not of course make finding a solution any easier. Part of the problem lay in the immense difficulties of trying to pacify let alone reconcile ethno-National antagonism. For communal violence tends to entrench political positions and cement passionately held prejudices. It polarizes and alienates communities from one another. In the process neighbours are demonized and transformed into mortal enemies, their culture a deadly threat to the survival of the 'other's' way of life. In such an environment the world is black and white, gain for one is loss for the other, while concession looks like surrender and moderation like weakness. It is a zero-sum relationship. Arguably these sentiments are a source of strength and unity when the community is under attack. When, however, the task is to search for an accord, they are an obstacle and one not easily surmounted. They operate like a drag-anchor upon their leaders' ability to manoeuvre, compromise and bargain: attempts to do this leave those leaders vulnerable to ambitious demagogues outbidding them by playing up tribal fears. For, as political scientist Richard Rose observes, 'to seek friends amongst one's enemies is to risk making enemies of one's friends'.[7] The inevitable result is that leaders in an ethnically divided community find 'it is more rewarding to pursue the conflict than to pursue accommodation'[8] and to fall back on traditional and safe sources of communal backing. Resolving such tensions and pressures is therefore an extremely delicate operation, the long-term success of which will require nothing less than a wholesale 'redesigning and reconciling the parties' relationship with each other',[9] or what another political scientist has called a 'decommissioning of mind-sets'.[10]

Decommissioning mind-sets in Northern Ireland will take more than a political agreement between leaders from both communities to accomplish, though it undoubtedly is a very good start. Part of the difficulty is that the conflict has lasted many centuries and thus has put down deep emotional and cultural roots. Even its most recent manifestation has been running since 1969 and has claimed the lives of 3,633 people, with a further 42,000 injured. Such suffering, over a long period, has created 'vast inventories of historical recrimination'[11] that in turn have deepened resentment, hardened attitudes and widened the communal gulf. Such inventories have meant that despite the signing of the Good Friday Agreement (GFA) in 1998, the causes of the conflict survive. Ingrained tribal loyalties, self-legitimating traditions and myths, tight communal separation and socio-economic exclusion continue to divide the communities and represent significant barriers to normalization. Community reconciliation remains a cherished aspiration rather than measurable development, with traditional anxieties, mistrust and hatreds never far below the surface of life in the province and often erupting into public view, as with the Holy Cross school stand-off during the autumn of 2001. Politically inspired violence may have receded, but that is hardly saying much when paramilitary turf wars, blast-bombs, sectarian rioting, house evacuations, intimidation and punishment beatings continue as a regular feature of life in the province. It seems one type of violence has been exchanged for another. Though even then political violence still casts a shadow, admittedly a pale one, across the region given the fact that various Republican splinter groups operate outside the Provisional IRA cease-fire of 19 July 1997 and remain committed to violence, a threat scarcely eased by the number and variety of weapons that still lie hidden throughout the region. The Troubles may have gone but Northern Ireland remains a troubled society and the current 'peace' in Northern Ireland can look at times unmistakably like no peace. Although it is now three years after the signing of the GFA, many observers are still not sure whether we have peace or just a lull in the fighting.

If the durability of ethno-National conflict has made solving the problem difficult, then the search for a solution has hardly been aided by disagreement over what the problem actually is! Hardline Republicans argue that it is the British presence in Northern Ireland that lies at the heart of the conflict. If the 'Brits' withdrew, the conflict would end as Unionists would come to perceive their natural home within a united Irish Republic. Unionists, unimpressed with such wishful thinking, focus upon the violence, and particularly that of the IRA, as the main issue at stake. Only by extinguishing this and removing the means to return to violence can the province achieve real peace and reconciliation. Constitutional Nationalists tend to view violence as a symptom of a deeper malaise, the systematic discrimination of Catholics and frustration of their political tradition. Only by addressing these issues will the violence be removed and peace generated. Alternatively, more extreme Unionists argue it is the very survival of this Nationalist political tradition amongst Catholics in the north, plus mixed signals from the British and unofficial recognition from the Republic, that has generated violence in the north. What is required to end the violence and return the province to peace and stability are tough counter-terrorist measures, alongside a clear endorsement by all that Northern Ireland is permanent and inviolable.

Given the sides cannot agree on the problem, the search for a solution was always going to be complex and arduous. So arduous, in fact, that many were sceptical a solution existed at all. Writing in 1976, Richard Rose sounded a despondent note when he reminded his readers that 'the existence of a political problem is not proof that there is a solution'.[12] This did not deter politicians who, with a legion of schemes and initiatives, from the Darlington conference of 1972, to the Sunningdale experiment of 1973–1974, the Constitutional Convention of 1975–1976, the constitutional conference of 1979–1980, rolling devolution 1982–1986, the Anglo-Irish Agreement 1985, the Brooke/Mayhew initiative of 1989–1992 and the IRA cease-fire of 1994–1996, attempted to solve the problem. Yet the fact that the Troubles *still* endured and 30 years of conflict has resulted in no more than a catalogue of fruitless discussions, broken deals and political collapses was surely testament that no solution was possible. Like some Hobbesian nightmare, war and conflict were thought the natural order of things in Northern Ireland. And any survey of the previous 300 years could make a strong case for seeing violence, bloodshed and disharmony as typical, with moments of peace and quiet merely periods of temporary exhaustion, regrouping and re-equipping.

On the other hand it might be argued that the problem in Northern Ireland was less that there was no solution than that there were too many of them. 'The trouble was,' A.T.Q. Stewart has noted, 'that the crisis in Ulster was regarded as a kind of puzzle, which could be solved if the right answer were found. The blunt truth was the opposite. The "solution" was the chief cause of the problem, and was constantly inflaming it.'[13] In his book on the peace process, Tom Hennessey has listed nine possible arrangements for the region, ranging from the full integration of Northern Ireland into the UK, to a United Ireland with a clutch of confederal, federal, joint-authority and devolutionary schemes in between.[14] Without a settled future and always awaiting the next Secretary of State for Northern Ireland armed with his latest plan, insecurity and instability became enmeshed into the very fabric of Northern Irish politics and society. And from insecurity sprang violence. Alternatively it might be that the solution existed all the time and the arduous process was actually bringing the leaders of the different groups and parties (or at least some of them) to that realization. The peace process as a journey towards enlighten-ment rather than a complex mathematical conundrum. The obvious similarities between the Good Friday Agreement and the Sunningdale experiment of 1972, immortalized in the now

66 Any survey of the previous 300 years could make a strong case for seeing violence, bloodshed and disharmony as typical 99

famous quip from former Deputy First Minister Seamus Mallon that the GFA was 'Sunningdale for slow learners', supports this notion of a slowly maturing enlightenment.

Whatever the nature of the problem (and indeed the solution), the complexities of the situation certainly help explain why the road to a political settlement in Northern Ireland has proved to be both long and forbidding. Bringing all sides into a form of dialogue, sometimes through mediators or on a unilateral basis, proved a highly delicate exercise in painstaking diplomacy. Indeed, the exercise gave birth to a new term, 'talk about talks', now common currency in diplomatic language. Progress was always an extremely fragile creature, vulnerable to disruption on the 'inside' by walkouts, posturing or histrionics, and to 'out-side' events be they a bomb, an election, a parade, political crisis at Westminster or just an insensitive speech. At all stages, the journey was characterized as much by delay, suspension, stale-mate, fragmentation, obfuscation and reversal as it was marked by measurable advance. Yet even then momentum in the process could be sustained only by 'sleight of hand' and flexible terminology, to enable leaders to elide over what seemed unbridgeable differences while preserving their fixed 'public' stance. And a terminology, we might add, capable of marrying mutually exclusive attitudes, or language able to hide subtle but significant shifts of position while projecting a continuity of approach for supporters.

A good example is the idea of a *fragile cease-fire*. This gave rec-ognition, for those who needed it, that a cease-fire still existed while simultaneously admitting to others that it was regularly breached. And the phrase *peace process* was the essential linguis-tic tool for camouflaging irreconcilable Unionist and Nationalist objectives. Unionists concentrated on the *peace* aspect of the Peace Process as an end to violence and a settled, water-tight and finalized agreement that by dint of being final has consoli-dated the Northern Irish state and Partition. 'I have risen from this table,' David Trimble declared on signing the GFA, 'with the Union stronger than when I sat down.' The SDLP and especially Sinn Fein highlight the *process* part of the Peace Process, a staging post in a still incomplete journey, the final destination being a united Ireland. Thus more about process than about the peace (or process and peace together) because for them, true, lasting peace will come only with unification. Indeed, one suspects that linking the word 'process' to 'peace' was the necessary sleight of hand required to persuade the more militant republicans to lay down (though not to hand in) their weapons. There operated, then, a plasticity of language and terminology that permitted forward motion even when the parties and political actors stood far apart.

A similar plasticity or ill-defined quality can be seen with the settlement itself. To a large extent this was unavoidable and even perhaps necessary, given Northern Ireland's zero-sum politics. In these circumstances it was essential that the Good Friday Agreement pointed both ways, offering security for the Union while advancing the cause and possibility of a united Ireland. Unless both communities saw in it a victory, it would not acquire a broad consensus of support. However, the reality was that the GFA was a compromise, a complex network of trade-offs involving Northern Ireland, Britain and the Irish Republic, in a society where the very idea of a compromise and trade-off meant defeat and surrender. To compensate for this the different parties placed upon the settlement their own conflicting inflections; indeed, they even referred to it differently. For Nationalists it was the Good Friday Agreement, stressing the powerful motifs of Easter and resurrection. Unionists, on the other hand, called it the Belfast Agreement, the locus of Unionist power and home of Stormont, a neo-classical reminder of a once dominant Unionist polity. Within the terms of the agreement, Unionists focused upon the guarantee that Northern Ireland would remain part of the UK as long as its people desired it, the creation of a devolved Northern Ireland Assembly and executive and the removal of the Republic's constitutional claim to the north in articles 2 and 3 of their Constitution. Nationalists stressed the recognition of their Irish identity and tradition in article 2 of the GFA, the sharing of power in the executive, the

> 66 Unionists focused upon the guarantee that Northern Ireland would remain part of the UK as long as its people desired it 99

North-South Ministerial Council and various implementation bodies dealing with all-island matters and the reformed British–Irish Inter-Governmental Conference. Refracted through the lens of their own political objectives, the agreement appeared to mean all things to all men/women. Elsewhere in the settlement, contentious or unbridgeable issues were suspended or 'farmed out' to various independent commissions, as with police reform and decommissioning. Even then particularly sticky areas were left blurred and vague, perhaps hoping for a softening of views or an altered political context in the future. The thorny question of weapons decommissioning is a good example. For some, the relevant passages in the GFA *obliged* all political parties to the actual demolition of terrorist arms, weapon by weapon. For others it reads more like a general *commitment*, necessarily gradual and without time limits, and connected to the simultaneous removal of all weapons within Northern Ireland – taking the gun out of Irish politics, whoever owned or wielded it.[15]

Unfortunately this inherent ambiguity in the agreement, though vital for providing each side with 'its' victory, has stored up difficulties for the future, difficulties that some three years after the GFA are only now being confronted with predictably destabilizing consequences. The subsequent 'stop-start-stop' record of the new Northern Ireland executive, the boil of decommissioning that *still* awaits lancing and the knotty questions of police reform, British de-militarization and the Saville inquiry into Bloody Sunday all loom like ice-bergs on the horizon and testify to the limitations of the 1998 Agreement. It also furnished those elements that stood outside it with an easy, soft target. Such flexible and multiple readings of the GFA enabled the DUP (and a growing number of Ulster Unionists) to claim it was not really an agreement at all. For them it was a sham, a mere tactical realignment by Republicans looking to continue their struggle by other means, and gullibly supported by naive British and Unionist politicians. Sections of the IRA would probably view 'the peace' in a similar way as an option to run with and, when exhausted, discard if nothing concrete materializes. In other words, the very nature of the peace agreement appeared indefinite, contested and ambiguous. It was a malleable, even moveable, agreement rather than a fixed and finite one. Though, arguably, it was these very qualities that allowed a settlement to be agreed in the first place. And a flawed peace is surely better than no peace.

HOPEFUL SIGNS

In light of these observations, a book on making the peace in Northern Ireland could seem a trifle rash, if not downright foolish. We might even wonder whether there was a book here at all. Certainly there have been moments during the last year when doubts have got the better of me. Reading the morning newspaper turned from a pleasant daily ritual into an act of anxious scrutiny. The raised eyebrow or glassy stare of a colleague, having enquired into what I was currently working on, was sufficient to register a wider sense of disbelief that I would reach the end of the project. It is therefore imperative at the outset to clarify the focus and rationale of the text. In this respect much depends on what is meant by 'peace'. If peace is assumed to mean an end to violence or an end to communal conflict, then the peace has not been made, for Northern Ireland clearly does not reside in a blissful state of peace. By this definition there has been no conflict resolution, let alone conflict reconciliation, and the best we might say is that a framework for 'managing' the conflict has been put in place. However, if peace is interpreted as an end to politically motivated violence and the agreement of a co-operative and inclusive political framework for organizing the life of the region, then peace has been made. By this reading of events the Good Friday Agreement has put in place a settlement that provides a mechanism and an impetus for the region to move towards a longer-term resolution of its conflict and ultimately reconciliation. It has opened the gates to the castle, and though the conflict persists (and may even worsen), we can say with a degree of confidence that the Troubles in their current manifestation have been brought to an end.

Making the Peace therefore examines how this process unfolded and was brought to fruition. It investigates why and when that political structure was put together. It explores the slow, agonizing path towards a settlement, charting moments of reverse and advance, and illuminating the dynamics of change. It will also analyze the role of the chief architects and builders of the political superstructure, upon what foundations they built, where they found the materials with which to erect their edifice, and who were the 'sappers' looking to destroy it. The Good Friday Agreement is represented here as a watershed, a moment of far-reaching change when something long thought unimaginable materialized, even if potentially hazardous problems continued beyond 1998 and deep communal divisions survived the post-agreement euphoria. Not all would see the GFA as a fundamental transformation, though even the most limited and pessimistic interpretation would agree with David McKittrick that in 1998 'it has (now) become safe to join the optimists'.[16]

Taking the latter minimum interpretation we might try to get some sort of perspective on the Good Friday Agreement, some measurement of that optimism, by comparing the circumstances of 1998 with, arguably, the best previous attempt to achieve peace, the Sunningdale experiment of 1973–1974. Then, as now, a new Northern Ireland Assembly and power-sharing executive were established, with a cross-border Council of Ireland finally agreed by the various political parties. Unfortunately the experiment collapsed after just five months, under pressure from a massive Unionist backlash that brought the province to a standstill. Disregarded and apprehensive, the Unionist majority broke the back of Sunningdale, forcing the executive to resign and the assembly to collapse – a mass popular revolt that registered its disapproval in the February 1974 general election, when anti-Sunningdale Unionists won 80 per cent of the *Unionist* vote and took 11 of the 12 parliamentary seats. Closer analysis of the events of 1973–1974 point to other contributory factors, for instance, deeply acrimonious Anglo-Irish relations, the absence of paramilitary cease-fires, the lack of outside involvement, in particular from the USA which

❝ The Good Friday Agreement is represented here as a watershed, a moment of far-reaching change when something long thought unimaginable materialized ❞

was still preoccupied with the fallout from the Watergate scandal, and a British general election that inflamed political attitudes at just the wrong time.

By contrast, few of these complications were prominent at the time of the GFA, nor have they subsequently manifested themselves. Though Unionist reactions remain a deep concern, the likelihood of a backlash on the scale of 1973–1974 seems unlikely. At the 1998 assembly elections the UUP, the main party of Unionism and supporters of the GFA, won 43 per cent of the overall Unionist vote, a figure that compares favourably to the 20 per cent that pro-Sunningdale Unionists were able to garner from their community at the 1974 general election. This substantial support for the agreement has been assisted by fragmentation in the Unionist movement, with six different Unionist parties fighting the 1998 assembly elections, compared with just two in 1974. In other words, a Unionist reaction of the same magnitude or degree of unity as in 1974 seems a remote possibility. Of equal significance, the past decade and a half witnessed a considerable strengthening in Anglo-Irish relations. This proved to be a vital combination in the search for a solution, for by working in tandem Britain and Ireland were able to broker deals, soothe party concerns, highlight realities, guide opinion, and mildly warn and gently compel politicians of both sides at different moments. By standing together they were able to encourage the political parties to go further than they might otherwise have gone, while denying those who were unwilling to 'fellow-travel' their support. Something of the latter had already been revealed in the aftermath of the 1985 Anglo-Irish Agreement when the forces of Unionism failed to face down the opposition of resolute British and Irish governments. Another missing ingredient in 1973–1974 but of immense importance by the 1990s was the American connection, and in particular the constructive part played by President Clinton. At pivotal moments the US administration performed a useful 'greasing' role in the political process, helping to ease tension, facilitate movement and resume progress. Again in contrast to 1973–1974, all the main paramilitary groups were on cease-fires from 1997 onwards, while those groups still outside it were mere splinters of a faction (though no less deadly), without popular support or substantial financial resources. Last, whereas the general election in 1974 undermined the political settlement, appeals to the people in 1997 and 1998 stabilized the peace process. The Labour victory in the 1997 general election gave negotiations a much-needed jolt, while the May 1998 Referendum provided the agreement with an indispensable democratic sanction.

We might add to this catalogue of differences several beneficial 'cultural' developments unique to the 1990s, which made peace a more likely prospect than at any previous time. One was a favourable international climate, following the end of the Cold War, the fall of the Berlin Wall and co-operation in the Gulf War. In an atmosphere of renewal and hope, politicians set about removing the vestigial problems of the twentieth century, such as Apartheid in South Africa and the violence between Israel and Palestine, which in turn focused attention on Northern Ireland. The 1990s also heralded what for some was an 'end of ideology', a blunting of the insular and absolutist ideals that had driven events for much of the twentieth century, against the onslaught from Europeanization, globalization, rapid technological advance, increased secularization and the collapse of Soviet communism. These changes, though with hindsight less clear cut, weakened the appeal and relevance of older convictions, forcing those more irredentist attitudes (within Unionism, Nationalism and Republicanism) to adopt a more accommodating, inclusive and consensual outlook. The 'end of ideology' was also marked by the triumph of liberal-capitalist values and the victory of the 'market', pressures that played a constructive role in highlighting the value of peace to Northern Ireland, what might be termed the economic dividend, of inward investment and financial regeneration that a political settlement might bring. More prosaically, the 1990s brought a sense of weariness, even exhaustion, to those on all sides of the Northern Ireland conflict. A British MI6 agent reflecting on the situation in 1972 did not 'think either community had suffered enough to want peace, to make peace an absolute imperative'. By 1998, after 30 years of conflict, things were now very different, not least because yesterday's teenagers were today's parents. 'Please don't let any kids suffer the history I have,' wrote the convicted murderer Billy Giles in his suicide note, 'I didn't deserve it and they certainly don't. Please let our next generation live normal lives.'[17]

In other words, we can find qualitative differences between 1974 and 1998, in terms of both the details and manner in which agreement was reached and the context in which it was agreed, that give us some confidence that a political solution to the Northern Ireland question has finally been found. On many of the 'big' questions (ownership, relations with Britain and the Irish Republic, an end to political violence and government based on cross-community support) the GFA has put compromises in place, some fairly stable, others tentative and fragile. Political leaders on both sides have emerged willing to risk everything (quite literally) for peace. Once sworn enemies now nestle (uneasily it has to be said) within the Northern Ireland executive. In a number of areas and at different levels, cross-party participation has taken root, while the various political structures established in 1998 have operated with varying degrees of success and stability. One clear success has been the devolved assembly, where tangible progress and a real sense of co-operation have emerged, as evidenced during the recent foot and mouth crisis. But perhaps above all else the guns have remained (largely) silent. And though the IRA has not gone away and there has been only a cosmetic surrender of weapons by them (something we should remember the IRA did not do in 1923 or in 1962) the International Commission on Decommissioning confirms that a 'decommissioning' is well under way.[18] Ironically, the return of violence to the Middle East may help concentrate minds in Northern Ireland, offering a glimpse of what the future might hold if leaders continue to prevaricate and bellow rather than 'work' together. In light of these factors it seems reasonable to conclude that some form of watershed in the history of the province was crossed in 1998.

> " By 1998, after 30 years of conflict, things were now very different, not least because yesterday's teenagers were today's parents "

Unfortunately when focus is on day-to-day matters, the distance Northern Ireland has travelled can easily be overlooked. It is sobering to recollect that as late as 1990 a representative of the IRA could state 'absolutely, on the record, that there will be no cease-fire, no truce, no "cessation of violence" short of a British withdrawal. That, as blunt as that, is our position'.[19] In 1993 John Major still felt it would 'turn his stomach' to sit and talk with Gerry Adams, while David Trimble could storm out of a TV studio in 1995, declaring 'we do not share platforms with Sinn Fein/IRA'. In worrying how far there is to go, we forget just how far we have come. Moreover, frustration at the slow pace of change since 1998, the episodic violence, the reversals and nagging obstacles all engender a scepticism that peace has really been achieved. In an age of instant action and fixed targets, of government task-forces and measurable progress, we expect immediate results.

But on these things Northern Ireland is quaintly old fashioned. It operates along different parameters and according to a different pace and tempo. Its rhythms are measured not in months and years but in generations. Its realities do not easily succumb to media makeovers or political repackaging. Its politicians cannot quickly abandon the language of 'cold war' for the idiom of peaceful co-existence. The task of unclogging the sedimentation of centuries of bitterness will take a long time. Tribal loyalties, fear and suspicion have deep roots in Northern Ireland. People will still hate and mistrust for years to come. Violence will still occur. Politics will remain polarized. The executive will stop and stall for periods. Full reconciliation might only ever be partial or it might not occur at all. But the essential difference of 1998 is that Northern Ireland now has a political structure, a settlement, which it might build upon and with which it might deepen the peace it has already, rather tentatively, constructed. In the words of Seamus Mallon, 'there may be heavy cloud, there may be flak, there may even be hijackers on board. But we can see the lights on the runway'.[20] This book will look at how the 'lights on the runway' came into view. But to chart these developments we need to understand the nature of that conflict.

NATURE OF THE BEAST

At the heart of the Northern Irish conflict lies a polarized society, divided upon the question of possession. One community, the smaller Nationalist or Republican one, desires the transfer of sovereignty over the region from Britain to the Irish Republic. Their goal is (crudely) to harmonize the geographical boundary of the island of Ireland with the political boundary of the Irish nation. The larger, Unionist or loyalist community is determined to resist assimilation into the south and preserve Northern Ireland as a part of Great Britain. Their political home lies within the archipelago of regions and identities known as the United Kingdom. At its core, then, the Northern Irish conflict is a problem of ownership, and any stable solution will need to address this question. This basic rivalry is complicated by the respective 'mother' states, whose policies and outlook have helped fortify the rival national claims to the province. This is obviously the case with Unionism, since Britain has remained the authority over Northern Ireland, guaranteeing its status in the 1949 Ireland Act and holding direct (if at times faltering) control of the region since 1972. But to a lesser extent Dublin, as the ideological home of Irish Nationalism, has helped sustain northern Nationalists, providing public sympathy and political recognition via clauses 2 and 3 of De Valera's 1937 Constitution. Some Dublin ministers even went further by offering military aid to northern Nationalists. Northern Ireland is therefore an internal conflict of competing nationalities, nourished and endorsed by rival external powers. Any solution to the conflict requires both 'external referents' to reposition and redefine themselves with regard to the Northern Irish state.

Settling the question of ownership of Northern Ireland would be laborious enough. But when that basic rift is overlaid (and re-inforced) by other, equally antagonistic rivalries, the adjective 'intractable' seems all the more appropriate. Religious loyalties, for example, fortify the territorial dispute, with Nationalist support emanating from largely Catholic communities, and Unionism dominant amongst Protestants. This close correspondence has encouraged some to regard the conflict as primarily a religious one, and undoubtedly religious identities have infused and shaped political loyalties. But few northern Nationalists desire unification with the south in order to create a theocratic Catholic state in the north. A second antagonism underpinning the clash of national claims is an historic distinction between native and settler or colonized and colonizer. The former regard themselves as the original (and so in their eyes legitimate) population of the region, the latter represent the seventeenth-century immigrants of mostly Protestant

> **At its core, then, the Northern Irish conflict is a problem of ownership, and any stable solution will need to address this question**

origin. Those claiming 'native' status tend to be Catholic, Nationalist and Irish: those of 'settler' ancestry generally conform to a Unionist, Protestant and British identity. However, these representations have problems. Locating an original, pure people, analogous to the label native, is all but impossible, while the term settler barely encompasses the constant traffic of people in and out of the north-east of Ireland both before and after the seventeenth century. Economic disparities also overlap the dispute over ownership. Catholic and Nationalist communities tend to be the more impoverished and economically dispossessed than the generally more affluent Protestant and Unionist communities. Lastly, ethnic differences are a fissure bolstering the territorial dispute. The Nationalist and predominantly Catholic minority embrace or aspire to a Gaelic Irish identity, the Unionist and mostly Protestant majority claim a British one. In short, the superimposition of religious, economic, colonial and ethnic differences onto competing national claims has exacerbated communal segregation. If Northern Ireland is to establish stable political institutions, then such community divisions will have to be reconciled eventually. For in the end only a political structure founded upon the support of both sides will be durable and effective.

This is evident in those societies that similarly embrace religious, ethnic or cultural divisions yet have managed to successfully reconcile them. Holland, for example, incorporates Walloons and Flems with few ethnic problems. The large

Catholic and Protestant communities of Switzerland and Germany reside calmly together, while the mix of French and English cultures in Canada is a source of vitality, not violence. Northern Ireland, however, has not reconciled its differences for the reason that its various communal fractures *overlap* with each other rather than *crosscut*. So, for example, while Holland's religious distinctions bear no relation to her economic differences, in Northern Ireland they do. Hence, instead of experiencing competing loyalties that serve to dissipate tensions, the province has mutually reinforcing ones that embed and strengthen divisions still further. Moreover, failure to reconcile differences stems from the absence of and indeed resistance to cross-communal contacts. In housing, in education, at work and in all areas of social activity, Nationalist and Unionist communities tend to look inwards, to their own estates, schools, church, pubs, jobs, clubs and shops. Communities live side by side yet remain quarantined from each other.[21] As a result a mere 9 per cent of marriages in the province are mixed.[22] In residential terms, Belfast at the end of 1972 saw some 70 per cent of Catholics living in all-Catholic streets[23] and 78 per cent of Protestants in all-Protestant streets[24] (although outside Belfast this level is considerably lower at 35–40 per cent). In education, 71 per cent of pupils in 1976 went to a single denominational school.[25] Even the great modern crosscutting allegiance, football, divides loyalties upon pre-established lines.

This process of estrangement has been sustained through the eagerness of each community to plunder the past in search of their own self-legitimating, self-justifying history – a history that furnishes communal solidarity, engenders group loyalty and kindles hostility towards the other community. For Nationalists their story is one of 'victimhood and resistance',[26] of *Irish* claims oppressed by centuries of British/Unionist prejudice, betrayal and discrimination. For Unionists, their tale is one of siege, self-reliance and eternal vigilance against the acquisitive designs of an Irish, Nationalist, Catholic majority. Perhaps like nowhere else the past hangs heavily over the present in Northern Ireland, indeed 'in Ireland the past and present were indistinguishable. There, history was too important to be left to historians'.[27] Unfortunately, with such conflicting and exclusive narratives, little common ground or sympathetic understanding can emerge between the two communities, generating in its place mutual ignorance, suspicion, fear and ultimately violence.

Much of the violence between the two communities has been carried out by self-proclaimed community defence groups. These were originally organized at a street or neighbourhood level, guarding against invasions and policing the communal boundaries. Mixed neighbourhoods became areas of acute territorial friction as each group tried to establish control through intimidation, harassment and ultimately burning families out of their homes. The defender groups regarded themselves as the legitimate protectors of their people and at a wider level as champions of their national claims. Accordingly their violence could be deeply symbolic or propagandist both in targeting and in intent. More often, however, it was nakedly sectarian or designed to maintain support within their community that drew upon an older tradition of 'public banding'. This can be seen on the Unionist side in the various loyalist paramilitary groups, such as the Shankhill Defenders, the Protestant Action Group, the Red Hand Commandos and the revived UVF, all of which emerged as counter-revolutionary, defence forces during the late 1960s. In September 1971 many of these groups federated under an umbrella organization, the UDA, which at its height claimed 50,000 members. Their violence was directed at the Catholic community and sometimes against the Irish Republic, both of which they accused of sustaining the IRA, with the objective of preserving the Union with Britain.

> "Much of the violence between the two communities has been carried out by self-proclaimed community defence groups"

From the Nationalist community, various community defence and protection groups had emerged during the sectarian troubles of 1969–1970 to protect Nationalist communities under fierce attack from loyalist mobs and part-time policemen. As the conflict escalated the once moribund IRA slowly revived, though not before splitting into the Official and Provisional wings. Though late starters, it was the Provisionals who most energetically took up the task of organizing community defence from the summer of 1970. And so successful were they that from late 1971/1972, they broadened their tactics towards a more offensive, Nationalist strategy. Their remit was no longer simple defence but the destruction of Stormont and a British withdrawal, after which, they believed, a united Irish Republic would materialize. The new tactics involved targeting the police, economic interests and British soldiers, active in the province since August 1969. This in turn altered the role of the British authorities in Northern Ireland, from a policy of benign neglect and separating the two communities to an all-counter-insurgency campaign, honed and perfected in Malaysia, Cyprus and Aden but inappropriate for the more media-sensitive Northern Irish conflict.

Conflict between these three 'players' has over the past 30 years resulted in the death of 3,633 people. Against the backdrop of the 1990s with its multiple genocides in Croatia, Rwanda and Kosovo, and bloody wars in Chechnya, Sri Lanka, Israel/Palestine and Indonesia, this appears unexceptional and meagre. Amounting to an average of 121 deaths per annum, far more are killed each year in Britain in road accidents and ten times more die from heart disease. Over half of all deaths (some 1,817) occurred in the six years between 1971 and 1976. If we remove the figures for these six years, the annual death rate for the remaining 24 years drops to 75, a level commensurate with the number of yearly deaths from food poisoning. The worst year for the Troubles was 1972, with 496 people killed, a mere *twentieth* of the number who died that same year in the Nicaraguan earthquake in Managua and the same number as are murdered each *month* in Rio de Janeiro. The majority of deaths occurred in ones and twos, in narrowly defined and recognized areas (45 per cent in Belfast alone) and according to communally understood and established codes of engagement and activity. This left most parts of Northern Ireland free of conflict and for 'most of the time, for most of the people, nothing untoward happened'.[28] Even the manner in which we describe the conflict (the 'emergency', the Troubles, the Northern Irish 'problem', or a 'security situation') suggests an episode of marginal, almost trifling significance. One British Secretary of State for Northern Ireland even denied it was a conflict at all.[29]

However, raw statistics and political spin more often disguise meaning and significance than liberate understanding. Much depends on how you package the facts/statistics and with what you make comparison. For example, by positioning the events of Northern Ireland within a European context it reveals the region as, at least until 1994, not only the most politically violent place in the EEC but having witnessed more people killed by political violence than the rest of the community *put together.*[30] Indeed, one eminent political scientist has gone further, claiming 'Northern Ireland was by far the most internally politically violent of the recognizably continuous liberal democracies (in the world) during the period 1948 to 1977, both in absolute numbers killed and relatively'.[31] We also need to be aware of the relative smallness of Northern Ireland. With a population of just one and a half million, the ratio of deaths represents about one in every 400 people. Comparatively, this would correspond for Great Britain as a whole to over 150,000 people killed, and for the United States a massive 600,000: it is sobering to remember the Vietnam War claimed the lives of 52,000 US soldiers, just over a tenth of this figure, while World War Two saw 274,000 casualties. Perhaps even more revealing is if we add the number of deaths (3,633) to those injured as a result of the violence, estimated to be a little over 42,000.[32] Startlingly, this suggests that one in every 33 people has been touched, in a direct and often agonizing way, by the conflict.

> 6 6 Quite literally, every family in Northern Ireland has been a victim of the Troubles 9 9

Quite literally, every family in Northern Ireland has been a victim of the Troubles. Yet it has not only been Northern Ireland which has felt the impact of the conflict. Violence has spilled over onto the British mainland, where 124 deaths have occurred, the Irish Republic, with 118, and Europe, with 18 (British Army bases in Germany and Gibraltar). If we include the funding and supply of weapons (the USA, Libya, Bosnia), the Northern Irish conflict takes on near-global dimensions. In other words, however slight 3,633 deaths seem, comparatively speaking, on a wider scale and in human terms this was a tragedy of enormous proportions, as publication of *Lost Lives* (a compilation of biographical sketches of all the victims and the manner of their death) makes woefully clear.

NOTES

1   J. M. Cohen, *Dictionary of Modern Quotations* (Penguin, 1971) p 16.

2   R. Rose, *Northern Ireland: A Time for Choice,* (Macmillan, 1976) p 139.

3   White House aide on hearing news about the Good Friday Agreement in C. O'Clery, *Ireland in Quotes* (O'Brien Press, 1999) p 253.

4   A. T. Q. Stewart, *The Narrow Ground* (Faber, 1977) p 3.

5   M. Ignatieff, *Blood and Belonging* (Vintage, 1994) p 2.

6   Ibid, p 2.

7   R. Rose, op. cit., p 16.

8   D. Horowitz, 'Conflict and the incentives to political accommodation' in D. Keogh and M. Haltzel (eds) *Northern Ireland and the Politics of Reconciliation* (CUP, 1993) p 176.

9   D. Bloomfield, *Peacemaking Strategies in Northern Ireland: building complementarity in conflict management theory* (Macmillan, 1997) p 69.

10   D. Whittaker, *Conflict and Reconciliation in the Contemporary World* (Routledge, 1999) p 90.

11   'But a resolution of the decommissioning issue – or any other issue – will not be found if the parties resort to their vast inventories of historical recrimination', in *Report on the International Body of Arms Decommissioning,* by G. Mitchell, J. de Chasterlain, H. Holkeri, 22 January 1996.

12   R. Rose, op. cit., p 6.

13   Stewart, op. cit., p 7.

14   T. Hennessey, *The Northern Ireland Peace Process* (Gill & Macmillan, 2000) pp 185–7; pp 7–9.

15   Ibid, pp 185–7.

16   D. McKittrick, *Nervous Peace* (Blackstaff Press, 1996) p 3.

17   P. Taylor, *Loyalists* (Bloomsbury, 1999) p 11.

18   Fergal Keane used this phrase in the *Independent.*

19   D. McKittrick, op. cit., p 5.

20   Seamus Mallon on 22 January 1999 in O'Clery, *Ireland in Quotes,* p 266.

21   S. Farren and R. F. Mulvihill, *Paths to a Settlement in Northern Ireland* (Colin Smythe, 2000) pp 83–101.

22   R. Sales, *Women Divided: Gender, Religion and Politics in Northern Ireland* (Routledge, 1997) p 7.

23 All in this context is taken to represent over 91 per cent.

24 J. Whyte, *Interpreting Northern Ireland* (Clarendon, 1990) p 33.

25 Ibid, p 43.

26 P. Arthur, *Special Relationships: Britain, Ireland and the Northern Ireland Problem* (Blackstaff, 2001) p 62.

27 A. T. Q. Stewart, op. cit., p 2.

28 K. Toolis, *Rebel Hearts: Journeys Within the IRA's Soul* (Picador, 1995) p 4.

29 J. McGarry and B. O'Leary, *Explaining Northern Ireland* (Blackwell, 1995) p 2.

30 B. O'Leary and J. McGarry, *The Politics of Antagonism: Understanding Northern Ireland* (Athlone Press, 1993) p 12.

31 Ibid, p 13.

32 S. Elliot and W. D. Flackes, *Northern Ireland: A Political Directory, 1968–1969*, 5th Edition (Blackstaff Press, 1999) p 638.

2

BRITAIN AND IRELAND, 1600–1920

'Whatever the status and political structures of Northern Ireland eventually arrived at, it seems likely its future will be determined by those patterns which are so deeply ingrained in Irish history.'

A. T. Q. Stewart[1]

'The present is so clearly the result of the past that historians cannot ignore the historical dimension of the Ulster problems.'

D. G. Boyce[2]

COLONIALISM AND PLANTATION, 1600–1800

AT THE START OF J. C. BECKETT'S CLASSIC *THE MAKING OF MODERN IRELAND* he quotes an English civil servant writing in the sixteenth century. 'It is a proverb of old date that the pride of France, the treason of England and the war of Ireland shall never have end. Which proverb, touching the war in Ireland, is like always to continue, without God set it in men's breasts to find some new remedy that never was found before.'[3] The English, it appears, have a long tradition of seeing Ireland (or parts of it) as an area of permanent conflict and feeling themselves burdened with finding a remedy to it. God, they believed, was an Englishman and had charged England with solving the Irish question and bringing peace and stability to her endemic discord. Of course it was, arguably, English meddling that created Ireland's problems in the first place: the trouble with the Irish, runs an old Irish adage, is the English. And what the English *actually* meant by bringing peace to Ireland, variously referred to as civilizing the Irish or stabilizing a strife-torn region or injecting modernity into a place of backwardness, was securing her own political and strategic interests. These were, it was thought, threatened by the position of Ireland, lying just off her western seaboard and thus offering a potential invader a springboard into the heart of her kingdom and a danger to her trading routes to the Americas and the Indies. But it was further complicated by the bitter religious disputes of the Reformation. As England moved towards Protestantism from the 1540s, Ireland kept her Catholic faith, so becoming deeply suspect. Catholicism was not only a heresy clung to by the unpatriotic and the traitorous but more threateningly the religion of England's imperialist-minded European enemies. In a Europe divided along religious lines, Ireland was England's backyard, the most likely point of entry for Catholicism in its stated aim of bringing the English back to the true faith.

Against the backdrop of these perceived threats and religious differences, England's earliest attempts to bring peace to Ireland involved colonial subjugation and marginalization of Catholics. This was achieved from the sixteenth century by gradually extending her authority over the region. Irish land was confiscated and redistributed to Tudor cronies of the Anglican faith, the Catholic Church was weakened, the king of England was made the king of Ireland, and Ireland's Parliament was subordinated to Westminster. Subordination turned to confiscation and penalization during the seventeenth century. The military campaigns of Oliver Cromwell (1649–1650) and then William of Orange (1690) left their own bloody mark on Catholic communities and provided them with powerful myths to organize and justify their anti-British, anti-Protestant

> 66 As England moved towards Protestantism from the 1540s, Ireland kept her Catholic faith, so becoming deeply suspect 99

views. Land was seized from rebel nobles and distributed to loyal Anglicans, so whereas in 1641 Catholics owned 61 per cent of land, in 1776 that had fallen to a mere 5 per cent.[4] Without land, the Irish Parliament was denuded of its Catholic representation and fell under the control of a new Anglican ascendancy. Under the ascendancy restrictions were placed on the priesthood and Catholic worship. Catholics were excluded from political office, government posts, judicial positions, commissions in the army and from many professions, if not by legal restraint then through institutional prejudice. Ireland was to be a Protestant state for a largely Catholic people. Here then were discriminations that drove an enduring sense of grievance and a feeling of victimhood deep into the Irish Catholic psychology – perceptions that would survive within Catholic communities through a vibrant oral tradition, so keeping alive a powerful sense of injury from one generation to the next. The sixteenth and seventeenth centuries provided a store of historic 'oppressions' that during the nineteenth century could be dusted down and reworked into a ready-made 'past' that would furnish a Nationalist political agenda with the legitimacy to challenge British authority in Ireland.

Just as British policy helped lay roots to a Nationalist identity, so it helped construct a Unionist one as well. One particular aspect of stabilizing Ireland was to be of immense significance to the future development of Unionism, and Northern Ireland more generally, namely the schemes for plantation from the early 1600s. Here, English and Scottish Protestants (particularly Dissenting Presbyterians) were 'planted' in the north of Ireland, where they dispossessed Catholic tenants of their land. Their charge was to defend and diffuse loyalty to the crown, the Protestant faith and British culture, in a region of treachery. They were a colonial garrison defending the border between loyalty and perfidy, civilization and barbarism, heresy and godliness, Britishness and Gaelicness, a border they have believed themselves to be defending ever since.

Plantation had several profound consequences. First, despite a long tradition in which Ireland had blended peoples from different regions and cultures, even previous colonial plantations, *these* arrivals drove a permanent wedge through the religious, political and cultural life of Irish society. Instead of succumbing to the familiar process of assimilation, both native and settler communities clung tenaciously to their separate identities, and so society became segregated. Second, despite the original purifying goal of colonial plantation, the Catholic Irish were never completely driven from their land. The result was a jumbled pattern of settlement, where settler and native communities found themselves living side by side and in some cases literally street by street. Such close proximity was compounded, for the settlers, by the numerical superiority of the native Catholic population. Instead of drowning Catholicism, as was intended, the plantation of Protestants gave them no more than a light dowsing. Thus settlers not only lived amongst their enemy but were outnumbered by them. A nervous defensiveness amongst the settlers was born of these geographical and demographic realities.

The failure of plantation to create peace and harmony was evident in the frequent escalation of tensions between the two communities into sectarian violence. In 1641, 1650, 1688–1689 and again during the revolt of 1798, against a backdrop of political instability in Britain, royal intrigue and attempts by the Irish Parliament to assert its power, inter-communal tension intensified into full-blown insurrection and sectarian bloodshed. Dispossessed Catholics in Ulster turned on their Protestant neighbours in a violent attempt to reclaim their land. Many Protestants were put to the sword, in awful circumstances, though perhaps not as gruesomely as Unionist propagandists have suggested. Whatever the reality, the events were used to embellish a settler representation of Catholics as treacherous, vengeful, covetous of Protestant land and eager to reclaim Ireland for the Pope. A Catholic stereotype entered the Protestant/settler mind-set that has helped to shape Protestant attitudes and define their own identity ever since. In addition, the failure of the insurrections and stories of Protestant resolve provided their own morality tales for future generations of Protestants. The siege of Londonderry of 1689 when a Protestant city stood firm against the forces of Catholic James II and ignored the advice of the Mayor, Lundy, to negotiate with the king was one such morality tale in which resistance, hardship and death were preferred to surrender. This furnished the Protestant/settler identity with a triumphalism, a steely fortitude and a sense of mission about resisting the Catholic hordes.

But it was not only the Catholic threat that shaped Unionism, for religious penalization was also a policy applied by Westminster against the dissenting Presbyterians. Though born of the same doctrinal mother, the radical independence of Presbyterianism and other dissenting sects made them suspect in the eyes of Anglicans (though not heretical as with Catholics), so warranting a degree of religious control and limitation by the state. Marginalized by their co-religionists on mainland Britain and deeply mistrustful of their Catholic neighbours, the Presbyterians of Ulster learnt early on the lesson of self-reliance and 'ourselves alone'. Their nervous defensiveness now combined with a siege mentality and an independent spirit to craft an identity clearly recognizable within today's Unionist communities. It was an identity sensitive to threat from within and from without, that craved security and was determined to maintain a constant vigil against the hostility of allies, the cowardice of comrades and the treachery of their Catholic neighbours.

> **"An easy-going, moderate approach was thought preferable to over-control from Westminster for keeping Ireland quiet"**

The bloodletting of the seventeenth century gave way during the eighteenth century to a relatively peaceful balance between the Anglican elite, the Catholic majority and the Presbyterian communities of the north-east. An easy-going, moderate approach was thought preferable to over-control from Westminster for keeping Ireland quiet. Economic progress, increased trade, rising investment, urban growth and agricultural change brought a degree of social contentment that was reflected in a swelling Catholic middle class and a diminution of communal tensions. One might have been momentarily forgiven for thinking that peace had finally arrived in Ireland. But all changed rapidly thereafter. The American Wars of

Independence and the outbreak of war against Revolutionary France (1793–1815) unleashed powerful ideological, economic and political pressures that injected instability into Irish society. Initially this instability found expression not in communal or sectarian conflict but in a flowering of republican sentiment with a rising of the politically and socially disenfranchized in 1798. It sought an Irish Republic that would break the links with Britain and, in the words of one of its leaders, Wolfe Tone, 'substitute the common name of Irishman in place of the denominations of Protestant, Catholic and Dissenter (Presbyterian)'.[5] Reality proved somewhat different as the rebellion slid into a sectarian bloodbath. Ancient grievances and long-nurtured prejudices resurfaced in an atmosphere of collapsed authority and revolt. Catholics and Protestants once again turned on each other with a great deal of violence, the destruction of property, the seizing of lands and attacks upon churches, a spasm of outrage matched only by the brutality with which Britain repressed it.

For Catholics, the events of 1798 fit snugly within their ancestral rhythms of grievance and subjugation by the British, and created a whole new cast of martyrs to be venerated and aped by future generations. Pre-eminent amongst the handful of such worthies was Wolfe Tone, whose suicide while he sat rotting in jail awaiting execution was constructed into a David versus Goliath tale of a man willing to make the ultimate sacrifice as a noble gesture of heroic defiance against a stronger foe. For Unionists, the events of 1798 fell comfortably within an established discourse of Catholic treachery and rapacity, so fortifying their need for eternal vigilance and security. For the British, 1798 reinforced all their prejudices about the Catholics as innately untrustworthy, sectarian and traitorous, and their strategic concerns about Ireland following French landings on the western coast in 1796 and again in 1799. Events also pointed to the bankruptcy of their own policies for creating long-term stability in Ireland. Plantation, coercion and penalization of the seventeenth and early eighteenth centuries were designed to eradicate disloyalty but in fact had merely added to a Catholic sense of grievance. On the other hand, the more moderate, balanced outlook of the late eighteenth century, though generating short-term peace, had only a limited impact in creating support for the British connection amongst the opinion-forming Catholic middle class and was always vulnerable to basic religious differences, as events of 1798 revealed.

THE ACT OF UNION, 1801–1886

Britain now turned to a policy of more direct rule for Ireland, hoping to create that illusive peace and stability from enlightened and modernizing administration. In the Act of Union of 1801 the British government took command of Ireland's affairs. Her Parliament was shut and its representatives moved to Westminster, the Church of Ireland was joined to the Church of England and her taxation and financial systems were harmonized with Britain. For the Protestant ascendancy, though denied their political independence, union did at least offer a powerful bulwark against what it imagined as the implacably disloyal and covetous Catholic masses. Even Presbyterians, no friend of Anglicanism, could recognize the defensive value of union as a pan-Protestant alliance within the UK, that once and for all would inhibit Catholic ambitions. Ironically, Catholics were initially sympathetic to the new arrangement, happy to be rid of the overtly sectarian ascendancy Parliament. But Britain's failure to accompany intervention with policies to end discrimination and to emancipate Catholics quickly lost the new regime their support (miscalculations the British would repeat in 1969, having deployed the Army in Northern Ireland). Not until 1829 did the British begin to address discrimination against Catholics, by which time they were already thoroughly sceptical about the value of union. By such means, the union came to define Irish politics, dividing supporters from opponents, Unionists from Repealers or Unionists from Nationalists. By falling along established religious fault-lines within Irish society, political loyalties added a further and extremely powerful (indeed dominant) layer to community separation. Politics, therefore, became a matter less of individual preference, or class distinction, or even regional preference than of communal and religious endorsement. In Ireland, politics became something more than just politics.

Despite this, British governments during the nineteenth century were increasingly aware that to make union work and so bring peace and stability to Ireland, sections of the Catholic community had to be accommodated. This meant reforms in education, the tithe, land holdings and tenants' rights, the poor law, the electoral system, and to the structures and finances of the Anglican and Catholic churches. It also meant trying to govern impartially, holding the ring between the different religious factions. Unfortunately, many Catholics never forgot it was a Protestant hand that held the ring, especially when horrors such as the Great Famine appeared to draw an indifferent response from the British government, with even the 'whiff' of smugness from officials at what looked like for some the just deserts for centuries of disloyalty and heresy. And later during the agrarian crisis of 1879–1882 the image of harsh Protestant landlords, backed up by the British authorities in the protection of property, suggested that her governance was unavoidably partial. For Catholics this perpetuated and confirmed a long-held representation of British rule as oppressive, with the union simply the latest technique in a long line of British attempts to control, limit and subjugate Ireland.

What made this all the more dangerous for the British, from the early nineteenth century onwards, was that this perceived legacy of persecution and oppression was politicized into the language of national self-determination currently in vogue amongst liberationist movements across Europe. Nationalism came to Ireland and found within the Catholic culture a rich seam of ancient myths and folk memories that could be galvanized into an historic right for Ireland to rule itself – a belief that Ireland's resources, her aspirations and her potential could be best realized under a government elected and run by her own people. So potent was this appeal that from the 1860s Nationalism was able to mobilize such large numbers of Catholics of all classes behind a Home Rule political party that from 1880 returned between 80 and 86 of Ireland's 104 representatives to Westminster. It appeared by the early 1880s that far from stabilizing Anglo-Irish relations, 70 years of union had generated a strong, confident Catholic Nationalist constituency that looked to its 80-odd Parliamentary representatives to win some form of self-rule from Britain. Other Nationalists held less faith that Britain would ever satisfy their national claims, preferring instead to place their hopes on driving the British from Ireland. Through physical force – acts such as dynamiting, assassination, 'ale-house' risings and various assaults on the symbols of British power – this tradition received periodic homage from a number of different groups, from Young Irelanders of the 1840s, Fenians from the 1850s onwards and the Invincibles of the 1870s.

> ❝ While impartial British government proved to be a contradiction in terms for Nationalists, for Unionists impartiality threatened the very purpose and rationale of union ❞

While impartial British government proved to be a contradiction in terms for Nationalists, for Unionists impartiality threatened the very purpose and rationale of union. For them there was little point accommodating Catholics or Nationalists since history showed they were inherently perfidious. Reforms to ease their plight would not placate them but simply encourage Nationalists to 'up their demands' and so bring the nightmarish vision of an independent Ireland that bit closer. For Unionists, an independent Ireland left them at the mercy of those who in 1641 slaughtered their kin and stole their land, who in 1688–1689 sided with the traitorous James II and who in 1798 turned on their neighbours. An independent Ireland would place political power into the hands of their enemies, the Catholic majority and their Catholic representatives. This in turn would endanger Protestant property, threaten Ireland's position within the British Empire and place their Protestant faith under the domination of the Catholic Church, which would limit their freedom of worship and religious expression. The prospect of such consequences made union for Unionists not something you could be partial about; it was a social, economic and religious imperative, 'a psychological necessity'.[6] Hence they regarded British attempts to accommodate the 'disloyal' as

acts of weakness and folly, suspecting that the British establishment held an increasingly flexible attitude towards union. For
the British, Unionists thought, union was simply a means to
ensure national security, religious toleration, economic benefit
and political stability. If these could be established or preserved
by other means, perhaps even by a degree of self-rule for Ireland,
then union was expendable. Unionists began to feel they faced
the open treachery of Nationalists and the concealed treason of
a British government.

It was clear, then, that by the 1870s the basic topography of
Irish politics seemed well established. The majority generally
aligned behind a Catholic, Nationalist and Gaelic position,
while the minority configured to a Protestant, Unionist and
British attitude. At moments, as with the years 1895–1905, this
binary could appear weak and even open to attempts to find
common ground, echoing the earlier eighteenth-century period
of moderation and balance. But the basic division never disappeared. Given this environment it could hardly be claimed that
union had lived up to its name or established the same degree
of stability and unanimity as the union with Scotland and
Wales. It had not delivered political stability or social contentment. It had simply provided a mechanism for managing the
various problems in Ireland – and a rather ineffective mechanism at that – not a method for resolving them.

HOME RULE, 1886–1918

The British Prime Minister William Gladstone responded to
these deficiencies in the union with a policy of Home Rule for
Ireland in 1886. It aimed to refashion the union in a direction
more likely to transform the stubbornly disgruntled majority of
the Irish population into loyal members of the empire, by
devolving power from Westminster to an all-Ireland Assembly.
Long-term peace and stability between the two countries would
be more effectively secured through trust and self-reliance than
from the firm control of her affairs from London. The Irish
assembly would remain subordinate to the authority of the
British Parliament, thus safeguarding minority groups from

discriminatory or confiscatory legislation, though Unionists saw little safeguard here and believed Westminster would always back down in the face of Irish resistance – a calculation that proved accurate when it came to Britain not intervening at least until 1972 in a Unionist-dominated Northern Ireland. Gladstone justified his sudden endorsement of Home Rule on the grounds of majoritarian consent, 'the will of the people', as registered at the general election of 1885, when the Nationalist party won 85 Irish seats – though, coincidentally, this was exactly the number he needed at the time to gain a majority in the Commons and to form a government. So was born the Liberal-Nationalist alliance, a 'union of hearts', that helped keep the question of Home Rule for Ireland at the centre of British politics for the next 40 years.

For Unionists, Gladstone's recommendation of Home Rule amounted to naked treachery. The union was being bartered and sold by a British government on the altar of domestic political calculation. They believed Home Rule was not a means to make union work more effectively but an irreversible step to independence. And regardless of the support it won from the majority of Irish voters, they were determined to destroy it. For this they could draw upon 20-odd Unionist MPs, a small but highly vocal unit. In the Lords, still with the power to veto legislation, Unionist Peers as well as most of England's peerage were Unionist to a man; should a Home Rule bill ever get to the upper house, they were prepared. Unionists retained local influence and financial power throughout Ireland, enabling them to marshal press support and fund loyalist committees. They also drew assistance from the Conservative Party, which was eager for a cause to break the Liberal stranglehold over government and whose reverence for Empire, the Anglican Church, the integrity of the UK and national security made them obvious allies. It was no coincidence that in 1886 the Tories became the Conservative and Unionist Party of Great Britain.

It is a moot point whether Gladstone's Home Rule plan would have set Britain and Ireland along a trajectory of long-term stability, close co-operation and mutual advantage. The course of the subsequent 40 years (and indeed well beyond that) certainly give it the feel of a missed opportunity. But if indeed it was such a moment, then in 1886 few shared Gladstone's foresight. Powerful obstacles lay in his path, not least within his own party, where 93 MPs rejected Home Rule and joined the Tories and Unionists to defeat it, a decision that was subsequently endorsed by the British voting public who threw Gladstone out of government in July 1886. In 1893, Gladstone introduced another Home Rule bill and although his party this time remained united, the bill foundered amidst the massed Unionist ranks in the House of Lords. To have missed the turning for Damascus twice was too much for him and he retired in 1894. With the domination of government by the Tories from 1886 until 1906, the Union appeared safe for the foreseeable future.

❝It was no coincidence that in 1886 the Tories became the Conservative and Unionist Party of Great Britain❞

Yet Home Rule did not die with Gladstone. In Ireland the Nationalist party remained dominant and returned substantial pro-Home Rule majorities at election after election. For Nationalists, their legitimate claims to self-rule were being frustrated and the will of the Irish majority ignored, though because Ireland was part of the UK, British governments denied that Irish will had majority status since the UK as a whole had voted for union. The Liberal Party also retained a sentimental attachment to the cause, though given they were out of government until 1906 (apart from the brief period 1892–1895), they could do little to further this sentiment. Indeed, it was not until after the 1910 general election that they were in a position to seriously consider another Home Rule bill, with their government's reliance upon the 86 Nationalists. Ironically, given the fate of the two previous Home Rule bills, the prospects of the third one, once the Prime Minister Asquith finally introduced it in 1912, were rather good. The Liberal government had a substantial and stable majority in the Commons, while the House of Lords had lost their power to veto legislation in 1911, preventing a replay of 1893. Moreover, the Tories were in a fractious and divided state, many uninterested in Irish affairs or, worse, willing to grant a degree of self-rule under the euphemism of federalism. British public opinion was well and truly sick of Irish issues and it was thought unlikely that the public would rally against a government that legislated Home Rule: if anything, finally removing the 'Irish Question' from British politics could well have gained votes. If any moment in Britain and Ireland's long and bloody past seemed propitious for the grant of a degree of self-governance, it was the early 1900s as a period of calm, peace and relative prosperity.

Of course, the Unionists in Ulster saw things differently, believing peace and prosperity were reasons why Home Rule should not be brought in. Yet Unionists were never happier than when their backs were to the wall and they were facing a formidable opposition. Moments of danger, whether real or imagined, seemed to unlock their sense of purpose and being, and the moment in 1912 certainly bristled with historic resonance and echoes of ancient struggles. As Asquith geared himself for a third attempt at Home Rule, the Unionists in Ulster steeled themselves to remain 'under the Union Jack' and resist inclusion into a Catholic-dominated, Home Rule Ireland. It was 1688 or 1798 all over again, though with one very significant difference: the Protestant/Unionist cause would now be primarily fought by the Unionists of Ulster. Ulster as opposed to all-Ireland Unionism had acquired a clearer sense of its own identity and political power during the course of the late nineteenth century. This growing distinctiveness was born of the demographic concentration of Protestants in Ulster's nine counties, though most heavily condensed into four, unlike Unionists in the rest of Ireland who were scattered and isolated. This furnished Unionism in Ulster with a regional power base, organized from 1905 through the Ulster Unionist Council, that was able to sustain a political presence of approximately 18 Westminster MPs. This political presence was enhanced by a settler mentality of inflexibility and self-reliance, rooted in a version of their past as one of dogged survival and 'epic' endurance, against the grasping designs of an Irish, Nationalist, Catholic majority. Together, regional political power and communal heritage combined explosively from 1912 onwards in a campaign of resistance to Home Rule.

Given their relative numerical weakness within Parliament and without the veto powers of the House of Lords to fall back on, the Ulster Unionist leaders took their campaign onto the streets and into the village halls of Ulster. Here they organized hundreds of petitions, meetings and large set-piece rallies. At one such rally, thousands of Unionists signed a Solemn League and Covenant, a contract to defeat Home Rule 'by all means necessary', in order to convey to the British government the intensity of their outrage at the prospect of residing under a Home Rule Parliament. Their leaders spoke of repelling Home Rule, of not paying taxes, of ignoring the new assembly and, if need be, repulsing a British army sent to coerce them into it. To make good their pledge they made plans for a provisional government and raised a paramilitary army, the Ulster Volunteer Force (UVF), that by spring 1914 was openly drilling some 100,000 volunteers, and with many units well armed after guns were imported from Germany on the evening of 24–25 April 1914. Ulster's was a 'patriotic' rebellion, taking arms against the government to stay *within* the UK and the British Empire, yet it was every bit as treasonable as Wolfe Tone's of 1798 or the Fenian rising of 1867. For here was a minority looking to dictate terms to the Irish majority and in defiance of British Parliamentary government, with a leader, Sir Edward Carson, similarly courting infamy and martyrdom by brash declarations to fight to save Ireland from Home Rule. These declarations were making themselves felt by the autumn of 1913 as certain ministers in the Liberal government began to contemplate a degree of autonomy for the Ulstermen or even partitioning Ulster from the rest of Ireland as a way out of the crisis. Partition, many felt, would give Nationalists three-quarters of their goal, while for Unionists, aware that all of Ireland could no longer be saved for the union, it might at least 'save' those parts where they enjoyed a high concentration of support and a degree of political power.

So by 1914 the contours to a possible political settlement in Ireland were slowly becoming visible. On the one hand, the

> **Ulster's was a 'patriotic' rebellion, taking arms against the government to stay *within* the UK and the British Empire**

grant of self-government for Ireland, on the basis of Home Rule, looked inevitable; indeed in September 1914 it was put on the statute books before being suspended for the duration of World War One. But so, too, did some type of separate treatment for Ulster Unionists, who had successfully bulldozed their claims into the debate on Ireland's future, while quietly acknowledging that little could be done to save their compatriots in the rest of Ireland. These competing claims came into sharper relief at the Buckingham Palace Conference of July 1914, when leaders of the Nationalist and Ulster Unionist parties, as well as Liberals and Tories, met to discuss the situation in Ireland. At the conference, discussion centred on the details of a compromise, not upon the issue of Home Rule itself, and revolved around what precise form of separate treatment a compromise solution might take. The government preferred some form of local autonomy for the Ulstermen within a united Ireland, 'Home Rule within Home Rule', a solution the Nationalists also begrudgingly accepted. The Ulstermen demanded the permanent exclusion of the 'loyal' north from a Home Rule Ireland, something Nationalists would not accept. Beyond these immediate difficulties, separate treatment for Ulster raised other questions. Would an excluded north be fully integrated under Westminster or have a devolved Home Rule assembly of its own or would it be fully independent? Where was the partition cut to be made and according to what criteria: ethnic location, religion, geography, historic borders or political support? And what would happen to those Nationalists and Unionists who found themselves on the wrong side of the divide, residing in an alien political unit and desiring linkage with the other part? Politicians on all sides realized passionate struggles lay ahead on these and other knotty questions and were probably relieved to be dragged into the Great War at the beginning of August.

War forced the Irish question onto the political backburner and suspended any decision on its future until the end of hostilities. For Nationalists this looked like another example of Irish claims sacrificed to British self-interest and a 'sell-out' to the Unionists, raising again the whole question of British impartiality in its approach towards the different groups in Ireland. The fact that the War Office refused to allow the early flood of recruits from southern Ireland to be called the Irish Brigade, whereas UVF recruits took the label the Ulster Division, further fuelled the idea that Nationalists would never get fair, equal treatment from a British government. The perception of Britain constantly frustrating Nationalist aims prompted a small clique of radical republicans, revolutionary socialists and militant Gaelic revivalists, led by Patrick Pearse, to take the initiative by seizing the centre of Dublin at Easter in 1916 and declaring themselves the provisional government of an *all* Ireland Republic. In this they drew their inspiration from the Ulstermen, who had demonstrated that a British government listened hardest and ceded more with a gun at its head. The rebels also believed their action would shake Ireland from its present state of torpor. Unfortunately most Irish people were rather happy with their state of torpor. And the only thing shaken was central Dublin, much of which now lay in ruins. Moreover, the needless death of 450 soldiers, young rebels and innocent civilians generated for the rebels not admiration but resentment and contempt. As with the Ulstermen, so again with the 1916 rebels – a minority was trying to impose its wishes onto the majority by hijacking Irish affairs, and, as would become clear, doing it reasonably successfully. Though few could see it at the time, the Rising provided the pretext for a dramatic transformation in the whole situation and a shift in the tone and direction of Nationalism.

66 The rebellion itself went the way of other symbolic if futile Republican gestures, towards irrelevance and oblivion 99

The rebellion itself went the way of other symbolic if futile Republican gestures, towards irrelevance and oblivion. However, thanks to the British counter-reaction that involved harsh measures to re-impose law and order, including martial law, curfews, road-blocks, limits on public meetings, stop and searches and a host of small 'needling' inconveniences, Irish opinion was sufficiently irritated and alienated to turn its resentment for the rebel action into sympathy and even admiration. The execution of 15 leaders, in particular, looked for many like acts of spite rather than necessity, while mass arrests dragged in the innocent and the uninvolved, for whom several months of prison turned into committed and hardened rebels. Nationalist opinion, already frustrated at delays to the implementation of Home Rule and what looked like the pro-Unionist leanings of the British government, now felt the 'whole community' basis to many of the punishments by the military smacked of teaching the traitorous Irish a lesson. When the military authorities then moved to introduce conscription in Ireland early in 1918, the alienation of the Nationalist community from the British was all but complete and registered itself in growing support for Sinn Fein, a once obscure extreme Nationalist group that until 1916 had resided on the margins of Irish politics.

The British authorities had, then, by their actions in the aftermath of 1916 helped to re-invigorate Nationalism into a more determined, martial and less soporific force. Ancient myths of English oppression and Ireland's eternal struggle for national 'freedom' were given life and resonance by events. The sacrifice of Pearse was placed in 'apostolic succession' to other Irish leaders such as Tone who had paid the ultimate price for challenging the British, so fitting 1916 into an unbroken and unalterable thread of resistance running through Ireland's past. What Conor Cruise O'Brien refers to as Ireland's 'ancestral voices' found a ready response from another young generation of Irish men and women.[7] However, Ireland's ancestral voices were also heard on the other side of the communal and political divide. For while Dublin smouldered in the wake of the Rising, thousands of Ulstermen made their own 'blood sacrifice' during the opening salvoes of the Somme offensive. Coming just months after the Easter Rising it underlined in a most dramatic way not only the extent of their own loyalty but the disloyalty of the Catholic Nationalist community. The death of so many young UVF men in the service of the British Empire left a deep mark upon the tightly knit Ulster Unionist community and created their own 'dead generation' whose memory could not be tarnished through betrayal and surrender. And such a sacrifice, so many believed, meant that no British government could now force Ulster into a united Ireland.

PARTITION, TRUCE AND TREATY, 1918–1921

The Great War left Ireland more politically polarized than at any time since the late eighteenth century, a polarization registered by the general election of December 1918 where of the 105 seats available, Ulster Unionism scooped 25 (so doubling its representation), while militant Nationalism, under the banner of Sinn Fein, gained 73, reducing the once all-powerful Nationalist Party to just six seats. The result in the south and west created a stand-off between Sinn Fein and the British, with Sinn Fein willing to accept nothing less than a republic, a demand the British government would never grant despite the overwhelming backing for it from the Irish electorate. Such rigidity on both sides guaranteed that the crisis would evolve into some type of military option in order to break the logjam. Before mid-1920 that military struggle amounted to little more than small, localized assaults by groups of Republicans, styling themselves the Irish Republican Army (IRA), who undertook isolated assassinations, symbolic acts of defiance, intimidation, beatings and 'sniping'. However, events soon escalated towards a more orthodox guerrilla engagement, with the IRA perfecting techniques for ambushing British Army patrols, the disruption of communications, the destruction of property (especially isolated police stations), the intimidation of tax officials and the rooting out of pro-British elements in local communities, what the IRA termed 'spies and informers'. Victory would be achieved through simple survival, by rendering Ireland ungovernable and so making it too costly for the British to stay, not through defeating its substantially larger forces.

The government met republican guerrilla warfare in kind. Although it claimed to be fighting a 'policeman's war', its methods pointed to a classic counter-insurgency campaign, including counter-terror tactics (such as the infamous Black & Tans), official reprisals, motorized patrols, tight restrictions on movement, curfews and martial law over large parts of the south and west. The irony was that such methods destroyed what little moderate Irish opinion still existed, which in turn fortified the position of Sinn Fein and strengthened the demand for a republic. Rigour and intransigence in Ireland rarely rebound with favour onto a British government (a 'rule of thumb' Mrs Thatcher characteristically ignored during the prisons protest of the early 1980s). Counter-terror tactics also raised both domestic and international condemnation, particularly the American and Dominion opinion they had hoped to mobilize against Sinn Fein. Condemnation forced the government to blunt the full intensity of its military campaign, but that in turn ruled out ever achieving an outright victory against the IRA. In other words, the British were increasingly caught between a rock and a hard place, unable to prosecute the 'war' to the full and yet still sufficiently brutal to alienate Irish opinion.

Developments in the north between the Ulster Unionists and the government followed a very different course. The 25 Ulster Unionists elected at the 1918 election took up their seats in Parliament and became a vocal and influential body of opinion to speak and advise upon Irish matters. They were all the more influential since they were the only representatives from Ireland, given Sinn Fein's decision to abstain from Westminster and convene its representatives as an independent assembly, the Dáil Eireann. While consistent in terms of principle, Sinn Fein effectively left the expression of Irish 'opinion' to the Ulster Unionist contingent and under the guidance of Sir James Craig they used it to bolster their position. The appointment in 1919 of the strongly Unionist Walter Long to chair the Cabinet's Irish Committee was an early indication that Unionists had the ear of the government, a government that in any case was dominated by sympathetic Tories under the more than sympathetic Bonar Law. That said, when Long and the committee announced their findings, they favoured a federal solution to the Irish question, with the province of Ulster having its own regional parliament within a wider Irish federal state, occupying a position analogous to an American state and the federal capi-

> 66 The British were increasingly caught between a rock and a hard place, unable to prosecute the 'war' to the full and yet still sufficiently brutal to alienate Irish opinion 99

tal of Washington. Craig was quick to show his disapproval for this, informing Long that a federalist structure was unacceptable since it still gave a southern government based in Dublin with power and influence over Ulster. Moreover his preferred choice was not all nine Ulster counties since that would contain too many Catholics but a more manageable six counties with a clear Protestant majority.

If the government had been tempted to make a stand against the Ulster Unionists over this, events on the ground in the north convinced the Prime Minister Lloyd George otherwise. From April 1920 sectarian violence escalated steadily in the province, reaching its usual summer apogee in attacks upon Catholic workers in the Belfast shipyards and communal rioting in Londonderry. The rise of violence reflected, as it often would in Northern Ireland, a growing sense of insecurity amongst Unionists bred of a concern for their future status and position. As an immediate and initially temporary remedy, the British government authorized the creation of a Special Constabulary, drawn largely from the old UVF, that was organized and deployed by late 1920. But what was really needed to calm anxieties was some form of political settlement and that finally came in December 1920 with the Government of Ireland Act, better known as the Partition Act. The Act created two Home Rule Parliaments, one for the 26 counties of the south and west, the other for six of Ulster's counties. The latter would take the title 'the Northern Ireland Assembly' and consisted of 52 seats from which a Northern Ireland Executive would be selected. Elections to the new assemblies would be held in May 1921 and opened the following month, although in the end only the northern Parliament was opened since Sinn Fein refused to convene themselves as a British-created Home Rule Assembly.

Home Rule was not the favoured option of either the Unionists or Sinn Fein, so it was far from clear whether the government's offer of such to both would succeed. Laffan writes, 'Nationalist Ireland was no longer being denied what it no longer wanted, while Unionist Ulster would be forced to accept what it had always opposed'.[8] After all, the Unionist intention had been to defeat Home Rule and to remain firmly under the Westminster Parliament. In addition, devolved power, though leaving Parliament with the right to intervene in affairs and even the right to reverse devolution, did project a sense of difference that Ulster though British was not *that* British and was actually a place slightly apart. On the other hand, devolved government did at least provide Unionists with a degree of security, and perhaps more realistically Craig recognized it as possibly the best deal they were likely to get. Indeed, six-county Home Rule for the north represented a 'firming up' in the definition of separate treatment, beyond what had been discussed at the Buckingham Palace conference in 1914 and the Irish Committees' initial ideas for a federalist structure. Given these advantages the Ulster Unionist Council voted to support the measure, though aware that in doing so they were deserting Unionists in the Ulster counties of Cavan, Monaghan and Donegal. Having taken the decision, Ulster Unionists set about preparing for the elections to the new assembly in May 1921 where, against a backdrop of deepening inter-communal violence, they captured 40 of the 52 seats, with the old Nationalist party taking six and Sinn Fein taking the remaining six. Unionists would now dominate the government of Northern Ireland, with Sir James Craig, architect of the 1912–1914 resistance to Home Rule, selected to become Northern Ireland's first Prime Minister and indeed the first Irish leader of a Home Rule parliament.

Unionist dominance did not bring unalloyed joy to the British government. It raised the reality of institutionalized sectarianism, something the government had been aware of and had tried to limit by insisting elections at both a local and regional level were by proportional representation and included a clause outlawing religious intolerance and discrimination. But looking further ahead Britain realized that the best course would be for north and south to weld back together into some type of close relationship, which she sought to facilitate by including in the Act a Council of Ireland. The Council of Ireland would be composed of representatives from both north and south that over time might become the institutional vehicle or focus for a united Ireland. Its inclusion reflected the British government's belief that the best guard against possible sectarian or irredentist tendencies developing in either the new northern or new southern polity was to ensure a broad and varied religious and cultural mix that could be achieved only by uniting both parts. Partition, therefore, was not to be a permanent solution but a temporary palliative, a necessary 'quick fix' to take the anger and poison out of the immediate political situation, with the hope that co-operation and coalescence would occur in the future. So when George V opened the new assembly in Belfast in June 1921, the irony was that the government hoped it might not last for ever.

Indeed, George V hinted as much in his speech that day in which he implored both north and south, as well as Irish and English, to extend the hand of friendship to each other and heal old wounds. In the circumstances of 1921 there was little likelihood of this happening between the north and south, even if it was clear whose southern hand was to be grasped. On the other hand, George V's speech did provide the pretext for an attempt to break the stalemate between Britain and Sinn Fein, with Lloyd George using the king's call for friendship to make tentative overtures to Eamon de Valera, President of Sinn Fein and of the Dáil, that from July resulted in a truce between the two sides. However, moving from cease-fire to agreement was never going to be easy. For one, it quickly became evident that despite a year and a half of military engagement, both sides still stood a long way apart. The British government remained resolute against a republic, while Sinn Fein declared it would accept nothing else. Moreover, violence had weaned hardmen for whom compromise meant a betrayal of dead comrades and venerated ideals. It was clear that an agreement under such conditions would require a Herculean effort. Nevertheless, several key reassessments did seem to point politicians in the right direction. The British military, by 1921, understood that the 'war' could not be won without flooding

> 66 When George V opened the new assembly in Belfast in June 1921, the irony was that the government hoped it might not last for ever 99

Ireland with troops, a costly enterprise in terms of money and lives and something neither public opinion nor the parsimonious Treasury would tolerate. At the same time Irish Republicans realized their low-intensity engagement could never defeat the British, and indeed it was doubtful whether they could sustain any type of engagement for much longer. With both sides exhausted, demoralized and weary of fighting, the military option had all but driven itself into the sand by 1921, leaving politics as the only course open to either side to achieve its ends.

However, soldiers and ideologues do not (generally) make good politicians, and unfortunately by the summer of 1921 there were plenty of each on both sides. What was needed to ease the process of bargaining and concession were pragmatic, flexible, even rather 'slippery' individuals. Ones who could comfortably retreat from fixed positions, who would settle for the obtainable rather than the desirable, and who would risk a great deal to surmount the initial and most forbidding hurdle of actually making an agreement. Luckily, at this crucial moment such leaders emerged on both sides. Lloyd George, Winston Churchill and Lord Birkenhead, for the British, all of whom would have cheerfully sold their grandmothers for political advantage. For the Irish, Arthur Griffith was a known moderate and Michael Collins, the de facto leader of Irish Republicanism, was also, thankfully, a hard-headed realist. The slipperiest of them all, Eamon de Valera, leader of Sinn Fein and President of the (yet unrealized) Irish Republic, stayed at home to re-invent himself as a die-hard republican. With such men locked in discussion during the autumn of 1921, a victory for the pragmatists over the ideologues was finally achieved with the signing of the Treaty on 6 December 1921.

The Treaty was a compromise between the Irish demands for a self-governing republic and the various imperial, security and symbolic requirements of the British. The Irish emerged with Dominion-style government over the 26 southern counties, called an Irish Free State to disguise what it was in all but name and symbolism: an independent republic. Britain withdrew, bringing to an end her formal involvement in Ireland, though keeping the south loosely within the Empire, along with a few naval installations. Peace it seemed had finally arrived in Ireland.

NOTES

1   A. T. Q. Stewart, *The Narrow Ground* (Faber, 1977) p 12.

2   D. G. Boyce and A. O'Day (eds) *The Making of Modern Irish History: Revisionism and the Revisionist Debate* (Routledge, 1996) p 217.

3   J. C. Beckett, *The Making of Modern Ireland, 1603–1923* (Faber, 1966) p 13.

4   R. Foster, *Modern Ireland, 1600–1972* (Penguin, 1988) p 211; also S. Farren and R. F. Mulvihill, *Paths to a Settlement in Northern Ireland* (Colin Smythe, 2000) p 3.

5   R. Kearney, *Postnationalist Ireland; Politics, Culture and Philosophy* (Routledge, 1997) p 30.

6   R. Foster, 'Anglo-Irish relations and Northern Ireland: historical perspectives', in D. Keogh and M. Haltzel (eds) *Northern Ireland and the Politics of Reconciliation* (CUP, 1993) p 20.

7   C. C. O'Brien, *Ancestral Voices: Religion and Nationalism in Ireland* (Poolbeg, 1994).

8   M. Laffan, *The Resurrection of Ireland: The Sinn Fein Party, 1917–1923* (CUP, 1999) p 333.

3

BRITAIN AND NORTHERN IRELAND, 1920–1968

'that Norman, Ken and Sidney signalled Prod,
And Seamus (call me Sean) was sure-fire Pape.
O Land of password, handgrip, wink and nod,
Of open minds as open as a trap,

Where tongues lie coiled, as under flames lie wicks,
Where half of us, as in a wooden horse
Were cabin'd and confined like wily Greeks,
Besieged within the siege, whispering mores'

Seamus Heaney, *Whatever You Say Say Nothing* in North
(Faber, 1975)

THREATS AND DANGERS, 1920–1922

FOR MANY, THE PARTITION OF IRELAND IN 1920 and then the Treaty with the south in 1921 had finally solved the Irish Question. Achieving a settlement had been far from painless and had involved many sacrifices on all sides. Yet to most informed observers the problem of satisfying the conflicting claims of British Imperialism, Irish Nationalism and Ulster Unionism, which had dogged governments since the 1880s, if not before, appeared resolved. Unfortunately what looked like the end of a tragic story was actually just the start of another bitter chapter. For events on both sides of the newly crafted border suggested forecasts of 'closure' were premature. In the Irish Free State many Nationalists felt so cheated by the fact that a 32-county republic had not been part of the Treaty that they organized into a determined anti-Treaty movement that helped steer Ireland into a bloody civil war by the summer of 1922.

> 66 The strength of this narrative meant the half a million Catholics left inside Northern Ireland could never be regarded by Unionists as anything but a potential menace to the state 99

In the north various pressures and dangers also generated profound instability and threatened the very survival of the fledgling state. So serious and menacing were these threats that for most Unionists the years 1920–1922 became (or were made to resemble) a modern-day siege of Londonderry, the re-enactment of tales learnt at a grandparent's knee about British duplicity and violent Catholic/Nationalist designs.

The most enduring of these tales, of course, was the legend of the 'enemy within', of Catholic neighbours who beneath a façade of quiet co-existence harboured an undying thirst for revenge and recompense that in 1641, 1688–1689, 1798 and 1920–1922, turned violent. The strength of this narrative meant that the half a million Catholics left inside Northern Ireland could never be regarded by Unionists as anything but a potential menace to the state. And perhaps with some reason, for their political loyalties gravitated southwards while they regarded partition and Northern Ireland as little more than illegal British constructs. They wanted unity with the south as their recognized political and cultural homeland, attitudes that simply, then, confirmed long-standing Unionist prejudices about Catholics. It is important to remember, however, that the size of the Catholic presence left behind was the result of Unionist policy. Unionists had wanted a state that was politically viable and internally stable. Arguably a four-county unit would have offered the best chance of this, given a Protestant majority in just four of the nine Ulster counties. Such a cut would have produced what many Unionists desired, which in the words of Sir James Craig was a 'Protestant state for a Protestant people'. But a state of just four counties was thought economically unsustainable and would necessitate the political sacrifice of several hundred thousand Unionists in the remaining five counties of Ulster, including the historic city of Londonderry. These considerations encouraged Unionists to demand a bigger cut from the government upon either a six- or nine-county basis. However, a Northern Irish state based upon all nine counties would have rested upon a perilously narrow Protestant/Catholic ratio of 56/44, leaving the future of Northern Ireland vulnerable to a demographic 'takeover'. Between, then, the threat of demographic change and the shame of sacrificing too many Unionists, Craig saw little alternative to a six-county statelet that guaranteed a 'safer' Protestant/Catholic split of roughly 67/33, though still with large Catholic communities in Londonderry and Belfast as well as Catholic majorities in Fermanagh and Tyrone. Ulster Unionists ditched the Catholic 'heavy' counties of Cavan, Monaghan and Donegal, and in so doing accepted the sell-out of Unionists in these three Ulster counties to their desertion of Unionists in the rest of Ireland. Yet with six counties they at least believed they had a state more economically viable than just four and one with a more stable and permanent Unionist majority than all nine.

In retrospect, however, a six-county state was the worst of all worlds. For the Catholic population left within Northern Ireland was still large enough for Unionists to imagine them a *real* threat (unlike just four), yet small enough to prevent them from *actually* offering any effective resistance to a bullying Unionist government (unlike all nine). It was a case of too large to ignore yet too small to challenge and so fear and instability were embedded into the structure of the state itself. This fear and instability might have receded if the Catholic communities had been accommodated and included within the state itself. This required altering or diminishing their political aspirations, providing equal access to economic, political and social rewards, eradicating discrimination and introducing various cultural and institutional mechanisms to crosscut ethnic differences – what Carson urged on the Northern Ireland state as 'displaying in their acts of government a tolerance, a fairness, and a justice towards all classes and all religions of the community'.[1] Unfortunately, this type of liberal, inclusive and tolerant approach from a Unionist government was probably unlikely at the best of times and in the menacing atmosphere of 1920–1922 almost impossible. Escalating sectarian violence, with the death of 40 over the summer of 1920 and simmering disorder in Londonderry and Belfast, stoked inter-communal suspicion and set the tone for the Northern Ireland regime.

What gave the idea of the 'enemy within' greater immediacy was the enhanced political presence of the Catholic/Nationalist minority as a result of the British insisting upon proportional representation for both local and assembly elections. At the 1920 local government elections, 25 out of the 80 local and county councils returned a Nationalist majority, all of whom subsequently pledged their loyalty to the Dáil. Some results struck at the heart of Unionism. Ulstermen lost 17 seats on Belfast city council, reducing their hold to 35 seats out of 60. Londonderry, a potent symbol of defiance against Catholicism, returned a Catholic majority and elected a Catholic mayor. Nor did Nationalist politicians help the situation when they pledged their council's loyalty to the Dáil, so raising suspicion and further hardening Unionist attitudes. Similarly, the elections to the new Northern Ireland Assembly, in May 1921, though returning a Unionist majority of 40 out of 52 seats, did see six Sinn Feiners and six Nationalists elected, with a combined vote of 165,000 votes or 40 per cent of the poll. Yet by abstaining from involvement in the Northern Ireland Assembly, they not only disempowered 33 per cent of the population and again reinforced Unionist prejudices about Nationalists. Those who rejected the state, so Unionists argued, now deserved little authority or standing within it.

What made these Nationalist electoral performances more dangerous was the steady advance of the Northern Ireland Labour Party and independent activity on the Unionist fringes. These signs of fragmentation within Northern

Unionist politics threatened to undermine the dominance of the Ulster Unionist Party. At the 1920 Belfast city election when 35 'official' Unionists were returned, opposition parties made gains of 13 Labour seats, 10 Nationalists and 2 independent Unionist. This combined total was quite capable of amalgamating into an anti-official Unionist coalition in the future. This drift away from the Ulster Unionist Party was again evident in the 1925 assembly results for Belfast, when the official Unionist share of seats dropped from 15 to 8 while Labour took 3 and independent Unionists 4. For the Ulster Unionist leadership, the enemy within now referred not just to Catholics but to 'aberrant' Protestants who placed class concerns above loyalty to the union.

> ❝ Widespread IRA persecution of Protestants in the south offered a less than felicitous picture of life for Unionists within a future united Ireland ❞

The Unionist concept of the 'enemy within' was given even greater relevance after 1921 by the growing threat from the 'enemy to the south'. Irish Republicanism refused to accept the legitimacy of partition in 1920 or the new Northern Ireland state from 1921, and imagined the north and all its people (including Protestants) as part of a 'seamless', non-sectarian Irish nation, artificially divided to protect British political, economic and strategic interests. Unfortunately, rather than gently woo the north back, Republicans sought to bludgeon them into a united Ireland, methods that badly misunderstood (or disregarded) the history and mentality of Ulster Unionists. Republican rhetoric 'demanded' the north as of right and in terms that dismissed Unionism as illegitimate and irrelevant. As evidence of this the Dáil chose to simply ignore the new Northern Irish government by paying the salaries of Catholic school teachers in the north. It also imposed an economic boycott on goods and materials from the north, to hit back at Unionist violence and weaken the state. Moreover, widespread IRA persecution of Protestants in the south offered a less than felicitous picture of life for Unionists within a future united Ireland. In County Cork, for example, where Protestants formed just 7 per cent of the population, they accounted for 34 per cent of civilians shot by the IRA and 85 per cent of those burned out of their homes. Sectarian violence was not limited to just one side of the border, reinforcing a Unionist determination to resist unification with the south.

Unionist anxieties deepened with intensification of the IRA campaign in the north from 1921. It was aimed at protecting northern Catholics and destabilizing the new state through the destruction of roads, bridges and telegraph wires, bombing Unionist businesses, assassinating police, attacking government offices and kidnapping local politicians, and was most intense along the newly created border. The campaign also looked to influence London by convincing the British that the northern state was non-viable. Here again was that familiar Irish strategy of combining military threat with political pressure, something perfected by the Ulstermen between 1912 and 1914 and applied by Sinn Fein during the 1980s and 1990s. The immediate result of these actions, then as in the 1990s, was simply to heighten Unionist apprehension, so that the Unionists in turn directed their ire against those they thought responsible or at least complicit: the Catholic community. Loyalist paramilitary groups, such as the Ulster Protestant Volunteers, emerged to spearhead sectarian attacks in the name of defending their community. Of the 557 people killed between July 1920 and July 1922, well over half, 303, were Catholic. The same period witnessed 10,000 Catholics expelled from their jobs, and 23,000 driven from their homes, by Unionists looking to impose a degree of control and uniformity over the mixed, jumbled pattern of housing and employment in the north.[2] Many Unionists had come to regard their Catholic neighbours as part of the extended arm of the IRA, a reservoir for recruits, resources, sanctuary and legitimacy. A bloody circularity was at work here. As loyalist attacks upon Catholics grew more violent, so in turn the IRA became more aggressive, killing 254 Protestants, soldiers and policemen between 1920 and 1922, so provoking a yet more aggressive reply from the loyalists. A similar cycle of violence would periodically spin into life during the 1970s and 1980s.

A third danger to the Northern Irish State came from the British government. Ulster Unionists realized that the 'enemy across the water' had long mistrusted what it imagined to be the bigoted sectarianism of Ulster Unionists. The Partition Act of 1920 had accordingly contained several safeguards to ensure the fair, impartial and tolerant operation of government by a Unionist-dominated administration. To Britain these were sensible (if retrospectively rather weak) precautions, but for the Ulstermen they looked, at best, like distrust, even disdain, for their administration and at worst, dangerous pro-minority sentiment, sure to encourage instability in the province. The British government's perceived misgivings about a Unionist ministry were born of a lukewarm commitment to the idea of a separate 'Ulster' state. Partition had never been its favoured option and was merely a temporary step, with a more permanent unified solution to the Irish situation evolving, they hoped, out of the All-Irish Council, possibly embracing a wider federal reconstruction of the UK or a degree of regional autonomy for Ulster. One of the abiding Republican myths of the Troubles is that the establishment of Northern Ireland served (or sustained) British interests. On the contrary, partition saddled her with an area that increasingly became a financial drain on the Exchequer. British defensive concerns had largely been dealt with in the Anglo-Irish Treaty of 1921. A unified Ireland would have contained large Unionist and Protestant communities, capable of blunting the strong irredentist direction and anti-British tone that southern Irish governments subsequently adopted. And having a discontented Nationalist minority trapped inside a Unionist statelet, under British sovereignty but with only limited powers of influence and control over it, not only stored up domestic problems for the future but was a recipe for international opprobrium – especially from the United States, where a discontented Nationalist enclave could always play on and up Nationalist sense of grievance in order to draw sympathy and financial support for Catholics in the north. Anglo-American relations were more important to Britain's strategic interests in the twentieth century than Anglo-Unionist ones, and would have been better served by a united Ireland. These reservations for partition certainly dented the confidence of Unionists in their 'mother state'.

Their fears intensified during the period of the truce and treaty negotiations. As part of the truce from July, the Special Constabulary that had been established back in October were stood down, though temporarily as it turned out. More worrying were the heavy hints dropped to Sinn Fein by Lloyd George during the treaty discussions that a more flexible approach on the republic would produce an equally pliant response from the British on the issue of unity. He even tried to persuade Craig to accept some form of autonomous position for Ulster within an Irish Dominion, the old idea of Home Rule within Home Rule, but to little effect. Saved from the fate of a united Ireland by the 1920 Government of Ireland Act, Unionists had little incentive or desire to trade in partition for any type of connection with the south, however persistently the British sought to persuade them otherwise. Yet Unionist anxieties continued and came to a head when the treaty terms were finally delivered to Craig early in December. In the treaty the Northern Ireland Assembly was given the choice of joining the Irish Free State or opting out of it, but the latter option was tied to the creation of a Boundary Commission, charged with the task of reexamining the border settlement. For Unionists, only too aware of the border's inconsistencies, even its absurdities in dividing villages, this was a direct threat to partition. And all the more so given Nationalists both north and south of the border regarded the Boundary Commission as the means by which Ireland would eventually be unified. With its clear Unionist majority, the Northern Ireland Assembly was quick to opt out of inclusion in the Irish Free State but in so doing was forced to live with a reexamination of the border settlement within the next few years.

> **❝ Anglo-American relations were more important to Britain's strategic interests in the twentieth century than Anglo-Unionist ones, and would have been better served by a united Ireland ❞**

CONSOLIDATING UNIONISM, 1922–1928

This combination of threats and dangers created deep apprehension within the Northern Ireland government and pressed upon Craig the immediate task of establishing the security and stability of the new state. One early defensive measure was to respond to the weakened position of the Ulster Unionist Party by destroying the political opposition. A Local Government (Emergency Powers) Act of 1921 gave the minister of home affairs the power to dissolve a local council and transfer its duties to a local commissioner. The introduction of an oath of allegiance to the king as qualification for political and civil service office ensured that power and government in the province would at all times reside in loyalist hands. In 1922 a Methods of Voting and Redistribution of Seats Act scrapped proportional representation (PR) in local elections (a mechanism that boosted minority parties), in tandem with a wide-ranging redrawing of local wards and electoral boundaries. This gerrymandering of constituencies was the most blatant exercise in political manipulation for the manner in which it maximized Unionist votes. In Belfast, for example, while it took 30,000 Catholic votes to win an assembly seat, it took just 18,000 Protestant votes. Similarly, in Antrim the 56 per cent Protestant population were able to collect 75 per cent of the assembly seats for that county, but in Fermanagh the 56 per cent Catholic population were able to win only 33 per cent. Tyrone told a similar story, where 70,000 Catholic votes won 9 seats but 57,000 Protestant votes acquired 18. In addition to reconfiguring the electoral map, plural voting was extended, limitations were placed on the franchise, such as the removal of non rate-paying voters, and in 1927 PR was abolished for the Northern Ireland Assembly.

Electoral manipulation was backed up by the construction of a powerfully repressive state apparatus. This was a response to a growing fear that the Irish civil war might spill over the border with an expansion of the IRA's northern campaign and an anxiety about how much support it would receive from the Catholic community. At the heart of this lay the Special Powers Act of 1922. The Act continued the wartime measures for maintaining civil order, which included guarding public buildings, curfews, closing roads, internment, the imposition of martial law and flogging. It also gave the minister of home affairs, Richard Dawson-Bates, what amounted to a legal blank cheque, 'to take all such steps and issue all such orders as may be necessary for preserving the peace and maintaining order'.[3] Such tough measures were put to good use by a new police service, the Royal Ulster Constabulary (RUC), and its part-time and overtly sectarian side-kick, the 20,000 strong 'B' Specials. Indeed, through 1921 and early 1922 the B Specials were the shock troops of Unionism, engaging with and defeating the IRA's northern campaign and earning for themselves a hallowed position within the Unionist pantheon. Taken together, the electoral manipulation and a tough state apparatus provided Ulster Unionists with the type of one-party state and hegemonic political power that the British government had tried to avoid.

That said, Craig was unable to evade Northern Ireland's treaty obligation to participate in a Boundary Commission. Since 1921 this had hung like a guillotine over parts of Northern Ireland, indeed over the whole state if its territorial dimensions were reduced too much, because in such circumstances, so Michael Collins believed, 'the north would be forced economically to come in' (to a united Ireland).[4] Despite Craig's bravado that he was 'not going to give away one inch of soil',[5] even the most optimistic Unionist forecast of the Commission predicted Northern Ireland would lose large tracts of land and population. A revision based on votes by county would have transferred Tyrone and Fermanagh to the south, reducing Northern Ireland to a four-county enclave, about the size of Devon. A revision according to population would have further reduced that enclave by also shaving off parts of south Armagh, north Antrim and the second city of Londonderry, though returning Protestant sections of Tyrone and Fermanagh back into the north. Given this prognosis, Nationalists both north and south looked expectantly to the commission's findings.

However, several things worked to thwart the Commission's work and preserve the border as it had been cast in 1920. One was the imprecise wording of article 12 of the Treaty that dealt with the remit, functions and objectives of the Commission – an imprecision of drafting that though useful in 1921 in order to squeeze all to an agreement was an obstacle and source of dispute when it came to sorting out the details for convening the body. More immediately, Craig sought to frustrate proceedings and delay the convocation of the Commission for as long as possible in the hope that the longer the border remained as it was, the more established it would become within the community and so the harder it would be to alter it. In this he was, ironically, aided by the south where the continuance of the Irish civil war distracted the attention of the Free State government until 1923. The death of Collins, in August 1922, also removed someone at the heart of the southern government with a considerable interest in revising the northern situation. Nor were circumstances helped by a series of general elections both in Britain and in Northern Ireland between 1922 and 1924 that further dragged things out. And just when all governments finally began to turn their attention to the Boundary Commission by 1924, the Ulstermen dragged their feet and refused to appoint one of the three Commission members. Alongside this Craig threatened resignation and moved large numbers of B Specials into Londonderry, raising the political pressure on the Commission not to tamper with things on the presumption that ownership was nine-tenths of the law. Against this onslaught the Commission dropped its proposals and the border stayed as it was. Keen to maintain good relations, Britain released the Free State of its National Debt commitments in the Treaty in return for which the Free State formally recognized the border.

> 66 Against this onslaught the commission dropped its proposals and the border stayed as it was 99

A NERVOUS STATE: NORTHERN IRELAND 1928–1962

To all intents and purposes, by the late 1920s Northern Ireland appeared relatively secure and settled. The border was now an established fact that no amount of Republican whingeing about illegality could undo. The IRA, having 'dumped arms' in 1923, had quickly become a pale shadow of its former self, with little direction, no support and a shrinking volunteer base that seemed to be constantly fragmenting and splitting. The political institutions of the north, having been 'cleansed' of disloyal elements and with the self-imposed abstention by many northern Nationalist politicians, functioned smoothly if not very effectively or impartially. And behind the state and border were the organized forces of the RUC and the B Specials, proven defenders against IRA violence and intensely popular within Unionist communities. The result of stabilization was that sectarian violence receded, with some commentators even suggesting that communal relations steadily improved in this period and that 'there was much more harmony than appeared on the surface'.[6] Dealings with Britain recovered, helped by the Conservative Party's dominance of government for much of the inter-war period and by Westminster's inclination to ignore the affairs of the province. This was born of the experience of 1922–1923 when Britain refused to ratify the Local Government (Emergency Powers) Act, on the grounds that it undermined a key component of the 1920 Partition Act: proportional representation for local elections. In protest Craig threatened the resignation of his cabinet, a move that would have necessitated re-integrating the region into the UK. With hindsight, such a response would have been a beneficial development, creating a more pluralist, open society and lessening the institutionalization of discrimination and sectarianism from where the Troubles came from. But having just got rid of the Irish Question, few within Britain wanted to bring it back. So the government caved in to Craig's demands, allowed the Act through and in the process provided Unionists with yet another invaluable lesson in power politics by showing just how effective threats and bluster were in moving a British government.

The drift of the Free State towards irredentism during the 1920s and 1930s enhanced the sense of repose in Northern Ireland. De Valera's governments, from 1932 onwards, seemed all too willing to prove correct longstanding Unionist prejudices about life in a united Ireland. His 1937 Constitution might have been specifically designed to upset and alienate the north in making the Free State a republic in all but name. Amongst its features that so alarmed Unionists were its 'claim' to the north in articles 2 and 3 and the grant of a 'special position' within the state to the Catholic Church in article 44, both of which had been absent from the 1921 Treaty and its offspring, the 'Liberal-Democratic' Irish Free State Constitution of 1922.[7] This special status, when placed alongside the illegalization of abortion and divorce, the imposition of Gaelic as the national language and growing ecclesiastical censorship, highlighted the gulf that separated the north and south. Beyond the Constitution of 1937, other actions by Dublin seemed more like clumsy affronts. The refusal, for example, of the Irish cabinet to attend the funeral service of Douglas Hyde, the first Irish President, because it took place within an Anglican Church. Or the episode in 1957 when a boycott of Protestant businesses in Wexford was called by the local priest, to force a Protestant wife in a mixed marriage to send their children to a Catholic school. To Unionists the south had become (and perhaps always had been) a 'foreign' place, separated by stark differences of culture, religion and identity, differences that in turn reinforced Northern Ireland's sense of place and purpose. In the process they became more British, or Ulster-British, and less Irish.

Above all else this sense of strengthening Britishness and separation of north from south was the product of World War Two. Northern Ireland made a significant contribution, with its shipyards, its port facilities, its role in the Atlantic naval war, its common experience of mass aerial bombing and its 38,000 volunteers. The war had a profound impact on Unionism. It triggered deep-rooted Unionist ideals and resonated with past deeds; the defence of the British Empire, standing alone, besieged by aggressive powers, resisting tyranny and upholding 'civilization' against 'evil' forces. That resonance was all the more powerful given southern Ireland's neutrality, a line supported by northern Nationalist politicians who together orchestrated an anti-conscription campaign in the north. These actions threw into sharp relief differences between a loyal Unionism and a traitorous Nationalism; for Unionists, neutrality and disloyalty were much the same sort of thing. And by generating a clearer sense of Britishness, stronger bonds were also forged between

Northern Ireland and Britain. This was seen in Britain's response to Dublin's declaration of a Republic in 1949 and exit from the Empire. Whereas De Valera's 1937 changes had prompted a relatively mild response from the British government, in 1949 Attlee's Labour government replied with the 1949 Ireland Act in which Northern Ireland was finally guaranteed as part of the UK as long as its Parliament desired it. This clear declaration of support was precisely the type of undiluted assurance needed to calm Unionist anxieties but which had been absent from both the 1920 Partition Act and the 1921 Treaty.

By the 1940s and 1950s Northern Ireland appeared a stable and tranquil society. War had generated closer ties to Britain, the gratitude of America and a more secure future rooted in the 1949 Ireland Act. Of course, image and reality were two very different things, and the lack of headline-grabbing violence and communal friction was not evidence of its absence. For beneath the heavily censored and manufactured images of baying cows, lush green hills and neat terraced houses of so many tourist guides to the region,[8] deep communal divisions and sectarian tensions festered. Few cross-community links operated, and even the brief rise of 'class' politics in 1932 never came close to dislodging sectarian politics. Despite their political dominance, Unionists never lost a deep and profound distrust for their Catholic neighbours. They continued to see themselves surrounded by enemies and thus in a state of perpetual siege, requiring a constant vigil in case of rebellion and necessitating the removal of Nationalists from positions of authority and influence in the state. Also a vigil against treason by soft leaders beguiled by Nationalist promises or against the treachery of dissembling British governments. The Ulster Unionist Party was charged with this vigil, and given the sacred duty to stamp out conspiracy, defend Unionist interests and above all else to uphold the status quo. In such an atmosphere and environment change itself became a threat as something liable to weaken the Unionist position, while reform was imagined not as a technique to strengthen but as a means

> " By the 1940s and 1950s Northern Ireland appeared a stable and tranquil society "

to destroy. So a profound anxiety continued to lurk at the heart of Unionism, reminiscent of the fragile, nervous dominance of various East European 'People's Democracies' in the 1970s and 1980s.

These sentiments helped extend discrimination from the political sphere into the social one. At the workplace, in education and in housing, Protestants were prioritized over 'disloyal' Catholics as a method of shoring up Unionist political support. Catholics were made into second-class citizens, occupying the worst housing, forced into the meanest jobs, educated in the poorest schools, and as a community suffering the highest rates of poverty. Discrimination in housing was a particularly sensitive issue, given its historic echoes of previous Nationalist struggles for land and ownership. For example, between 1945 and 1967 of the 1,048 houses built in Fermanagh, 82 per cent went to Protestants, despite the county having an overall Catholic majority. In employment the picture was very much the same, with Catholics filling a disproportionately small number of professional occupations yet a disproportionately large slice of the unskilled jobs. Catholics were also 2.6 times more likely to be unemployed than Protestants, which against the backdrop of a steadily declining industrial base meant that if things were tough for many working-class Protestants, they were even tougher for working-class Catholics. Such discrimination was not government policy, and was often the result of local council 'clientalism' or a private employer's concern to employ co-religionists. However, the rhetoric and inaction of ministers did little to address (and much to encourage) the economic and social *apartheid* within Northern Ireland. The supreme irony of all of this was that by discriminating against and demonizing the Catholic communities, Unionist prophecies became self-fulfilling. Political exclusion and social prejudice produced the disloyal minority they sought to eradicate.

Generally these pressures and discriminations remained latent, shelved by the daily grind to make a living, find a job, turn a profit, bring up kids and pay the rent. However, on occasions they could ignite into violence. In 1935, the silver jubilee celebrations of George V sparked several days of sectarian rioting in

Belfast that resulted in 13 deaths and the forced relocation of several hundred Catholics. Not only did communal tensions have the potential to disrupt the cosy and contented image Unionists created for their state, but developments outside the province could also shatter their illusion of permanence and security. The Anglo-Irish Trade Agreement of 1938 sent bolts of anxiety through the Northern Ireland government that the border was about to be phased out. More dramatic were rumours of a deal between London and Dublin, in the dark days of May–June 1940, to trade Irish neutrality for partition, and evoking a stinging response from Belfast. This posed a tantalizing dilemma for the Northern Irish government: did they place British interests, clearly best served at that stage by Irish entry into the war, before Unionist ones of maintaining partition? In the end De Valera, who had done so much to preserve the clarity, unity and strength of Unionism, came to its rescue by refusing the offer. And although Attlee's Labour government from 1945 to 1951 had 'guaranteed' the union in the 1949 Ireland Act, Unionists could never forget the pro-unity leanings of the Labour Party, especially with an active backbench group, the Friends of Ireland, openly championing their sympathy for unification.

Discrimination also helped sustain anti-partitionism within the Nationalist communities. This sentiment was aided by developments to the south where in 1946 Clann na Poblachta was founded as an aggressively republican party under the leadership of the former IRA Chief of Staff, Sean MacBride. Two years later MacBride was to be found in Costello's coalition government as Minister of External Affairs and an important influence the following year in Ireland's declaration of a republic and exit from the Commonwealth. Of more concern to Northern Ireland was Clann na Poblachta organization of an anti-partition league in alliance with northern Nationalists. These events helped generate a brief flowering of militant republicanism during the early 1950s. Support for Sinn Fein came to a dramatic head at the 1955 Westminster elections when they won two seats and over 150,000 votes for their traditional platform of ending partition, an all-Irish Republic, a British withdrawal and abstention from Westminster. The surge in support for republicanism in turn revived the fortunes of the IRA, which in 1956 launched an operation against the border. The campaign involved 150 IRA men crossing into Northern Ireland looking to destabilize the state by attacking various communications, administrative and strategic strong-points, such as police stations and military bases. The Border Campaign achieved some damage, a number of deaths and much publicity, but was largely ineffectual and quickly defeated, primarily by a lack of support within Catholic communities and co-operation between Northern Ireland and the Republic over the internment of IRA suspects. Unionists reacted as they had before and would again by stepping up their vigilance and control over their Catholic neighbours, as with the 1954 Flags and Emblems Act, effectively banning public displays of Republican emblems. The coercive resources of the state, notably the B Specials, were also deployed with efficiency and success: there was little to teach a Unionist government about meeting force with force. Unionists now positioned Republican violence alongside northern Catholic disloyalty and southern Irish irredentism, as one large 'green' coalition.

> ❝ The Border Campaign achieved some damage, a number of deaths and much publicity, but was largely ineffectual and quickly defeated ❞

O'NEILL AND REFORM, 1963–1966

The 1960s unleashed pressures that challenged the rather stuffy, restrictive atmosphere of many regimes throughout the world. A sense of hope and renewal pervaded Western culture, seen most strikingly in a turn to radical activism to confront the established order, whether it be in Czechoslovakia, Poland, Yugoslavia, Paris or London. Technological and communication advances offered opportunities for economic restructuring and growth. Wealth filtered downwards in societies, enriching new social groups and individuals. Once rigid social barriers and mores controlling class, sexuality, background, gender, race, religion and ethnicity began to relax. Ecumenicalism blunted religious passions. Marginalized social groups sought empowerment and inclusion, be they women, gays, blacks in South Africa or the USA, and Palestinians in Israel. Welfare and education policies spread knowledge, raised living standards and improved the health of citizens (especially in Northern Ireland where two decades of British welfare prompted a fall in the level of Catholic emigration from the province and created a prosperous, well-educated and socially ambitious Catholic middle class). Moreover, established conservative elites throughout the Western world were giving way to a younger generation of leaders, imbued with liberal values and with a reformist, modernizing agenda – a generation that was also comfortable in front of the new and increasingly intrusive medium of television.

Like everywhere else, these were pressures Northern Ireland needed to respond to. However, in addition to these the province was confronted by its own localized challenges. One was the arrival of a Labour government in Britain in 1964 under Harold Wilson, a known supporter of a united Ireland and with an active backbench pressure group, the Campaign for Democracy in Ulster. A second challenge was a revival in popularity for the Northern Irish Labour Party that, as in the early 1920s, threatened the electoral dominance of the Ulster Unionist Party. The advance of Labour was all the more menacing given the decision by Nationalists to involve themselves in Northern Irish politics. For the first time since 1921 they were relinquishing their stance of abstaining from the Stormont assembly to play a more constructive oppositional role inside it. By implicitly recognizing the Northern Irish State they were now determined to achieve real reform from within, instead of fruitless anti-partition gestures from without. This tactical change materialized in the National Unity Party and later the National Democratic Party, dedicated to correcting the economic and social grievances of Catholics. Alongside these a plethora of local action groups, housing trusts and citizen leagues also sprang up demanding more equal treatment in public housing. By 1964 these had federated into the Campaign for Social Justice (CSJ), which sought redress across a range of areas, including voting and employment reform. The switch from a traditional anti-partitionist stance towards practical reform and community rights was encouraged by improving relations with the south following the election of the modernizing Sean Lemass as Taoiseach in 1959. Participation in Northern Irish politics was also a consequence of the IRA's failure to generate popular support during its Border Campaign of 1956–1962, a failure that shredded the Republican movement into a host of insignificant backroom cliques, such as Wolfe Tone societies, or aligning themselves to the Communist Party or trades councils. What was left of the IRA dumped its arms, mothballed its belief in an ultimate military victory, and by the mid-1960s was busy reinventing itself as a non-sectarian Marxist 'workers' party under its Chief of Staff, Carthal Goulding.

> **The ferment within Northern Irish politics during the early to mid-1960s presented the Ulster Unionist Party with a series of tactical questions**

The ferment within Northern Irish politics during the early to mid-1960s presented the Ulster Unionist Party with a series of tactical questions, though one thing seemed clear enough: straightforward sectarianism was no longer sufficient. Unfortunately for the party the septuagenarian Lord Brookeborough, Prime Minister since 1943, appeared singularly ill-equipped to find an alternative response. The task of dragging Northern Ireland into the twentieth century fell upon the young minister of finance, Terence O'Neill, who 'emerged' as Prime Minister in 1963. O'Neill responded to developments by thawing relations with the south, becoming the first Prime Minister of Northern Ireland to visit Dublin and to receive the Irish Taoiseach, Sean Lemass, in Belfast in 1964. On the economic front he introduced a programme of modernization that included regional planning, infrastructural change, local government reform, improved social services and an increase in house building to stimulate growth and undercut the growing electoral strength of the Labour Party. More controversially he emitted a softer, more inclusive tone towards the Catholic communities, in place of Unionist triumphalism. He sought to 'build bridges between the two traditions' by offering Catholics a place in what would be his new vibrant Northern Ireland.[9] These sentiments he backed up by visiting Catholic schools, meeting members of the clergy and in 1963 by sending condolences to Cardinal Conway on the death of Pope John XXXIII. He even talked of Catholics joining the Unionist Party, an obvious step if they were now willing to work within the state. O'Neill was offering his own combination of *perestroika* and *glasnost*, of economic reforms and greater openness designed to strengthen the Northern Irish State, not to undermine it. It was preservative reform, consolidating the union by gradually extending its 'ownership' to all communities and citizens. As Brian Faulkner, the Minister of Commerce, explained: 'By raising the general level of prosperity for everyone, by making it possible for all our citizens to have a secure job and thus a good house and a decent standard of living, the traditional divisions in our community would soften and become blurred ... In fact we succeeded too well, for there were those who saw that with greater prosperity, and a greater gulf between living conditions north and south of the border, the United Ireland of their dreams was becoming more and more a mirage.'[10]

THE COLLAPSE OF O'NEILLISM, 1966–1968

Reforming a political system built upon sectarian divisions would prove a terribly difficult process. To succeed it had to satisfy sufficient numbers of Nationalists while at the same time retaining the support of a significant number of Unionists. A package, in other words, that would deliver the impossible of both a successful transformation *and* an essential continuity. Such a trick was difficult enough in a liberal-pluralist political system where leaders might collect votes from different groups, communities and interests. But when the leader was, as with O'Neill, unfortunately rather aloof and secretive, and when communal relationships were zero-sum where gain for one community was interpreted as loss for the other, successful reform looked a very distant prospect. At the start of O'Neill's premiership this structural tension was less visible, for at the 1965 Stormont elections O'Neill was able to increase the

Unionist Party vote while cutting the Labour Party's to 66,000 (remembering just a year earlier they had scooped 103,000 at the Westminster election). Even as late as December 1968 O'Neill and his reform plans were able to win the backing of Unionist MPs at Stormont and a great deal of support in the wider community, as evidenced by the 150,000 letters of endorsement for the 'I back O'Neill' campaign organized through the *Belfast Telegraph*.

Unfortunately the pull of communal suspicion and Unionist anxiety proved too powerful. A growing number of Unionists came to regard O'Neill's declarations of social inclusion and communal reconciliation as 'a policy of treachery' and the appeasement of the disloyal.[11] Their traditional watchword was eternal vigilance against the enemy within, not a blurring, bridging or softening of community divisions – especially when in 1966 that enemy so publicly celebrated the 50th anniversary of the Easter rebellion, an event regarded by Unionists as the republican stab in the back. O'Neillism was, they feared, 'Lundyism from above',[12] a suspicion that found an echo within his own government when in 1966 he uncovered a conspiracy led by cabinet colleagues Desmond Boal and John McQade. A year later he was forced to sack his agriculture minister Harry West for dissent. Anxiety towards O'Neill was also evident within the Unionist business community, concerned by the direction of his economic reforms and the threat they posed to their interests. Apprehension spread to local government, worried about possible curbs to their power and influence. But unease was also present amongst the wider Unionist communities and played up by 'politico-religious demagogues' such as Ian Paisley, only too willing to 'ride' the popular anxiety for political advantage.[13] Paisley stoked Unionist fears of a sell-out and an awakening Republican menace, channelling those fears into 'patriotic' organizations such as the Ulster Constitution Defence Committee (UCDC), the Ulster Protestant Volunteers (UPV), Ulster Protestant Action and Tara.[14] In 1963, when Belfast's mayor lowered the town hall's Union Jack to half-mast following the death of the Pope, it was Paisley who led a march of his National Union of

Protestants in protest. A year later he led loyalists against a Republican club in West Belfast that flew the Irish Tricolour in contravention of the Flags and Emblems Act, that resulted in several days of rioting. More ominously, in the Unionist heartland of the Shankhill in Belfast a small contingent of the UVF spluttered into life to carry out the first sectarian murders of the present Troubles in 1966. By the mid to late 1960s the once granite-like edifice of Ulster Unionism was fragmenting into reformers and resisters, radicals and hardliners, between those willing to adapt the present to the future and those desiring to fix it to the past.

❝ Disquiet within Unionism forced O'Neill to curtail his reformism ❞

Disquiet within Unionism forced O'Neill to curtail his reformism. But in so doing he encountered the wrath of Catholic opinion and especially those whose hopes had been raised by his rhetoric. O'Neill's inclusive, consensual words now appeared hollow and pragmatic, little more than 'flamboyant gestures', as one of his colleagues described it.[15] This hollowness was exposed when a key rail line to Catholic Londonderry was ended or when a new city was sited in Protestant Portadown or a new university was built in Protestant Coleraine or evidence emerged that development money was being concentrated in the Protestant east rather than the predominantly Catholic west. Even on those areas he had set out to reform, such as discrimination in voting, public housing and employment, as well as the coercive apparatus of the Special Powers Act, the Flags and Emblems Act and the hated B Specials, there appeared little movement. O'Neillism came to resemble no more than sectarianism with a smile and the experience and living standards of Catholics were little different to what they had been 20 or 30 years previously.

This quickly bred frustration. In Londonderry, where council house allocation was a particular source of bitterness for Catholics, a Derry Housing Action Committee was set up to advertise abuses and push for change. More significantly, in January 1967 the Northern Ireland Civil Rights Association (NICRA) was formed as an umbrella movement composed of the

CSJ along with the Labour and Liberal parties of Northern Ireland, Republican clubs, the Wolfe Tone societies and the Belfast Trades Council. NICRA co-ordinated a campaign of public protest, highlighting minority grievances but focusing on the issue of 'one man one vote' for local elections as the most tangible affront to democratic principles, thus likely to attract a wider international publicity. Some in the leadership went further, believing in the old IRA tactic of 'coat-trailing',[16] of provoking an over-reaction from the RUC to rally a genuinely mass movement amongst the Nationalist community and intensify media attention. The campaigns drew heavily upon the successes of the civil rights movement in the USA, where tactics of peaceful protest and appeals to the federal government had won a series of reforms outlawing discrimination in voting, education and public transport. Learning from this, NICRA took its protests to the streets with large-scale marches, peaceful in intent and geared to high media exposure in order to broadcast its grievances, one of the first being on 24 August 1968 when 2,500 people marched from Coalisland to Dungannon. Street protests and marches were taken up by another, more radical and confrontational civil rights group, People's Democracy, which developed out of a student body and contained a larger militant, socialist element to it.

Though born in an atmosphere of despair, the emergence of NICRA and People's Democracy reflected the rise of an assertive northern Catholic middle class, the product of 20 years of British educational and welfare provision that far exceeded what was on offer in the south. As a result this new middle class now felt itself more 'British' and thus *expected* and certainly *deserved* better treatment from the British state which it was finally willing to recognize. These developments were signs of progress and health. After 50 years Catholics were sidelining their traditional Nationalist abstention and incantations against the border for a more participatory role in the affairs of Northern Ireland. Once equal civil rights were established, their active engagement in politics could conceivably have led to the rise of a more pluralist political system, Catholic involvement in the Unionist Party and a weakening of the obstacles to community reconciliation.

Such developments presented Unionists with their best long-term solution, the legitimization of the union through the involvement of their Catholic neighbours.

Understandably, perhaps, many Unionists did not see it this way. Such a scenario could materialize only if the dominant position and power of the Ulster Unionist Party was curbed, yet many Unionists regarded the dominance of the Ulster Unionist Party as a sine qua non for the survival of the union. It was the party that had led the defence of the union during the previous 50 years of threat, struggle and siege. Unsurprisingly then, within a Unionist mind-set shaped by a sense of threat and siege, the emergence of civil rights groups was regarded more as a challenge and danger than a sign of health and hope, as an act of subversion rather than a development likely to strengthen the Union. Civil rights were imagined as a Trojan horse within which Republicans planned to discredit Stormont and destabilize the state. Behind the rhetoric of civil rights, a Catholic, Nationalist and Republican enemy still hankered and plotted for a united Ireland.

66 Enemies who marched 'outside' the Unionist citadel were easily smashed 99

Of course the Unionist Party had encountered challenges before and overcome them. What made these more dangerous was that they emerged at a moment of deep unease and weakness within the Party itself over the tone and direction in which O'Neill was taking it. Enemies who marched 'outside' the Unionist citadel were easily smashed. But when they combined with what some saw as enemies on the inside, in the form of an elitist liberal leadership, the threat was more serious. This, in turn, generated deep alarm at a grass-roots level and more widely amongst Unionist communities from 1967 onwards – an alarm that found a sympathetic ear from hard-liners within the Party, Harry West and William Craig, both sacked by O'Neill, and from outside the party by Paisley and his close associate, Major Bunting. Paisley offered a more visceral, defensive and nervous unionism, that connected past struggles to present fears, especially to the events of 1912–1914 when Carson and Craig had stood resolute against Irish Nationalist demands for Home Rule. Such a unionism resonated with the widespread anxiety within the community that the survival of their religious freedoms, their heritage and even the continuance of the Northern Ireland state itself were in serious danger. From within Unionist communities, groups of loyalists began to organize into the UPV and the UCDC, as vehicles that might take the defence of the state onto the streets and challenge the civil rights marchers themselves. Loyalist energies were channelled into a series of counter-demonstrations, orchestrated to disrupt protests and speeches and re-establish Unionist control. So began the wave of marches and counter-marches through 1968 and 1969 that made violent clashes all but inevitable and brought both communities into more open and bloody conflict with each other. The Troubles in Northern Ireland had burst into life.

NOTES

1 T. Hennessey, *A History of Northern Ireland, 1920–1996* (Macmillan, 1997) p 6.

2 Ibid, p 11.

3 L. Donohue, *Counter-Terrorist Law and Emergency Powers in the UK* (Irish Academic, 2001) p 21.

4 N. Mansergh, *The Unresolved Question: The Anglo-Irish Settlement and its Undoing, 1912–1972* (Yale, 1991) p 221.

5 Ibid, p 218.

6 R. D. Edwards, *The Faithful Tribe: An Intimate Portrait of the Loyal Institutions* (HarperCollins, 2000) pp 339–44.

7 P. Arthur, *Special Relationships: Britain, Ireland and the Northern Ireland Problem* (Blackstaff Press, 2000) pp 88–91.

8 H. V. Morton, *In Search of Ireland* (Methuen, 1949) ch 12.

9 O'Neill in 1963 in F. Cochrane, 'Meddling at the Crossroads: the decline and fall of Terence O'Neill' in R. English and G. Walker (eds) *Unionism in Modern Ireland* (Macmillan, 1996) p 153.

10 B. Faulkner, *Memoirs of a Statesman* (Weidenfeld and Nicolson, 1978) p 41.

11 Ian Paisley in 1966 in F. Cochrane, op. cit., p 152.

12 B. O'Leary and J. McGarry, *The Politics of Antagonism* (Athlone, 1993) p 141.

13 B. Faulkner, op. cit., p 39.

14 S. Bruce, *The Red Hand: Protestant Paramilitaries in Northern Ireland* (Oxford, 1992) pp 14–32.

15 B. Faulkner, op. cit., p 42.

16 S. Bruce, op. cit., p 28.

4

THE BIRTH OF THE TROUBLES, 1964–1972

'Those who urge that the Army should be more vigorous in its actions ignore the requirements of the law. They ignore the fact that the Army is operating in the UK among people who, though some might not thank me for saying so, are UK citizens. They ignore the likelihood that over-reaction to a relatively minor riot may influence it into something more violent. Also they ignore the fact that undue action by the Army is likely still further to alienate whole sections of the Northern Ireland community.'

Geoffrey Johnson-Smith, Parliamentary Under-secretary of State for Defence and the Army, in *Conservative Party Monthly*, January 1972

'ON THE DOORSTEP',[1] 1964–1968

THE LABOUR PARTY OF HAROLD WILSON ENTERED GOVERNMENT in 1964 determined to cast its reformist gaze across all areas of British society and politics after a decade and a half of stale, old-fashioned Toryism. That gaze did not at first rest upon the dark and murky recesses of the Stormont regime. Understandably for such a 'sensitive' politician, if a problem was not attracting public attention Wilson's predilection was to let sleeping dogs lie. Regardless of his public sympathy for Irish unity, he was never one to rake up a problem on principle. Irish unity, he thought, was something that would not be forced but would evolve naturally and over time through the logic of closer economic ties, political co-operation and European integration. However, events and personalities conspired to make Northern Ireland an unavoidable issue for him. In January 1964 the Campaign for Social Justice publicized discrimination of Catholics in housing, employment and elections. The findings found a receptive audience amongst Wilson's Labour backbenchers, and led by Paul Rose they organized themselves into the Campaign for Democracy in Ulster (CDU) to urge Wilson to press far-reaching reforms upon the Unionist government. With a slim Commons majority Wilson could ill afford to ignore their request. In any case, confronting the problem of discrimination against Catholics sat well with Britain's steadily improving relations with the Irish Republic, led since 1959 by the modernizing Sean Lemass, and in championing human rights and democracy throughout her old African colonies. It also seemed Wilson was pushing at an open door. The arrival in 1963 of O'Neill and his reformist rhetoric suggested the province was at last beginning to throw off the 'baggage of the past'. Politics in Northern Ireland were changing, to which Wilson had to respond.

Wilson initially sought to bolster O'Neill's reformist Unionism. At meetings with him in May 1965 and again in August 1966, Wilson offered assistance in dealing with the problems of discrimination in housing, employment, voting practices, local government and the thorny question of 'one man one vote' in local elections. Stormont was encouraged to put its own house in order.[2] The problem for the government was how, when O'Neill's rhetoric was finally exposed as hollow by 1967, it was to force Stormont into change. Especially since Northern Ireland had established for itself a remarkably high degree of autonomy. Westminster had few direct means of altering the policies of a Unionist

> 66 The arrival in 1963 of O'Neill and his reformist rhetoric suggested the province was at last beginning to throw off the 'baggage of the past' 99

government or intervening in the province, short of taking it over. And the idea of taking control to push through reform filled everyone with alarm. 'On no account,' James Callaghan, the future Home Secretary, was warned by his advisers, 'get sucked into the Irish bog.'[3] All Britain could do was engineer change through informal influence and meddling behind the scenes, by threatening to cut her financial commitment to the region or by reducing the voting rights of her MPs. But meddling created communal unease and political instability, and from political instability came violence. On 5 October 1968 a large NICRA march in Londonderry was stopped and dispersed by the RUC, using baton charges and water cannon. Events sparked several days of intense rioting in the Catholic Bogside and inter-communal disorder, with hundreds injured. For the RUC, whose 'premature uncontrolled and unnecessary'[4] tactics were caught on film by the large media presence that day, they were also a publicity disaster. Particularly dramatic were pictures of Gerry Fitt, MP for West Belfast, with blood streaming across his face having been batoned to the ground by zealous RUC officers. For the Home Secretary, Jim Callaghan, not only had 'Ulster arrived in the headlines'[5] but it had landed slap-bang in his lap.

The pictures shocked the Labour Cabinet, reinforcing their desire for far-reaching reforms but simultaneously denting their faith that O'Neill could actually deliver them. Events forced Wilson to shift from genial encouragement to what Faulkner regarded as a 'vaguely threatening posture'.[6] Under British pressure O'Neill now announced far-reaching reforms which included a points system for housing allocation, reform of local government, a review of the Special Powers Act and abolition of the Londonderry Corporation. He also removed 'obstructionist' elements in his cabinet by sacking his hardline Home Affairs minister William Craig, while in December 1968 he tried to rally moderate opinion from all sides with an upbeat and mildly defiant public broadcast. The government and O'Neill believed such a programme of change would be sufficiently radical to dampen civil rights activism yet sufficiently mild not to raise Unionist suspicions. Reform had to be sold as both change and continuity, as heralding a new future while simultaneously conserving a golden past.

Not surprisingly Wilson and O'Neill miscalculated on this. Increasing the rate and remit of reform did not stem the demand for civil rights legislation, indeed it may even have intensified it, so further deepening Unionist fears. On the other hand, however reasonable the reform package, Unionists regarded it as a threat to their way of life and an attack on the very institutions that had ensured them security and dominance for 50 years – an attack all the more galling for being carried out by one of their 'own' and at Westminster's bidding. These sentiments did little to enhance O'Neill's political standing and as a result his power dwindled. When he attempted to recover his position by announcing a 'snap' election in February 1969, he simply split the Ulster Unionist Party into pro and anti O'Neill factions.

Beyond the rarefied atmosphere of the party leadership, the quickening pace of reform had triggered a violent reaction outside. Power and initiative shifted to the streets and into loyalist housing associations, loyalist orders, Orange clubs, young Unionist associations and the Ulster Protestant Volunteers, many of whom orchestrated counter-demonstrations to confront the civil rights movement. During one infamous encounter in January 1969, at Burntollet Bridge just outside Londonderry, RUC officers were captured on film standing aside as a Protestant mob, itself composed of some off-duty B Specials, waded into marchers with clubs. The attack spilled over into rioting between the Catholic community and the RUC. In the evening, sections of the RUC carried out 'late night sorties' into the Bogside, attacking houses and forcing the Catholic community to raise barricades to protect themselves.[7] Decades of simmering sectarian mistrust erupted within a few hours into full-blown inter-communal conflict. Far from stabilizing the situation, British-driven reforms pushed the province into chaos. Yet still the government could see no alternative but to support Stormont's programme of change. Even O'Neill's resignation in April 1969, and his replacement by James Chichester-Clark, did not substantially alter this assessment.

The approach of the summer, however, filled everyone with alarm. Summers are periods of heightened communal tension in the province, a time when 'people ... not so much celebrate past history as relive it'.[8] The most obvious manifestation of this are the series of parades and marches undertaken by both communities to remember (perhaps even construct) ancient deeds, martyrs and communal victories. Amongst the oldest and largest of these parades was that of the Apprentice Boys in August each year, a Protestant celebration of the successful defence of Londonderry against Catholic James II in 1689–1690. What made the 'summer of '69' all the more dangerous was the evident and near total breakdown in community relations. Even Wilson, when he spoke of 'a stormy summer ... ahead', could not have realized quite how stormy![9] June and July had already witnessed sectarian violence in a series of bloody tit-for-tat clashes. Tensions continued to rise steadily through July fuelled by the funeral of Sam Devenny on the 16th, beaten in his home by RUC officers rampaging through the Bogside. By the start of August rioting had become a daily ritual that came to an inevitable climax with the Apprentice Boys march around the walls of Londonderry on 12 August. What started as a now familiar clash between Catholic Bogsiders and the RUC quickly grew into full-scale rioting. Barricades were thrown up to defend Catholic communities against loyalist and RUC invasion. By the 13th Londonderry was consumed in pitched battles, in what was fast taking on the appearance of a 'Battle of the Bogside'. That evening rioting spread to Belfast and elsewhere. Belfast probably witnessed the worst sectarian violence, as groups from both communities invaded and attacked each other in a 'turf war' that resulted in Catholic and Protestant houses being burnt and families forced to flee. The violence continued unabated for two days and nights. By 14 August the RUC were exhausted. As a force of just over 3,000 officers they were dangerously under-manned for the situation (the 1968 anti-Vietnam war riots in Grosvenor Square, London had alone seen over 8,000 police mobilized). Under-manning

> **Summers are periods of heightened communal tension in the province, a time when 'people ... not so much celebrate past history as relive it'**

made them prone to over-react, make mistakes or resort to blunt 'publicity-awkward' weapons such as CS-gas and gun fire. More disastrously, with a stretched RUC, Chichester-Clark was forced to call out the 8,500 part-time B Specials, the vicious part-time force loathed by the Catholic community. Armed with revolvers they went into action in the Bogside, the final, desperate throws of a Stormont government incapable of performing its most basic function of maintaining law and order.

Calling out the B Specials was akin to throwing petrol onto the sectarian fire, though matched in its inflammatory effect by a broadcast from Jack Lynch, the Irish Taoiseach, attacking partition and claiming the Republic would 'not stand by' and watch Catholics attacked. As substance to his claims the Irish army was mobilized to the Donegal border and field hospitals opened. Unbeknown at the time, several members of his cabinet were busy helping to smuggle arms to Republicans in the north. For Unionists it appeared southern Irish troops were mobilizing for invasion, a belief that well and truly 'put the fat in the fire'.[10] By the afternoon of the 14th, with no options left, Stormont asked the British government for troops. An hour later a battalion of the Prince of Wales' Own Regiment deployed itself onto the streets of Londonderry, to re-establish law and order, but particularly to offer protection to Catholic communities. The next day British troops entered Belfast to perform a similar role. An eerie calm now befell the province, through which the realization dawned on Britain that after 50 years of turning the other way, the Northern Irish Troubles had smashed their way back to the centre of politics. A melancholic Jim Callaghan reflected on the sheer intractability of the problem he was now being called upon to deal with: 'So GB was inexorably drawn back into the Irish Question, into a heady brew made up of pleas for specified rights for the minority coupled with the desire to upset the settlement of 1921 by others, and offset by the enraged response of many "loyalists" who felt that their police had been defiled and humiliated.'[11] Even more warily, Frank Cooper, permanent secretary at the MOD, spoke of 'a fear that you were going into an unknown mire and that you didn't know what was there. You didn't know what was going to happen to you when you were there and how you got out at the other side of the bog'.[12]

GRUDGING ENGAGEMENT: THE BRITS COME BACK, 1969

The deployment of troops onto the streets of Northern Ireland was the first substantial mobilization of British military personnel in Ireland since 1921. And if that unhappy episode was anything to go by, the future was bleak indeed. The British government had had little real choice in the matter. In front of the world's press, Northern Ireland appeared on the brink of civil war, with the Irish Taoiseach hinting at 'action' and the RUC overwhelmed and exhausted. Nationalist claims made at the time of partition in 1920 that the northern statelet would prove non-viable were finally coming true. Stormont had revealed an almost structural incapacity to reform itself, paralyzed between a Unionist community that felt it was moving too fast and a Nationalist one that believed it was not moving at all. In the face of mass communal unrest, the Northern Ireland government had visibly staggered. Its urgent request for soldiers was as much to save it from collapse as it was to restore order. Wilson was forced to comply with great reluctance, but in so doing admitted his policy of 'arm's length' encouragement of Liberal Unionist reforms could no longer be kept at arm's length. The issue was not just 'on our doorstep ... (but) ... in our house'[13] and so a bolder approach was necessary.

> **Two particularly bold initiatives, the reunification of Ireland or full independence to 'Ulster', were thought as likely to inflame civil unrest rather than eliminate it**

Agreeing to a bolder approach was not easy. Two particularly bold initiatives, the reunification of Ireland or full independence to 'Ulster', were thought as likely to inflame civil unrest rather than eliminate it. More practical policies were for Britain to abolish Stormont and fully integrate Northern Ireland into the UK. Or, more limitedly, assume temporary direct rule to push through far-reaching economic and political reforms before devolving power back to an elected assembly. Unfortunately both courses would have angered the Irish Republic and involved a degree of intervention few at Westminster were prepared to contemplate at this stage. The prevalent view remained 'for not trying to settle the affairs of Northern Ireland too directly from London'.[14] So Wilson and Callaghan went for none of these options and chose instead the course of least resistance but, as it turned out, of maximum long-term disadvantage – namely temporary military intervention to restore calm and allow reform to be implemented, but *without* assuming direct political control. It was a policy of more of the same plus the army.

This approach was enshrined in the first Downing Street Declaration of 19 August 1969. The Declaration, as with its namesake 24 years later, tried to address the concerns and ambitions of both communities. For Unionists came the reassurance that the region would 'not cease to be part of the United Kingdom without the consent of (its) Parliament', and affirmed that 'responsibility for affairs in Northern Ireland is entirely a matter of domestic jurisdiction'. Unionists would keep their beloved Stormont. For Nationalists 'the two governments (British and Northern Irish) reaffirmed that in all legislation and executive decisions ... every citizen of Northern Ireland is entitled to the same equality of treatment and freedom from discrimination as obtains in the rest of the UK, irrespective of political views or religion'.[15] In other words, to keep their Unionist-dominated institutions, Unionists would have to undertake moderate Nationalist policies. To keep his job, the gamekeeper would have to steal his own rabbits.

Callaghan had few illusions that this was a very difficult trick to pull off. It would take the fanciest of fancy footwork to marry the conflicting demands of each community in the aftermath of such violent communal tension. Yet his optimistic calculation was that if the *status* of Northern Ireland was no longer an issue, Unionists would not feel insecure and so could be persuaded to accept far-reaching reform. More difficult was to win the trust of the Catholic community and convince them that a reformed

Stormont could legislate with equality and fairness. To build this trust Callaghan visited the province at the end of August, pledging change, allaying community fears and tensions, meeting various local groups, and generally assuring the world's media that peace, impartial government and stability would now prevail. 'He arrived like some Kissinger before his time, breathing goodwill and understanding,' one leading Ulster Unionist noted acidly.[16] But uncle Jim could also act like 'Big Brother'[17] and Chichester-Clark found himself pressured into a whole raft of changes designed to appease Nationalist concerns and win back their trust. Two Whitehall civil servants were temporarily stationed at Stormont, 'as a good way of exercising real control without offending susceptibilities'.[18] Callaghan also constituted two inquiries, one under Lord Scarman into the events of August, and the other under Lord Hunt into reforming the RUC, a topic always likely to rouse Unionist anxiety. Sure enough, when the Hunt Report recommended the disarming of the RUC, the abolition of the B Specials and creation of a new part-time force, the Ulster Defence Regiment (UDR), Belfast exploded into two nights of intense rioting by Protestants, while Chichester-Clark's position was irreparably weakened.

Yet however delicate political relations with Stormont were, the first few months of British intervention were accompanied by high hopes of success. Nor were these hopes outrageously fanciful. Unionists, though suspicious of Labour's reforms, appreciated the calming effect and dip in violent activity that British troops initially brought to the province. Catholics welcomed the reforms, and especially the changes to the RUC and abolition of the Specials. Callaghan remained popular amongst their community leaders, who believed (wrongly) that the British government was now in control. And British troops experienced a 'honeymoon' period, warmly welcomed in Catholic communities, where the greatest danger they faced was drowning in a sea of tea and biscuits. This was due, in part, to a sensitive, 'softly-softly' approach from local army commanders, showing adeptness at avoiding potentially harmful entanglements and negotiating with local residents' groups to avoid friction and offence.[19] Indeed, during these first few weeks they acted more like a UN peacekeeping force than an army in defence of civil authority.

THE BRIAR PATCH, 1970–1971

The early promise turned out to be nothing more than misplaced optimism. In their eagerness to limit British involvement, Wilson and Callaghan failed to observe the fundamental flaws in their approach. One defect was a misreading of Ulster Unionism, believing they would passively accept a programme of reform if the status of Northern Ireland as part of the United Kingdom were copper-fastened. On the contrary, and despite this guarantee of consent, reform continued to unsettle the Protestant community. This was especially the case with police reform which left them feeling exposed and vulnerable. It appeared, somewhat ironically, that British intervention had actually strengthened Unionist insecurity. 'It was like an invasion. This was our own army coming in and it felt as though we were being invaded by them. They were fairly abusive towards us because they looked at the damage that had been done to the Nationalist or Catholic community.'[20] Nor was it just security. Reforms in housing, government administration and local political representation suggested the very framework of the 'Protestant' state was now being dismantled. And for what, since 'nothing was going to placate the Catholics', an officer in the B Specials commented, 'except union with Ireland. Throwing things like that (reforms) to the Catholics was just a bloody waste of time. All it did was depress the majority who felt they were being sold down the river.'[21] The fear of being 'sold down the river' pushed many Unionists into the hands of intransigent demagogues such as William Craig and Ian Paisley,

> It appeared, somewhat ironically, that British intervention had actually strengthened Unionist insecurity

only too willing to play on (and up) people's fears and insecurities, or into the hands of long-established community defender groups such as the UVF or more recent loyalist paramilitary outfits such as the UDA. Worried by mounting signs of

Unionist revolt, Wilson and Callaghan eased up their pressure on Stormont to push through reforms. Not for the first or the last time, Westminster buckled under the pressure of Unionist hardliners.

If the government misjudged the Unionist reaction, it badly miscalculated the Catholic one as well. Wilson realized that radical reform was the quid pro quo of Catholic acquiescence in Stormont. But by not taking political control in August 1969 he had left political responsibility over the pace, direction and speed of reform in the hands of Stormont. He had charged the very institution being transformed with overseeing the transformation: the poacher left to tend the rabbits. Such a woolly, liberal and rather quaint faith in the power of reason and rational action appeared misplaced in a context where power was a matter of life and death, and politics a struggle between survival and extinction. By treating Northern Ireland as if it were merely an errant county council, the government revealed just how little it understood the province and its people. All too inevitably, when radical reform did not materialize or came too slowly, in the face of mounting Unionist disquiet, so the Catholic community became frustrated and disillusioned, undermining their willingness to accept Stormont or even trust the British. The British government no longer appeared the gallant defender of minority interests but the defender of Unionist power; no longer the protector of Catholic communities but the protector of the Unionist government. And by not assuming political control, Britain saddled herself with all the bad publicity but with only a limited ability to do anything about it.

As relations between Britain and the Catholic community cooled, a third flaw embedded within British policy came into play, namely that 'no army, however well it conducts itself, is suitable for police work'.[22] Events of 1919–1921 had demonstrated the inappropriateness of soldiers acting like policemen, but especially soldiers and officers whose military experience was rooted in colonial conflicts. For as the army became embroiled in day-to-day matters, so it automatically responded to developments by drawing upon its experiences in various colonial conflicts where counter-insurgency methods had been used to quell it. In late September, for example, the army erected a 'peace line' in Londonderry, restricting access into the Catholic Bogside[23] and allowed only limited movement into the city centre. In February the army was accused of brutality when it tried to disperse Catholic protestors from outside the Guildhall with the use of batons,[24] though it was not until April and the Ballymurphy riots that the army decided to use snatch-squads and CS gas. These responses, though the stock-in-trade for the British Army in Malaya, Cyprus and Aden, simply generated hostility towards the army and alienated the Catholic community.[25] Soldiers once greeted as heroes by Catholics now found 'the tea had stopped flowing in the Falls'.[26] These developments suggested the army was an overly blunt weapon to use in the sensitive situation of Northern Ireland, though few could see an alternative.

Herein lay the final flaw. Wilson assumed British troops could act as neutral arbiters in a setting where they were far from neutral. Britain was, after all, operating in defence of a Unionist-dominated government. She also had special cultural and political links with the Unionist community, whether she cherished them or not, while carrying historic antagonisms with the Nationalist one. So whatever the army's intentions, this heavy baggage of Anglo-Irish history weighed against it ever performing an impartial role. As friction rose between the army and the Catholic community, and as communal violence escalated, as relations deteriorated, as petty inconveniences turned to bitterness and mutual animosities grew, so that historical baggage was unpacked and all the old fears, myths, traditions and prejudices gained new life and relevance. As a consequence demands for civil rights ripened into demands for 'Brits out' and reunification of the Irish 'nation'. Questions of reform and equality of status wilted as older questions of nationality, partition and the legitimacy of the state revived. The conflict transmogrified beneath Britain's feet, from a question of rights to a question of 'ownership', from the issue of reform to the issue of 'possession'. Ireland's 'ancestral voices'[27] began speaking once again to a new generation of northern Nationalists.

Those ancestral voices were heard loudest within the emergent Provisional IRA. PIRA, or the 'Provisionals', or simply the 'Provos', were a hardline splinter group from the larger Marxist-based 'Official' IRA. Formed in January 1970, it was a coalition of traditional republicans, pledged to establish an Irish republic through armed struggle, and hard-headed Catholic defenders rooted in the northern communities, who saw little point theorizing Marxism when their communities were under attack from loyalist mobs. The Provisionals were, then, a powerful mix of sectarian militancy, community defence and revolutionary fervour, whose aims in the short term were to defend 'their' people and in the longer term to undermine Stormont, force Britain out of Northern Ireland and establish a united Irish republic. These objectives were sacrosanct and beyond compromise and since all political activity entailed some compromise, they shunned politics altogether. Armed struggle was the only 'safe' route to achieve (and preserve) the purity of their ideals. But armed struggle was reliant upon arms. So through the spring and summer of 1970 the Provos carefully built up support and resources from inside Catholic communities, aided by the growing friction between the army and Catholic communities. Build-up, unlike previous IRA revivals, also now meant propaganda. The Provos carefully nurtured an image of themselves as a legitimate and largely defensive organization, reactive rather than pro-active, and engaged in a colonial conflict against an Imperial aggressor. Their first military action in June 1970, when they defended the small Catholic enclave of Short Strand in east Belfast, centred upon St Matthews Church, was expertly manipulated to convey just these images. Similarly they policed their 'no-go' areas, enforced a summary justice within the community, and increasingly orchestrated confrontations with the army to provoke retaliation (or better still over-reaction), to further legitimize themselves in the eyes of the Catholic community and to wider international and especially US opinion to which they appealed. By the autumn of 1970 the Provisionals went on the offensive. It began with a sniping and

> 66 The Provisionals were, then, a powerful mix of sectarian militancy, community defence and revolutionary fervour 99

bombing campaign across the province, claiming in August the lives of two RUC officers. Six months later they turned their guns on the British Army, killing their first soldier, Gunner Robert Curtis, in February 1971. In all, the emergence of the Provos exerted a 'multiplier' effect upon the developments unfolding in the region by intensifying Unionist insecurity, widening inter-communal divisions, diverting government resources from reform and turning friction between the army and the Catholic communities to hatred and loathing.

So by the end of 1970 weaknesses in British policy had under-mined attempts to impose peace and stability. Military inter-vention had been premised upon giving Stormont's reform programme time to establish a political consensus between the communities. Unfortunately it had resulted in escalating dis-order, a widening communal gulf, institutional weakness, Britain mistrusted and her army alienated from both communi-ties, but especially alienated from the Catholic community where old-style Nationalist politics and paramilitary activity were replacing the politics of civil rights. The likelihood of a compromise political settlement materializing under these con-ditions was a very faint hope.

AT SEA AND ADRIFT, 1971–1972

British political leaders seemed unable to imagine alternative courses. Despite scant improvement in the situation, there was no review of methods and strategy, let alone consideration of long-term objectives. The government still regarded a political solution as possible, though offered few ideas on how to achieve it. It continued to believe Stormont capable of delivering reform, even though two-thirds of the population wanted no change while the other third had no faith that it would happen. And it still would not countenance assuming overall political control, despite a conviction in Whitehall and at Westminster that it was fast becoming inevitable. All Britain would offer was more of the same. 'I think we felt,' a senior minister explained at the time, 'this would die down ... that if we showed enough resolution and force, they would pack up.'[28]

While politicians dithered, the army was only too willing to show resolution. In the absence of ministerial direction the military took the initiative, injecting a firmer touch and harder response into its duties, or as it liked to portray it, banging heads together and bringing the 'natives' to order. The movement towards a full-blown counter-insurgency campaign was rooted in the growing frustration at the persistent violence on the ground, and especially the mounting number of 'hits' against the army. A tougher response was also a consequence of changes at Westminster, where a Conservative victory in the June 1970 general election brought Edward Heath to power, with Northern Ireland thrust into the incapable hands of Reginald Maudling, the new Home Secretary. Tories did not bring a fresh understanding of the problem or any new ideas for solving it. But they did bring a sterner tone, a harder attitude, a deeper sympathy for the Unionist position and the union, and a stronger commitment to military methods. These produced differences of balance and priority. Where Callaghan had stressed reform, Maudling emphasized security. Where Labour probably sympathized more with the Catholics, Tories generally took the Unionists' side. And where Labour was hesitant and fretful over military options, the Tories gave 'the army its head to crush the rebels'.[29] Fortunately, with the IRA military campaign 'gearing up' by mid-1970, there were now recognizable, though not always locatable, 'rebels' for the British to crush.

Crushing rebels took many forms, from threatening to shoot petrol-bombers in April 1970, and actually doing so later, to house searches, more roads-blocks and stop-and-search measures. But giving the army 'its head' was not always a wise course and often 'getting tough' against terrorism could become self-defeating. This was apparent with the imposition of a three-day curfew on the Catholic Falls Road area of Belfast between 3 and 5 July 1970, as a pretext for soldiers to search for IRA weapons. The arms found proved significant but paled in comparison with the permanent ostracism of Catholic communities that followed the destruc-

> 66 Where Callaghan had stressed reform, Maudling emphasized security 99

tion of property, petty assaults, and the sense of invasion and injustice engendered by the operation. Since the Falls area was an Official IRA stronghold, the Provisionals emerged unscathed, with stronger community support and a flood of recruits into the organization. The Falls curfew would be the first of many British own-goals.

The lessons of the curfew were clear enough: the vital importance of having good intelligence, the precise targeting of suspects, the acute danger of over-reacting, the desirability of establishing and maintaining contacts with community leaders and the need to accompany toughness with political progress. Unfortunately, as disorder spiralled ever upwards, these lessons were quickly forgotten, with disastrous consequences. On 9 August 1971 British politicians and army leaders introduced Internment. In Operation Demetrius the army swooped on Catholic areas throughout the province, detaining without charge or trial hundreds of mostly innocent Catholics. Embarrassingly few Provos were caught in the operation and most of those arrested were innocent civilians who were then subsequently released, though with tales to tell of harsh treatment and now only too ready to aid the Provisionals. The very public 'whole-community' basis to the operation, reinforced by the failure to arrest a single Protestant, now led the Catholic communities to feel themselves at 'war' with the British, with the Provos as the legitimate defenders of their community. Violence, far from receding, ratcheted in an ever upwards direction, while those calling for peace and reconciliation were either marginalized or, like the newly formed constitutional Nationalist party, the SDLP, forced into a more partisan position to survive.

What made matters worse was that having alienated the Catholics, British 'get tough' policies did nothing to satiate Unionist insecurities. The escalating violence and the strengthening position of the Provisionals deepened their sense of 'besiegement' and impending catastrophe, the beneficiary of which was extreme Unionism. William Craig, with his eyes now firmly set on Carsonite martyrdom, responded by forming the Ulster Vanguard to agitate *inside* the Ulster Unionist Party for his brand of more emotional, hardline Unionism. Not to be out-'toughed', Paisley established the Democratic Unionist Party late in 1971 for similar ends. Insecurity also drove large numbers of Protestants from September into the UDA, which within months stood at 20,000, though peaking a year later at between 40,000 and 50,000. Its attraction was clear. If Britain and Stormont could not protect Protestant communities, they would do it themselves. Accordingly they established their own 'no-go' areas, their own patrols in Protestant estates, and retaliated to IRA attacks with attacks on Catholics. 'The situation had all the characteristics of the "security dilemma" in which one side's efforts to protect its own security only makes the other side feel more insecure and thus likely to take "protective" measures of its own.'[30]

THE FALL OF STORMONT, 1972

The result of these developments was that the eight months from the introduction of Internment, in August 1971, to the suspension of Stormont, in March 1972, witnessed some of the worst violence of the entire Troubles. On 10 August 1971 Gunner Paul Challenor became the 100th victim of the Troubles. Exactly one year later that total stood at 534. In the seven months up to August 1971, 34 people had been killed; in the five months afterwards, 140 died. Such figures suggest the region was teetering on the edge of all-out ethnic war.

One particularly nasty cycle of violence began on 23 and 24 October when the army shot dead three young Catholic men and two women of the Cumann na mBan, the women's wing of the IRA. In reply the IRA took its campaign to the British mainland and on 31 October exploded a bomb at the Post Office Tower in London. Back in Northern Ireland its campaign continued with the murder of four RUC officers and two off-duty soldiers between 1 and 11 November. In response, on 4 December, 15 people were murdered by the UVF in a bomb attack on McGurk's bar in Belfast, to which the IRA responded by planting a bomb in a crowded shop on the Protestant Shankhill, killing four people, one of whom was a seven-month-old baby. The province had reached almost unimaginable levels of barbarism and brutality, with the communities locked in cycles of revenge and retribution. Stormont appeared powerless to stem the slide towards complete social breakdown.

Events provoked a frantic debate on how to get to grips with the deteriorating situation. From the opposition benches Wilson suggested a 12 Point Plan that included a Minister for Northern Ireland to sit in Cabinet, an All-Ireland Council and the introduction of PR in elections. By November his 12 points had grown to 15 and included progress towards Irish unification if the Republic re-entered the Commonwealth. Faulkner saw this as 'fantasy' and thought Wilson mistrusted 'by almost the whole spectrum of Ulster Unionism'[31] – a far from comforting thought since he would be Prime Minister again within two years. Yet Wilson's fantasies found an echo within sections of the Foreign Office, the Northern Ireland Office, the Treasury, ever keen to save money, and even amongst some members of that once most eager of Unionist champions, the Conservative Party.

The army, on the other hand, favoured direct rule. Many officers, including the counter-insurgency expert Brigadier Frank Kitson, believed it would enable a political initiative to be mounted in support of the military one and so redress the pro-Protestant image of the British security forces. It would provide that 'something big ... to the Catholics in order to persuade them to support the IRA rather less' and thus would be essential for winning Catholic 'hearts and minds'.[32] Direct rule would also remove the chaos of overlapping chains of authority, the petty inter-service squabbles, the lack of co-ordination between the RUC and the army and between the civil and military arms that had characterized operations in Northern Ireland since the army arrived. Yet however militarily advantageous, direct rule remained politically unattractive. This calculation was based partly on a fear of the unforeseen consequences of being sucked into an intractable situation, partly on a misplaced faith that Stormont could, with time, restore stability and legitimacy, but

66 Events provoked a frantic debate on how to get to grips with the deteriorating situation 99

also on the realization that a primary aim of the IRA was to abolish Stormont. If Stormont was removed, the IRA, scenting victory, would step up its campaign while the Unionist communities, scenting betrayal and re-unification, would move wholesale into the arms of Paisley, Craig and the UDA. All-out civil war was as much a possibility of Britain assuming full control over the province as it was of withdrawing from it.

So like Wilson before him, Heath continued to hesitate over taking control of Northern Ireland. He did, however, believe Westminster needed to play a *larger* political role in the province, for without that he realized the status of Catholics would never be improved. On this problem he was already beginning to contemplate some type of power-sharing executive, as Maudling hinted in a Commons speech when he talked of 'an active, permanent and guaranteed place in the life and public affairs of Northern Ireland shall be available both to the majority and the minority community'.[33] Though unaware of its significance, Maudling was launching an idea that would dominate government policy over the next 30 years, though in private the Home Secretary and others were also predicting the imminent demise of Stormont. Despite, then, his constructive thinking, Heath remained committed to Stormont and shared the Foreign Secretary's view of 'anything but direct rule'.[34] It would clearly take something very big to shake the Tory government into assuming direct political control over Northern Ireland.

That something came on 30 January 1972 in Londonderry, when members of the Parachute Regiment shot dead 13 unarmed and largely peaceful protestors and wounded a further 14; Bloody Sunday. The events of Bloody Sunday transformed the conflict. Any lingering regard for the British Army by the Catholic community was shattered. The Provos' numbers swelled massively as new recruits flooded into the organization. Even more useful than recruits, the Provos were handed a propaganda coup they could only have dreamed of. A coup that enabled the events to be constructed into an Irish 'Amritsar' and the desperate act of an oppressive colonial power, a projection able to win money and support in the USA, the Republic, at the

UN, in the councils of Europe and on the British mainland. The power of this was felt immediately with the deluge of criticism in the USA and the burning down of the British Embassy in Dublin. At a wider cultural level Bloody Sunday left a deep, gaping scar within the Catholic community and an entrenched alienation from what was, after all, their own government. This was aggravated yet further by the overly rapid and overly partisan official inquiry into events under Lord Widgery that left a feeling of mistrust and a belief that gentle reform would no longer satisfy their expectations and political interests. The government was obliged to act – and to act quickly. 'Something must be done became the inevitable comment of the moment.'[35] Britain had to be seen to be taking matters in hand, getting to grips with the problem and trying to somehow placate the Catholic community, and in the circumstances direct rule seemed the obvious, indeed the only, course. So what had long been an unpalatable possibility had turned into an unavoidable certainty. 'We just found it very difficult to believe,' admitted the British government's representative in Belfast as he listened to the radio traffic, 'when three, then five and then seven deaths came in … when we got to seven, Howard and I looked at each other and said, "Right, that means direct rule". Of course, when it got to 13, direct rule was inevitable.'[36] There was also a military consideration here as well. For Bloody Sunday, by mobilizing mass support behind the IRA, had made a purely military victory a much more difficult prospect, suggesting the conflict was now going to be a very long and drawn-out process.

> **Bloody Sunday, by mobilizing mass support behind the IRA, had made a purely military victory a much more difficult prospect**

Contingency plans for direct rule had existed since Callaghan's time at the Home Office. However, the step was delayed while Heath finalized arrangements and prepared for the likely political repercussions from the Unionist community. Despite some last-minute manoeuvrings, Heath temporarily suspended the Northern Irish Assembly and its executive on 24 March 1972, though it would turn out to be a far from temporary initiative.

All powers, authority and responsibilities were transferred to Westminster, in a form of reverse devolution, taking back what she had given in 1920. Stormont, that had defended Unionist interests for 50 years, was gone and the province placed under the authority of a British Secretary of State for Northern Ireland. William Whitelaw was given the daunting task of solving the Northern Irish problem, a problem that was probably, at this stage, beyond solution. 'I am undertaking,' he told the Harrow Conservative association on the night of his appointment, 'the most terrifying, difficult and awesome task.'[37] Nor was he exaggerating.

NOTES

1 H. Wilson, *The Labour Government, 1964–1970: A Personal Record*, (Weidenfeld & Nicholson, 1971) p 675.

2 M. Cunningham, *British Government Policy in Northern Ireland, 1969–2000* (MUP, 2001) pp 1–11.

3 J. Callaghan, *A House Divided* (Collins, 1973) p 15.

4 C. Ryder, *The RUC: A Force under Fire, 1922–2000* (Arrow, 2000) p 105.

5 J. Callaghan, op. cit., p 7.

6 B. Faulkner, *Memoirs of a Statesman* (Weidenfeld and Nicolson, 1978) p 49

7 N. O'Dochartaigh, *From Civil Rights to Armalites: Derry and the Birth of the Irish Troubles* (Cork UP, 1997) p 40.

8 J. Callaghan, op. cit., p 34.

9 H. Wilson, op. cit., p 675.

10 Ibid, p 39.

11 Ibid, pp 45–6.

12 P. Taylor, *Brits: The War Against the IRA* (Bloomsbury, 2000) p 24.

13 H. Wilson, op.cit., p 693.

14 R. Jenkins speaking in 1967, quoted in P. Rose, "Labour, Northern Ireland and the decision to send in the Troops", in P. Catterall (ed) *The Northern Ireland Question in British Politics* (Macmillan, 1996) p 96.

15 J. Callaghan, op. cit., pp 191–2.

16 Ibid, pp 68–9.

17 Ibid.

18 J. Callaghan, op. cit., p 66.

19 N. O'Dochartaigh, op. cit., pp 130–40.

20 P. Taylor, *Loyalists* (Bloomsbury, 1999) p 70.

21 D. Hamill, *Pig in the Middle: The Army in Northern Ireland, 1969–1984* (Methuen, 1985) p 29.

22 M. Dewar, *The British Army in Northern Ireland* (Arms and Armour, 1985) p 38.

23 Ibid, p 156.

24 N. O'Dochartaigh, op. cit., p 171.

25 P. O'Malley, *The Uncivil Wars* (Blackstaff, 1983) p 206.

26 M. Dewar, op. cit., p 48.

27 C. C. O'Brien, *Ancestral Voices: Religion and Nationalism in Ireland* (Poolbeg, 1994) pp 156–60.

28 D. Hamill, op. cit., p 38.

29 C. Kennedy-Pipe, *The Origins of the Present Troubles in Northern Ireland* (Longman, 1997) p 52.

30 S. Farren and R. F. Mulvihill, *Paths to a Settlement in Northern Ireland* (Colin Smythe, 2000) p 47.

31 B. Faulkner, op. cit., p 133.

32 D. Hamill, op. cit., p 64.

33 B. Faulkner, op. cit., p 130.

34 Ibid, p 128.

35 W. Whitelaw, *The Whitelaw Memoirs* (Aurum, 1989) p 79.

36 P. Taylor, *Brits: The War Against the IRA* (Bloomsbury, 2000) pp 107–8.

37 W. Whitelaw, op. cit., p 83.

5

LONDON INITIATIVES:[1]
1972–1983

'I realized just why the Irish problem was said to be insoluble.'
The Whitelaw Memoirs, p 92

'Oh it's disgraceful, surely, I agree.'
'Where's it going to end?' 'It's getting worse.'
'They're murderers', 'internment, understandably . . .,'
'The "voice of sanity" is getting hoarse.'
Seamus Heaney, *Whatever You Say Say Nothing* (Faber, 1975)

CHAOS AND ANARCHY, 1972

WHITELAW WAS NOT THE MOST OBVIOUS PERSON TO UNDERTAKE the task of ending the violence and finding a solution to the Troubles. An avuncular, old Wykemist, patrician in manner, plummy in speech, with the florid countenance of an eighteenth-century squire and the embodiment of the British Establishment, he was arguably the most unlikely person to take charge of Northern Irish affairs since the philosophizing, effete Tory politician Arthur Balfour (collector of fine bone china and nicknamed 'pretty Fanny') was appointed Irish Chief Secretary in 1886. But Whitelaw, like Balfour and other similarly 'plummy' Tory Secretaries of State in the future, was to prove unexpectedly resourceful and politically courageous. He certainly needed to be. For the full intractability of the situation in Northern Ireland was only too apparent when he landed at Aldergrove airport in Belfast on 25 March 1972. Violence was spiralling out of control. Political extremists on both sides were growing in number and vitriol. Communal differences had become deeply polarized and bitter. The result of these pressures was, as Whitelaw quickly found, that government action became almost impossible for 'any moves which were likely to encourage the Catholics were almost certain to infuriate Protestants still further'.[2] It was zero-sum politics in its purest form, where a tough security policy alienated one side while the lack of toughness antagonized the other. Or a lack of political reform angered one community, while progress on political reform outraged the other. And so with the removal of Stormont, a move that delighted Nationalists but deeply alarmed Unionists, who interpreted Britain's action as a base betrayal and yet another slide along the slippery slope to unification.

Indeed, the assumption of direct rule appeared initially to do little more than strengthen the hands of paramilitary groups. Ending Stormont and forcing Britain to take over direct rule had, after all, been a principal aim of the IRA. It sharpened and clarified their anti-colonial ideology if the 'colonial' power had now assumed full control and could no longer hide behind Unionist 'collaborators'. It also provided better targets. Murdering fellow Irish men and women, even if they were mostly Protestant and wearing a police uniform, had always sat uncomfortably with the IRA's aspiration to liberate all the Irish people from colonial oppression; theirs was, by any standard, a very sectarian and rather permanent definition of liberation. Murdering the soldiers of what they could represent as an oppressive colonial regime held fewer ideological or propagandist difficulties. Most significantly, the end of Stormont filled IRA commanders with confidence. It encouraged them to believe that further well-targeted violence could win yet more political gains, if not actually force the British to withdraw from Ireland. After all, had not people scoffed back in 1970 when the IRA bragged it could collapse Stormont? Loyalist paramilitaries shared this Republican reading of the situation. The last obstacle to a united Ireland had been destroyed by Tory betrayal and little of substance now stood in its path; like most Unionists they had little faith that a British government would defend their interests. They had, after all, witnessed the striking and brutal effectiveness of the IRA campaign in forcing Heath into surrender. So to them it was clear, 'violence can pay . . . violence does pay, and those who shout, lie, denigrate and even destroy earn for themselves an attention that responsible conduct and honourable behaviour do not'.[3] And what was good for the goose was good for the gander. Loyalists proved able and quick in learning the political effectiveness of violence. Whitelaw found himself embroiled in a 'lose–lose' situation, looking like the limp red rag tied to the rope of a tug-of-war match.

Given the intractable nature of the situation, Whitelaw was extremely uncertain how he was to solve the problem. Indeed, the only things he was certain of were that direct rule was a stopgap, that a settlement had to be by agreement between both communities, and the one place it would be found was at the political centre amongst moderates within Unionism and Nationalism. Unfortunately, the middle ground had all but disappeared as communal differences had steadily widened over the previous four years. Since the introduction of Internment, moderate Nationalists of the SDLP had refused all political contact, a rather self-defeating tactic later repeated by the Ulster Unionists towards the Anglo-Irish Agreement. The Ulster Unionist Party was fragmenting and losing ground to the advance of a more uncompromising brand of Unionism, both outside its ranks in the form of Paisley's DUP and within them in the shape of Craig and his Vanguard movement. Even the recently formed Alliance Party, a cross-community body dedicated to moderate policies, could win only a marginal position within the politics of the region. Constructing peace on the middle ground of early 1972 was akin to erecting a house on quick-sand.

> 66 Loyalists proved able and quick in learning the political effectiveness of violence 99

Yet Whitelaw had no option but to engage in political jerry-building. His first task was to generate support amongst the Catholic community by reducing the sense of grievance upon which the IRA had thrived so prodigiously over the past two years. To this end he released some internees and lifted the ban on marches and demonstrations. He also gave limited 'special category' concessions to Republican prisoners. These gestures drew a positive response from the Catholic community but did not alter the stance of the SDLP as he had hoped. Sadly, as was so often the case, it took an act of brutality to jolt politics into movement. The murder of William Best, a young Catholic soldier from Londonderry, by the Official IRA led to such widespread revulsion within the Catholic communities that the Officials were forced to end their campaign. It also persuaded the SDLP to call off its 'boycott' of British officials and to use what channels of communication it had to try to persuade the Provisionals to follow suit. The 'mood of peace'[4] did indeed encourage them into a temporary cease-fire, from 27 June until 9 July, during which time they invited Whitelaw to Free Derry for talks. Whitelaw refused but did arrange safe passage to London for the IRA leadership, where he met them in secret at the Chelsea home of his Minister of State, Paul Channon. However, the context was all wrong for a deal with the Provos at this stage. The Provisional leadership was riding high after the abolition of Stormont and cocksure about its eventual victory. With this frame of mind the invitation to meet was not regarded as a bold political initiative to end violence but as a sign that the British wanted to disengage. So their approach to negotiation amounted to an issuing of demands and insisting upon agreement, rather 'like Montgomery at Luneberg Heath telling the German Generals what they should and shouldn't do if they wanted peace'.[5] The Provisionals' leadership, which included Martin McGuinness, the young Derry commander, and Gerry Adams, the young leader of the Ballymurphy command, were expecting little more than to finalize arrangements for a British withdrawal. As a process of discussion and an attempt to establish peace, the meeting was 'a non event',[6] not least because the Provos demanded a British withdrawal by 1975 at the latest.

Though a non-event for Whitelaw, news that the British minister was talking to terrorists was a cataclysmic event for the Unionist community. It represented the latest in a long line of 'appeasements' of the Catholic community in general and the IRA in particular. For Unionists 'Willie Whitewash' was pursuing a policy of gradual surrender and retreat, starting with the abolition of Stormont, the release of internees, the granting of special category status to people they regarded as murderers, and now an IRA cease-fire followed by talks with the British Secretary of State. And all the time IRA violence pushed Northern Ireland deeper into anarchy. A suspicious person – and there were a few within the Unionist community – could be forgiven for thinking that Britain, if not actually about to 'cut and run' was building up to something big and far from attractive. Whatever the government was planning – and the lack of transparency was itself a major source of instability – Unionists were on the march during the first six months of 1972. The UDA responded in the way it knew best by matching Republican violence with its own, following O'Brien's observation that 'if Catholic gunmen were seen to shoot and bomb their way to the negotiation table, Protestant gunmen would not be slow to emulate their performance'.[7] Loyalist 'killer squads' openly targeted Catholics with no IRA connections, with the strategic aim of forcing the Nationalist community to put pressure on the IRA to stop. Others, such as the newly formed Loyalist Association of Workers, responded by exploiting the strike weapon to advertise their dissatisfaction, while Paisley railed and rallied across the region, attacking treachery in London and feebleness within the Unionist party – a sentiment shared by a number inside the party given the growing sympathy for the more emotive and militant Unionism of Craig and his Vanguard movement. The fall of Stormont and apparent inability to influence government policy divided Unionists and seriously weakened Faulkner's position as leader of the Ulster Unionist Party.

If Whitelaw had been only mildly aware of emerging Unionist disenchantment, events of 21 July 1972, Bloody Friday, left him convinced of the need to act quickly to placate the Protestant community. In just over an hour the IRA detonated 20 bombs across Belfast, killing 11 people, all but two of whom were civilian, and injuring 130. With the inverted logic of someone capable of executing such an action, the IRA Chief of Staff, Sean MacStiofain, put the blame squarely on the British for not clearing the areas quickly enough: the acts of planning, making and planting bombs in a busy city centre were apparently perfectly innocent, guilt-free occupations. Yet just as Bloody Sunday was an own-goal for the British, so Bloody Friday backfired on the Provisionals as widespread revulsion took root on all sides, and not least from moderate Nationalists.

With 'the water ... beginning to turn a little unhealthy for the fish',[8] Whitelaw seized his moment to open 'a new phase of policy'[9] and win back sympathy within the Protestant community by addressing their central concern of security. Ten days after Bloody Friday the British Army launched Operation Motorman, the biggest military operation since Suez in 1956, aimed at breaking the no-go areas in Belfast and Londonderry and re-establishing British authority across all of Northern Ireland. The move had long been urged by Unionist political leaders as both a practical measure for undermining the IRA's sanctuary and as confidence-building for the Unionist community. It would also, Faulkner hoped, shore up his own weakened political position since the suspension of Stormont. The initiative worked and brought Whitelaw the support he needed from within Unionism – and crucially *without* alienating the sympathy he had earlier acquired from moderate Nationalists. Bloody Friday and Operation Motorman had delivered what many had long thought to be undeliverable: a strengthened moderate centre, composed of sections from both communities. From these delicate sentiments Whitelaw realized that a window of opportunity was opening for him to engage all sides in discussions for a political settlement. As he later reflected on this moment, 'we seemed at last to be set on the road back to political dialogue'.[10]

> **❝Yet just as Bloody Sunday was an own-goal for the British, so Bloody Friday backfired on the Provisionals as widespread revulsion took root on all sides❞**

'A VERY TENDER PLANT';[11] FROM DARLINGTON TO SUNNINGDALE, 1972–1974

Whitelaw moved quickly to take advantage of the apparently favourable conditions opened up by the events of the summer, with a frantic round of discussions with all the major leaders. Keen to establish a momentum, he invited them to a conference at the Europa hotel in Darlington in late September. The SDLP refused to attend with Internment still in operation but maintained a loose contact through position papers and various informal channels. Darlington did much good work in thrashing out ideas and establishing personal contacts and was certainly invaluable for Whitelaw in understanding what type of political edifice this emerging moderate centre ground would be able to sustain. His results were published on 30 October in a Green discussion paper entitled *The Future of Northern Ireland*, which enshrined the twin-peaks of British thinking towards the region for the next three decades. First, the union would continue as long as the people wanted it, what has become known as the 'consent' principle. Second, any form of governance must include an Irish dimension and some type of power-sharing executive, in Whitelaw's slightly pro-consular and mildly condescending words, 'responsible Nationalists and Unionists should work together to devise a practical form of government for the beleaguered communities for whom they proclaimed their concern'.[12] Although it would be another 26 years in arriving, here were the green shoots from where the Good Friday Agreement of 1998 would spring.

As expected, Whitelaw's Green paper drew sharp comments from Faulkner and the Unionist Party, who dismissed power-sharing in favour of government based upon a majority and expressed deep reservations about the Irish dimension. To placate them Whitelaw held a referendum on the Border, a largely meaningless and wholly predictable action given the Nationalist boycott, but significant for seeming to publicly legitimate partition and thus reassure doubting Unionists. From the other side, the leader of the SDLP, Gerry Fitt, though generally more supportive of the Green paper, had hoped for some type of joint authority over Northern Ireland. To placate him Whitelaw gave some heavy hints that Internment would be dropped. Undeterred by the evident but far from unexpected differences of opinion, the Secretary of State engaged in further consultation and carefully tweaked his ideas before introducing them to Parliament in March as a White paper, *Northern Ireland: Constitutional Proposals*, followed in April by legislation. The proposals combined long-term aims with short-term initiatives. Step one would create a new Northern Irish Assembly on the still warm ashes of Stormont. The new assembly would provide a launch-pad for negotiations between the party leaders to find an agreed basis for government in Northern Ireland. And once a new Northern Ireland executive was agreed and established, it could engage in talks with both the British and Irish governments to reach an agreement over north/south relations, the Irish dimension. Whitelaw's plan was for a settlement to evolve in stages and by general agreement. The key to its success was that as it evolved the leaders retained a majority of support from both communities or at least a sufficient amount to enable them to carry through the changes. It was the dilemma faced by every moderate Northern Irish politician: would the construction of a settlement at the centre scare their supporters back to the extremes?

Events got off to a reasonable start. On 1 March 1973 a new Irish government was elected, composed of moderate Fine Gael and Labour members, with a youthful Garret FitzGerald as Foreign Minister, replacing the more traditional Republican Fianna Fail. In addition, the New Year seemed to herald some improvement in the security situation, though that was hardly saying much with 263 people killed during 1973 and was more by comparison with the absolute bloodbath that had been 1972. Finally, the election outcome to the new Northern Irish Assembly in June 1973 was promising, with 'pro-White paper' candidates winning 52 seats against the 'anti's' 26. The results provided the necessary support in the new Northern Ireland Assembly and thus the springboard into the first ever multi-party talks from October between Faulkner, Fitt and Oliver Napier of the Alliance Party, with the brief to agree a structure for governing Northern Ireland. It was an historic and politically brave step by all the party leaders, and by Faulkner and Fitt in particular. For upon their shoulders sat powerful groups hostile to the very idea of talks and keen to collapse them. Anti-White paper Unionists led by Craig and Paisley were busy circling Faulkner like hungry vultures, while the Provisionals glared ferociously at the SDLP. Yet despite these political dangers 'they were prepared to sink their substantial differences in the interests of giving a constructive lead to all the people of Northern Ireland'.[13] There was 'that basic will'[14] on all sides to find an accord and this was enough for Whitelaw to work his magic for oiling over differences, marrying entrenched positions, soothing egos and mollifying antagonisms in order to move divergent interests towards a consensus.

With such an 'operator' at the helm and a general will to succeed, the talks made quick progress, and by the time of Whitelaw's imposed deadline of 22 November an agreement had been reached. It was a superb compromise whereby Nationalists got the power-sharing executive they had long wanted but Unionists were given a majority upon it, so enabling Faulkner to take up the position of chief executive, with Fitt as deputy. The immediate effect was one of relief and congratulations on all sides, so allowing arrangements to move onto their final stage, the convening of talks on the Irish dimension. Whitelaw was euphoric at the construction of an executive, though by a cruel irony, any basking in the after-glow of his great triumph was cut short by Heath who whisked him back to London, like some sort of political fireman, to work his magic on the problem of the miners. Yet Whitelaw was more than a touch premature when he reflected that 'we had broken the mould of Northern Ireland politics based on sectarian division and we had helped to provide an opportunity for Northern Ireland politicians across the divide to work constructively against the men of violence'.[15] Time would show that the mould was still very much in place

> ❝It was an historic and politically brave step by all the party leaders, and by Faulkner and Fitt in particular❞

and that the men of violence, far from put onto the defensive, were simply gearing up for a showdown.

So it was under increasingly dark and threatening skies and under the gaze of a new Secretary of State, Francis Pym, that representatives of the three governments met at the civil service staff college at Sunningdale in Berkshire on 6 December 1973. In three days of intense negotiations the representatives managed to establish an institutionalized presence for north and south relations. A Consultative Assembly would be formed of 30 members from the Northern Assembly and 30 from the Dail, empowered to debate issues but without legislative powers. A Council of Ireland was created, composed of seven representatives from the Northern Executive and seven from the Republic. It would have 'executive, harmonizing and consultative' powers on a limited number of areas, yet vitally for Unionists all its decisions were to be by unanimous agreement, in effect granting them a veto. And although Faulkner did not succeed in having articles 2 and 3 of the Irish constitution removed, he did get full 'recognition by the Republic of our (Northern Ireland) right to self-determination within our existing boundaries' and a commitment to remove the articles at the earliest opportunity.[16] It was a remarkable agreement and a triumph for the type of moderate consensual politics that for so long had eluded the region. It held the hope for a new political dispensation to emerge in Northern Ireland as the foundation stone for a period of co-operation, modernization, economic development and social stability. As all tucked into their turkey that Christmas 1973, the future looked bright.

'GOD HELP THOSE WHO GET IN OUR WAY':[17] UNIONIST BACKLASH, 1972–1974

Unfortunately, within little more than five months both the executive and the Council of Ireland had collapsed. Part of the explanation lay with an intensifying IRA campaign in the early months of 1974 with the intention of destroying institutions that were designed to strengthen and stabilize Northern Ireland. Much more central to their demise was the eruption of the frequently mentioned and long expected Unionist backlash. That is not to argue that Unionism before 1972 had been a shy, retiring creature. Far from it, and in the name of the union, loyalist groups had already murdered, bombed, revenged and retaliated as much as – perhaps more than – any violent Republican group, while extreme dissident Unionist leaders had for years given their cause a voice that even the deafest would find hard to ignore. But a full Unionist backlash, the 'rising' of a whole community, had like some mythical Scottish monster failed to materialize. All that the commentators had so far glimpsed was the misshapen shadow of a Paisley beneath the surface or the gnarled fin of a Craig silhouetted against the sky-line. However, from 1973, in an atmosphere of profound uncertainty about the future of Northern Ireland, with the recent destruction of Stormont and evidence of British 'appeasement' of Nationalists, the beast finally broke cover to stalk the land. The catalyst for this was Whitelaw's White paper of March 1973 with its intention of building a compromise upon a power-sharing executive and an Irish dimension. In opposition Vanguard and the DUP, coalesced with various Protestant workers' groups such as the Loyalist Association of Workers (LAW) and with sections of the UDA. Though sharing the same aim as the IRA, namely the destruction of Sunningdale, their objectives differed and embraced the return of Stormont and preservation of Unionist supremacy.

Just how much support this militant Unionism was able to attract became clear by the time of the elections for the new Northern Assembly in June. Although the pro-White paper forces won 52 seats, with the antis just 26, a mere 24 of those 52 were Unionists. In other words a majority of Unionists had voted against Faulkner and against entry into talks with the SDLP and Alliance, though not enough to divert Faulkner from his course. It was, however, a clear warning that many in the Unionist community were extremely alarmed by developments. If Faulkner needed any further warning then it came soon afterwards with his extremely narrow victory at a Ulster Unionist Council meeting, by just 379 to 369 votes, on whether to accept a power-sharing executive. Faulkner was stretching Unionist support well beyond the length it was willing to go. By early December, following the agreement at Sunningdale, that support snapped altogether when full-blown 'fisticuffs' broke out in the Assembly between pro and anti-White paper Unionists. 'There was a concerted physical assault *on the members of my party by the loyalists*', Faulkner observed, 'Peter McLachlan was rugger-tackled by Professor Kennedy Lindsay, fell over the bar of the House and was then kicked in the groin ... Herbie Kirk received a wound on the head which drew blood, and all around the benches members were trading punches and struggling. Basil McIvor was seized by the tie and half strangled before he hit his attacker so hard he almost knocked him down.'[18] Such behaviour more than justified Whitelaw's decision not to invite loyalist leaders to the Sunningdale conference that convened the very next day and so the tantalizing sight of Paisley wrestling with Heath on the conference floor became one of history's lost images. However laughable, even ludicrous, the vision of middle-aged Parliamentarians and otherwise stuffy academics 'swapping blows' inside the austere surroundings of Stormont, these were extremely worrying signs for Faulkner's leadership of his party and of the Unionist community as a whole. It was all very reminiscent of the final days of O'Neill, another Unionist leader who tried to squeeze Unionism along a path it was unwilling to travel down.

> ❝If Faulkner needed any further warning then it came soon afterwards with his extremely narrow victory at a Ulster Unionist Council meeting❞

Faulkner realized this all too late. Three days after the power-sharing executive took office, on 1 January 1974, the rug was finally pulled from underneath him. At a special meeting of the Ulster Unionist Council, party mavericks Harry West and a young John Taylor, egged on by powerful Paisleyite rhetoric of a 'sell-out', initiated a rejection of the Sunningdale agreement. Faulkner's line and leadership were overturned, forcing him to resign as leader of the Ulster Unionist Party, though able to remain leader of the executive with the support of his somewhat marooned and dwindling band of supporters in the assembly and the backing of Alliance and Nationalist members.[19] Ulster

Unionism had now split into a pro-Faulkner minority and an anti-Faulkner majority. Since the anti-Faulknerite section had the entire infrastructure, finances, experience, constituency offices and electoral agents of the Unionist Party, it was a moot point how long Faulkner could survive, which in turn placed a large question mark over the executive. If the power-sharing executive lost its ability to share through the implosion of one of the partners, it could no longer function. In these circumstances what Faulkner did not need, but which unfortunately transpired, was Heath's decision to call a Westminster election on 28 February. If anything was going to undermine a still weak executive, it was the radicalizing effect that accompanied any election in Northern Ireland. Heath, ignoring the advice of Whitelaw and Pym, entered the contest on the basis of a showdown with the miners on the question of 'Who Rules Britain?' The outcome of this particular contest was unclear, but in Northern Ireland it was demonstrated with brutal transparency that the anti-Sunningdale Unionists ruled the province. Out of a possible 12 Westminster seats, the combined forces of the DUP, Vanguard and other loyalists groups, under the banner of the United Ulster Unionist Council (UUUC), won 11. Since they ran on the slogan 'Dublin is just a Sunningdale away', the vote was a decisive and massive show of Unionist repulsion for the executive and Sunningdale, though because it was a Westminster and not an assembly election, Faulkner and his government could stagger on for the time being.

For how long was not clear. Faulkner desperately tried to shore up his position by hardening his tone and by attempting to extract a pledge from the Irish government to rescind articles 2 and 3. Whether this would actually have altered things is a moot point, but the failure of Dublin to at least attempt it for the sake of saving Faulkner and thus Sunningdale was at the very least extremely short-sighted. More controversially, he moved to delay implementation of the Council of Ireland, but that simply generated division within the executive. The new Labour Secretary of State, Merlyn Rees, even went so far as to hint at a possible British withdrawal from Northern Ireland if Sunningdale collapsed, a

Gerry Adams and Martin McGuiness of Sinn Fein. PA Photos.

The Claws of HISTORY

The HAND of HISTORY

Bono with David Trimble (left) and John Hume (right) during a concert in Belfast to promote the 'Yes' vote in the peace referendum in Northern Ireland, September 2001. PA Photos.

bold move designed to swing moderate Protestant opinion back behind Faulkner. But such eleventh-hour moves failed to strengthen Faulkner or to save the power-sharing experiment, and given the clear shift in the popular mood since the assembly elections of 1973, probably little now could. For the UUUC was claiming, with some force, that it reflected the 'true' voice of the people and the assembly was an unrepresentative body that made the power-sharing deal and the Sunningdale bargain contrary to the 'will' of the people. From here it was just a short step for the UUUC to demand fresh elections to the assembly, hoping to capitalize on its popularity within the Protestant communities. On 9 March, more than 2,000 UUUC demonstrators advanced on Stormont to demand fresh assembly elections, a demand repeated by the anti-Sunningdale members of the assembly on 14 May. The pro-agreement majority in the assembly stood firm and rejected the motion, but at the expense of provoking a general strike orchestrated by a newly formed Ulster Workers Council (UWC), which co-ordinated the activities of various Protestant workers, and the Ulster Army Council (UAC), which did the same for paramilitary loyalist groups.

> ❝ Loyalists brought the province to a standstill in a show of solidarity and grassroots power that overwhelmed the executive ❞

Loyalists brought the province to a standstill in a show of solidarity and grassroots power that overwhelmed the executive. High levels of violence accompanied the strike, one of the more atrocious being the loyalist car-bombs in Dublin and Monaghan three days into the strike that killed 33 people, still the highest number of deaths in one day throughout the entire Troubles. But the strike also represented something like a popular insurrection by three-fifths of the population, sustained by intimidation and a profound sense of anger and fear. Not even blunt threats from Wilson or Rees could humble the UWC, which in cutting oil, water, fuel, sewerage and electricity supplies as well as various public services, turned a standstill into a state of emergency. The army, fearing a war against both the IRA and the

UDA, a war on two fronts, was most reluctant to become involved in a struggle with loyalist paramilitaries, an eerie echo of events long ago at the Curragh. But without the full compliance of the army, the British government and the executive had no means of breaking it. And by refusing to negotiate with the strikers to reach a compromise, Wilson revealed himself a firm, if uncharacteristic, defender of parliamentary government, but also ensured no means of political escape from an ever-tightening vice. Without an exit and increasingly daunted by the reaction from his own people and within his own community, Faulkner resigned as chief executive of the power-sharing government on 28 May. With Faulkner went his Unionist colleagues, the power-sharing executive, the Sunningdale agreement and the Northern Ireland Assembly. The brave experiment in consensual government was destroyed in a tidal wave of Unionist opposition dressed up as democracy. The Ulster dog had done more than bare its teeth at Sunningdale – it had savaged the fledgling initiative to death.

WHAT NOW? 1975–1983

The collapse of the power-sharing executive and the Sunningdale agreement had a powerful impact on future attempts to construct a political settlement in Northern Ireland. Embittered Nationalists saw only weak British government, unwilling to stand up to undemocratic and overbearing Unionist behaviour in a further example of that all-too-familiar narrative of Britain accepting the legitimacy of the Unionist veto. Moderate Unionists saw an inflexible Dublin unwilling to give up its constitutional claim to the north and over-reaching itself with the Council of Ireland. Both have a degree of truth but are too simplistic. It is important to remember that none of the paramilitary groups were on a cease-fire, so violence continued to buffet political initiatives, with largely negative results. Far better in the future to hold talks when violence was suspended or at least declining. Furthermore, significant political groups – Republicans, Vanguard and the DUP – were either omitted or excluded themselves from the negotiations, which left their leaders angered, alienated and thus dangerous. Again it would be better in the future to have such characters, if possible, 'inside the tent pissing out, than outside pissing in'. In addition, the initiatives had collapsed because the viable centre ground spotted by Whitelaw in 1972 progressively weakened before disappearing altogether at the February 1974 election. Any future peace initiative would require a strengthened and sustainable political middle ground for it to stand any chance of success. Finally, whatever the politicians might decide, they had to carry *both* communities with them, or at least sizeable elements from both. In 1974 Catholics could see what they were winning from Sunningdale, whereas Protestants could not and indeed felt they were giving much more than they were getting in return. It was this particular spectre, the 'ghost of Faulkner's betrayal', that would haunt Trimble throughout the period 1996–1998.

The lessons of Sunningdale would prove useful for future attempts to find a negotiated settlement. Yet in the circumstances of 1974 and for some considerable time afterwards there was little chance or inclination for another attempt. Political sensitivities were too raw, egos remained badly bruised and mutual recrimination seemed a far easier diet to swallow than consensus politics. The parties of the extremes were in the ascendancy and so with little hope of advance, Northern Ireland sank back into a state of violence and political arthritis. This is not to argue that all stopped thinking about how the problem might be solved. Indeed, the period was rich and fertile in conflict-resolution strategies, the only problem being that they were all either impractical or likely to worsen the situation. One such scheme popular with the Tory Right and with sections of the Ulster Unionist Party was to fully integrate the region into the United Kingdom, as if Northern Ireland was some type of troublesome Surrey or Hampshire. Such a move would have alienated Nationalists both in the north and in Dublin, and further legitimized the IRA's position. Even less practical was the idea of a repartition, making Northern Ireland more ethnically homogeneous, through the transfer of huge numbers of people. The ancient demand of a united Ireland also reared its head once again, though in light of the loyalist strike this seemed even less a realizable ambition, if it ever really had been. While, the notion of a federal Ireland received little support and even less encouragement.

One idea that grew in attractiveness after the events of 1974 was the notion of a British withdrawal. This should not occasion surprise given the 'bloody nose' inflicted on the government by the Unionist backlash and with opinion polls in Britain regularly showing a popular desire to cut and run. Moreover, successive British governments since 1969 had all expressed their desire to withdraw from the region; military intervention in 1969 and then the suspension of Stormont had both been predicated upon a temporary basis. Hints and talk of withdrawal had also been useful tactics for helping to lull the IRA into a period of truce through much of 1975. The effect of this was to so seriously divide Republicans that the IRA came very close to collapse. Yet for the British to simply up tents and pull out would have plunged the whole region and perhaps the rest of Ireland into civil war. Britain could and would withdraw but only when a stable, cross-community system of government was in place to take over and thus when both communities, particularly the majority one, agreed to it. So ideas of 'troops out' and 'leaving them to it' amounted to no more than hypothesizing in shadowy Cabinet committees or muffled whispers in the corridors of the Northern Ireland office. It was never a practical policy. And so thinking the unthinkable or the unachievable brought British policy back to the unavoidable – direct rule – as the least obnoxious, least problematic path for all concerned.

> 66 The notion of a federal Ireland received little support and even less encouragement 99

Of course, recognizing the intractability of the situation and the policy constraints did not stop a series of British Secretaries of State attempting to do something, like a succession of knights looking upon Excalibur, knowing it was impossible to shift but aware that untold political riches awaited them if they could pull it off. Rees, late in 1974, established a Constitutional Convention of Northern Irish politicians to agree amongst themselves a governing structure. Unfortunately, the discussions were typified more by disagreement than consensus. When it presented Rees with a highly partisan scheme, reflecting the dominant Unionist presence within the conference, he threw it and its plan out. Several years later in 1979 a new Tory Secretary of State, Humphrey Atkins, convened talks between the various political leaders, again to thrash out a new constitutional future for Northern Ireland. When the Ulster Unionist Party refused to attend, and the DUP and SDLP disagreed over what to talk about, the Atkins initiative went the way of the Whitelaw and Rees ones. Two years later, in 1982, another Tory Secretary of State, Jim Prior, constructed a scheme composed of elements of Whitelaw's plan and elements of Rees' in what became known as 'rolling devolution'. A new Northern Irish Assembly was created in October 1982 with a system of committees, though as yet no power. 'In time, if sufficient agreement emerged between the parties to form a Northern Ireland administration, they could seek a return of legislative powers from Westminster.'[20] Power would roll from London to Belfast if Belfast could show it was able to use it responsibly and fairly. But without the involvement of the SDLP his scheme rolled nowhere. Attempts, then, through the late 1970s and early 1980s to resuscitate the power-sharing executive and Sunningdale agreement proved impossible. Politics were just too polarized, the centre ground too weak and the political will missing.

However, the lack of political progress was counter-balanced by success elsewhere. The war against terrorism, after a clumsy and naive start, had by the mid-1970s grown in sophistication. High-tech surveillance equipment was introduced to eavesdrop and monitor the province with an intensity that severely restricted the operations of the IRA. The use of spies and informants, particularly during the period of the truce, became widespread and effective, with some 400 suspects taken into custody during the first five months of 1976 as a result of their information.[21] To expedite the legal process the government introduced a raft of security legislation, extending its powers to investigate and detain suspected terrorists through the Prevention of Terrorism Acts of 1974 and 1976. More covertly, the SAS was deployed into the bandit territory of the border regions, south Armagh and south Tyrone, where both sides engaged in a more orthodox guerrilla style of conflict. And like any guerrilla conflict, propaganda and representation were as important as bloody conflict. So far British attempts to win 'hearts and minds' had met with limited success, while their control of the media through censorship and political influence had done little to improve their international standing. So from mid-1970, with the intention of raising her propaganda game, Britain introduced policies to 'normalize' the situation. As part of normalization came a programme of 'Ulsterization' in which the RUC and UDR took over frontline duties from the British Army. IRA targeting of soldiers now became more difficult and when it resorted to killing 'home-grown' policemen, its campaign lost its spurious colonial legitimacy and acquired a less attractive and unpopular sectarian flavour. In total the divisive effects of the truce of 1975, the introduction of high-tech surveillance, deployment of the SAS, Ulsterization and normalization had a grievous impact upon the capability of and support for the IRA. By the late 1970s, though still able to commit atrocities, the organization was a pale shadow of what it had been in 1972. The Republican movement was contained and seemed on the face of it to be destined to go the way it had gone after the 1920s and after the Border campaign of 1956–1962 – to rumble along at a low level of operations, on the margins of obscurity and irrelevance.

That it didn't and indeed that Republicanism grew to represent, by 1998, some 16 per cent of the population of Northern Ireland and play a leading role in establishing the Belfast Agreement, owed much to developments of the late 1970s. One significant development was the IRA's elaboration of a Long War philosophy as a means of counteracting the growing success of normalization and Ulsterization. This entailed the introduction of a new organizational structure based on self-contained (and thus more secure) units to replace the older system of companies and brigades that had proved so easy for British intelligence to infiltrate. However, though more secure, the cellular structure cut off the IRA from contact with the local community, which was vital to it for resources, support and recruits. Accordingly the

IRA was forced to construct alternative contacts with the local community by 'broadening the battlefield', an approach of engaging with the British in a variety of areas, the key ingredient of which was a movement into the political arena where propaganda could be more effectively managed and support for the IRA galvanized. The IRA therefore extended Republican Sinn Fein, or just Sinn Fein, into more high-profile activity, though its appearance was less that of a political wing of the IRA than a political feather, lacking a clear identity or a political agenda beyond the rather stale-looking Republican mantra of British withdrawal and a united Ireland. Indeed, Sinn Fein's only prominent role thus far had been the management of incident centres during the truce period. Yet from small acorns a powerful, community-based, media-sensitive and tactically astute Republican movement would develop.

Broadening the battlefield, or Total Strategy, also meant engaging the British wherever they could be engaged, a sort of flexible frontline policy, and by the late 1970s perhaps the biggest frontline, given the success of British counter-terrorism policies, was in the prisons. The withdrawal of special category status for all new Republican prisoners in 1976, in response to the IRA ending the truce, had long been advocated by British officials as an obvious and necessary part of 'normalization'. After all, the best way to normalize members of a self-proclaimed Irish Republican Army was to indulge in your own bit of self-proclaiming by denying they were prisoners of a war (with the implication that it was not a war) and categorizing them instead as criminals. Mrs Thatcher, newly arrived in Downing Street, decided to extend criminalization by removing special category status from all prisoners. Given the IRA was hemmed in on the outside, the change of prisons policy provided an ideal opportunity to take the war inside the prisons. The removal of special category status gave the Republican movement a cause and a 'protest' to try to rouse popular pathos, international support and generate community backing. We are

> **"The IRA was forced to construct alternative contacts with the local community by 'broadening the battlefield'"**

'an army of propagandists' was how Bobby Sands, the IRA commander of the prisoners, saw things.[22] And so the IRA engaged the British in a game of 'chicken', first in the form of a blanket protest, then moving on to a dirty protest, and from October 1980 a hunger strike, designed to humiliate the government if it backed down on special category status or to castigate it in international opinion if it did not. Either way the IRA would gain. The prisons protest offered the Republican movement a 'win–win' strategy. The one uncertainty was whether the prisoners could stand the awful conditions longer than the government could stand the adverse publicity.

The Republicans' choice of battlefield was well made. Prisons and prisoners have always had a deep significance within Republican sentimentality, loaded with historic poignancy and with the act of incarceration ifself symbolic of Ireland's oppression. And within this world of signs and symbols nothing held more power, verging at times on the religious, than the hunger strike. The idea of dying for Ireland resonated loudly and profoundly within a culture seeped in Catholic motifs and Republican metaphor. But Republicans were also fortunate to have Mrs Thatcher as their adversary. Probably any other postwar Prime Minister would have been more sensitive to international opinion and recognized the political naivety of involving themselves in a stand-off with Republicans. They would have, accordingly, offered a compromise, cut their losses and so pulled the propaganda rug from underneath the IRA protest. Yet instead of such eminently sensible pragmatism, Mrs Thatcher approached the dispute with the same mind-set of one of the Republican prisoners and, as with the Yorkshire mineworkers or the Argentinian Junta, as enemies of the state to be crushed. But Republican hunger strikers proved more resilient than shivering Argentinian conscripts or an unemployed miner desperate to feed his family, though even they were surprised at just how inflexible she was, it taking the death of ten men to bring that lesson home to them.

The outcome of the hunger strikes of 1980–1981 was a Pyrrhic victory for Thatcher. The protest was called off without compromise and the Iron Lady preserved her iron image. She performed no u-turn, though the speed with which concessions were then granted to the remaining prisoners suggests at the very least a three- or four-point turn. She had won the battle but, to draw on a much over-used quote, she lost the propaganda war. For if her intention was to smash the Republican movement once and for all, she had the opposite effect. Bobby Sands, was elected to Parliament in April 1981, bringing the protest and movement immense publicity and indicating that militant Republicanism could win political support and thus a genuinely broad-fronted campaign could be mobilized. Britain's international standing was severely dented, particularly in the USA where fund-raising for the IRA now grew rapidly. The fact that during the same period the IRA killed 22 prison officers and RUC men was all too easily forgotten by those who uncritically swallowed Republican propaganda.[23] Sands' subsequent death on 5 May 1981 saw 100,000–150,000 people turn out for his funeral, showing once again what the British had failed to learn from the nineteenth and early twentieth centuries: that a dead Fenian was more successful and more dangerous to the British than a live one.

> 66 Sinn Fein now entered mainstream politics with immediate and electric success 99

Sinn Fein now entered mainstream politics with immediate and electric success. At the 1983 general election it swept 13.4 per cent of the vote and saw the election of Gerry Adams as member for West Belfast. Thatcher had undercut the moderate Nationalism of the SDLP at the expense of providing militant Republicanism with a foot in the political door, while amongst the Unionist community the strength of more hardline parties, such as the DUP, surged as that of the UUP diminished. She had given the Republican movement what the 1974 loyalist strike gave to militant Unionism, an energy, a strength and a mass support that would block progress towards a political settlement for Northern Ireland. The hunger strikes were, then, a turning point in the history of the Troubles, the moment Sinn Fein leapt from obscurity to mainstream power-broker. When Adams and McGuinness finally entered the talks process in September 1997 and acquired a set of offices at Stormont, next to their portrait of Bobby Sands as the founding father of the modern Sinn Fein party they perhaps ought to have hung a portrait of Mrs Thatcher as their political midwife. Without her unshakable resolution they would arguably not have been at the talks at all.

NOTES

1 B. Faulkner, *Memoirs of a Statesman* (Weidenfeld and Nicolson, 1978) p 149

2 W. Whitelaw, *The Whitelaw Memoirs* (Aurum, 1989) p 92.

3 B. Faulkner, op. cit., p 156.

4 Taylor, *Provos: The IRA and Sinn Fein* (Bloomsbury, London, 1997) p 136.

5 Ibid, p 142.

6 Whitelaw, op. cit., p 100.

7 C. C. O'Brien, *States of Ireland* (Hutchinson, 1972) p 286.

8 Ibid, p 287.

9 B. Faulkner, op. cit., p 172

10 Ibid, p 172.

11 Whitelaw, op. cit., p 120.

12 Ibid, p 110.

13 Ibid, p 115.

14 Ibid, p 119.

15 Ibid, p 120.

16 B. Faulkner, op. cit., pp 237–8.

17 Bill Craig speaking at a Vanguard meeting on 9 February 1972 in S. Bruce, *The Red Hand: Protestant Paramilitaries in Northern Ireland* (OUP, 1992) p 81.

18 B. Faulkner, op. cit., p 227.

19 Though only two of his 20 Unionist supporters in the Assembly deserted him, James Stronge and William Morgan.

20 J. Prior, *A Balance of Power* (Hamish Hamilton, 1986) p 195.

21 P. Dixon, *Northern Ireland: The Politics of War and Peace* (Palgrave, 2001) p 168.

22 Ibid, p 183.

23 Ibid, p 185.

6

SHIFTING GROUNDS, 1984–1987

'The United Kingdom government again affirm that responsibility for affairs in Northern Ireland is entirely a matter of domestic jurisdiction.'

Downing Street Declaration, 19 August 1969

'Our position is clear and it will never, never, never change: the war against British rule must continue until freedom is achieved.'

M. McGuinness, 1986, Ard Fheis

'The future of the constitutional affairs of Northern Ireland is a matter for the people of Northern Ireland, this government and this Parliament and no one else.'

Mrs Thatcher, 20 May 1980

BY 1984 THE CONFLICT IN NORTHERN IRELAND HAD REACHED a stalemate. Looking back one saw 15 years of slaughter and turmoil, while looking forward one could envisage only more of the same. The recent political initiatives by Atkins and Prior had foundered. Moderates on both sides were unwilling or incapable of co-operating with each other for fear of driving their support into the hands of more extreme parties. And without that willingness a settlement within Northern Ireland looked as unlikely as snow on Christmas Day. Twelve years of direct rule and a host of plans, schemes, frameworks, institutions and political initiatives had brought no change and very little improvement. Indeed, things had probably worsened for Britain, with spiralling costs and mounting criticism from Dublin, the USA and Europe in the wake of the hunger strikes and the steady rise of Sinn Fein. Moreover, Britain's incessant search for a compromise settlement, though worthy of praise, probably made matters worse by reinforcing Unionist fears of a sell-out while simultaneously fuelling Nationalist concern that Stormont was returning in another guise. British efforts to do something had themselves become a source of the problem. Following his first visit to the region in 1983, the British Minister Richard Needham reflected the general sense of hopelessness. 'I went home on the shuttle that night, my mind filled with the contradictions I had seen and heard during my four-day visit to Ulster. I had known the problems were labyrinthine in their intractability, but I had not fully understood the depths of division or the narrow scope for compromise that existed in communities with such opposing national aspirations.'[1]

Political stalemate was mirrored by military deadlock. By 1984 the British Army was managing the violence at a politically acceptable level, establishing 'some sort of equilibrium' as one serving officer described it.[2] But it could not eradicate the IRA, nor could it insure against periodic 'spectaculars'. This was brought home to the security services in July 1982 with the opening up of a new campaign on the mainland. Bomb attacks in Hyde Park and Regents Park resulted in the death of 11 people. In December 1983 a bomb outside Harrods killed six people and a year later the Brighton Grand Hotel bombing nearly wiped out Mrs Thatcher and much of her government. Like some eerie echo of the Great War, the army's 'quick nip-in and nip-out job'[3] of 1969 had turned into a long-haul slog with little sign of light at the end of the tunnel. Both the IRA and the army were now locked into a Long War. On the other side although the slimmed-down and tightly structured IRA was able to maintain a steady level of operations, sustained by money from the USA and large quantities of sophisticated weaponry from Libya, it was no closer to forcing a British withdrawal. If anything the IRA's 14-year military campaign had entrenched Britain's presence in the region and made her even more determined not to give in to terrorism. 'Armed struggle' looked like an obstacle to Republican objectives, not a facilitator of them.[4] Yet however contradictory or self-defeating the nature of IRA violence, such arguments did nothing (yet) to stop the killing and of course as long as the IRA continued to kill, so loyalist paramilitaries continued to react with even greater and more random violence. Not since 1974 and the collapse of the Sunningdale experiment had the Troubles seemed so interminable and irresolvable.

ENDING THE COLD WAR: ANGLO-IRISH RELATIONS

By 1984 closer Anglo-Irish relations were thought to be the key to finding a political solution to Northern Ireland. However, between Thatcher, whose 'own instincts are profoundly Unionist',[5] and Charles Haughey's unreconstructed republicanism, relations had 'cooled to freezing'.[6] And they remained cool following very public disagreements over the hunger strikes and the Falklands war. Despite this frosty 'top soil', warm subterranean currents were beginning to flow between London and Dublin and leading in the direction of a rapprochement. The rapprochement can be traced back to the meeting between Thatcher and Haughey in December 1980 when their joint communiqué went beyond mere diplomatic niceties by speaking of a 'unique relationship' and willingness to discuss issues relating to 'the totality of relationships within these islands'. This willingness was formalized a year later by Thatcher and the new Taoiseach, Garret FitzGerald, with the creation of the Anglo-Irish Inter-Governmental Council. The council was to convene regular summits, convey ideas, generate cooperation and establish harmonious working relations, what we might call an Anglo-Irish process. Process was one thing, actually constructing an agreement was something very different

> ❝By 1984 closer Anglo-Irish relations were thought to be the key to finding a political solution to Northern Ireland❞

altogether. Thus it was left to a group of mandarins and civil servants, notably Sir Robert Armstrong and Dermot Nally, who away from the glare of public attention through 1982–1985 slowly chipped away at years of misunderstanding, entrenched views, ingrained prejudices and vested interests to move both countries towards an accord.

The search for an accord was never going to be easy, nor was the Anglo-Irish relationship ever going to be terribly close or very 'special'. Thatcher was dismissive of Irish politicians in general (as she was about much else) while they in turn imagined her as some sort of 'Paisley in high heels'. The Anglo-Irish relationship was a liaison without love, but rendered stable by a growing realization that in the circumstances of 1983–1984 they shared similar interests and felt common concerns. One of these concerns was a realization that acting separately had done little to advance the cause of peace in Northern Ireland and might even have fuelled the conflict. Another was that Northern Ireland endangered the stability of both states and the threat posed by a strengthening Sinn Fein impacted on Dublin as well as on London, an understanding brought home to the Republic after two hunger strikers were elected to the Dáil in June 1981. Lastly dawned the recognition that local politicians were probably incapable of agreeing a system of government for themselves. It was clear, then, that progress towards a settlement could work only if local people and their leaders were cut out of any debate on the future governance of Northern Ireland.

Alongside their growing commonality of interests, Britain and Ireland nurtured more selfish reasons for co-operation. Thatcher's primary concern was security and to tighten policing along the border where many terrorists found an all-too-easy escape route. She also hoped that doing something with the Irish would improve Britain's image abroad and especially in the USA, what Bew has referred to as 'fire-proofing Britain internationally'.[7] More ambitiously, Thatcher wanted the Republic to persuade northern Catholics to accept the Northern Irish state, by formally recognizing the right of the people in Northern Ireland to determine their own destiny and by dropping articles 2 and 3 of its constitution. Such changes Thatcher believed were vital to reassuring the Unionist community and for weakening political backing and community toleration for the IRA. Marginalizing Sinn Fein was likewise a major consideration for FitzGerald, less to beef up security in the north than to ring-fence the south against the spread of Republicanism while sim-ultaneously strengthening the SDLP. To this end FitzGerald took up the 'revisionist' Nationalist agenda then emerging from the New Ireland Forum. The New Ireland Forum was set up in 1983 as the brainchild of Hume and aimed at reinventing Irish nationalism from its traditional, deep-green, non-negotiable and rather exclusive variety, towards something more inclusive and inviting (theoretically speaking) for Unionists. Also to rethink the Northern Irish question by examining relations between the north, the south and Britain, and moving the debate away from notions of ownership and conquest, towards reconciliation and accommodation. In terms of Northern Ireland FitzGerald took up the Forum's recommendation of joint Anglo-Irish sovereignty of the north, something akin to 'joint custody'. This was a means of 'reducing the alienation of the nationalist minority',[8] so (in theory) nurturing responsi-bility and mutual respect. Thatcher, though aware she needed to trade something in the north for better security arrangements, would not accept joint custody. For her, Northern Ireland was the child of a single parent, with the Republic limited to the role of a governess, concerned with punishment and discipline but with no legal say over how the child was to be brought up.

THE ANGLO-IRISH AGREEMENT, 1985

The result of nearly four years of intense diplomacy, gentle back-room progress and blunt horse-trading was the Anglo-Irish Agreement of November 1985. The key sections of the treaty were articles 1 and 2. Article 1 *again* guaranteed that the status of Northern Ireland would change only with the consent of a majority of the people in Northern Ireland. And since the current majority was Unionist, that meant no change at present. However, 'if in the future a majority of the people . . . clearly wish for and formally consent to the establishment of a united Ireland', then both Britain and Ireland would 'give effect to that wish'.[9] Though signalled before, Britain restated its 'neutrality' on the union, as neither a 'persuader' for or against. Northern Ireland was now a 'conditional unit of the UK'.[10] What Britain guaranteed was majoritarian democracy for the Northern Irish people, not the union with Britain and certainly not the Unionist veto. Article 1 also formalized what Irish representatives had long said in private, namely that national reunification was a long-term hope and would come 'by consent and only by consent'.[11] Despite this healthy dose of reality, Haughey, now in opposition, still chose to reject the agreement as giving up on Irish unity and even FitzGerald's reformism did not stretch to the repeal of their 'claim' to the north in articles 2 and 3 of their constitution.

> 66 The right to meddle was highly symbolic in recognizing an Irish dimension within the governance of Northern Ireland 99

Article 2 of the agreement created an Inter-Governmental Conference, with its own permanent civil service secretariat based at Maryfield just outside Belfast. With this Britain 'accepted the Irish government will put forward views and proposals on matters relating to Northern Ireland within the field of activity of the conference',[12] but nervously stressed this was 'no derogation from the sovereignty of . . . the United Kingdom government'.[13] Ireland had acquired the power to meddle rather than joint authority. But the right to meddle was highly symbolic in recognizing an Irish dimension within the governance of Northern Ireland, what FitzGerald called 'an Irish resident presence in Belfast'.[14] Moreover, it was recognized that until a devolved cross-party government for the north was established, Dublin would 'represent' the interests of the Nationalist community. Northern Nationalism now had recognition for its national aspirations and protection for its interests, what might be termed long-term hope married to short-term support. It was 'direct rule with a green tinge',[15] but even just a tinge was thought enough to boost the position of the SDLP and undercut the appeal of Sinn Fein, which was one of the key strategic aims.

Of course, what for the signatories of the agreement was a tinge, for Unionists was a huge green stripe, winding remorselessly towards a future, if distant, united Ireland. Thatcher did not see it this way. For her, British sovereignty over Northern Ireland remained gloriously untarnished while limited Irish involvement had been more than compensated by a hoped-for improvement in the co-ordination of security with the south. The reality was that British sovereignty, while legally undiluted, was in practice 'qualified'. Moreover, the Inter-Governmental Conference was tacit acknowledgement by the British that they were unable to bring peace to the north on their own. The search for a solution or even just management of the conflict would now occur within the broader framework of Anglo-Irish co-operation and understanding, with input when required from the USA and perhaps even Europe. And herein lay the major success of the agreement – Anglo-Irish co-operation. Such co-operation would prove *the* essential ingredient in moving events and groups towards and through the Belfast Agreement of 1998.

This was not the prime intention of its architects. For hidden in the details of the agreement lay mechanisms they hoped would 'sling-shot' both communities towards a compromise solution, a system of carrots and sticks designed to cajole Unionists and Nationalists into a settlement. For example, in recognizing Nationalist sensibilities and grievances through the Irish dimension, the agreement gave the SDLP for the first time the political reassurance and support to engage constructively with Unionism without endangering its support in the community to Sinn Fein playing the 'green card'. For Unionists the incentive was a balance of evils. If they wanted to remove Dublin meddling in Northern Irish affairs and reduce their reliance upon the traitorous British, they had to sit down and discuss with constitutional Nationalists alternative structures. Until that time Britain spoke for Unionism, Ireland 'spoke' for Nationalists and the Inter-Governmental Conference remained a vehicle for Dublin to discuss policy in the region. With typical frankness Mrs Thatcher outlined the situation: 'The people of Northern Ireland can get rid of the Inter-Governmental Conference by agreeing to devolved government.'[16] All realized Unionists did not relish working with the SDLP, but it was thought a more appealing option than dependence upon Britain or the meddling of Dublin, while the chance to get their hands back on some power was thought too tempting to ignore. The agreement, then, had an evolutionary element to it that by containing the seeds of its own destruction aimed in the medium term at creating a viable and sustainable political middle ground.

FROM NO TO NEVER TO MAYBE: UNIONISTS RESPONSES, 1984–1989

The hoped-for 'sling-shot' towards a settlement initially looked more like a shot in the foot. Unionist outrage at the agreement quickly took on near rebellious proportions. For them it was a step along the slippery road to a united Ireland. Northern Ireland's position within the UK had been dangerously weakened and its union rendered 'conditional' rather than concrete. Union now had more to do with population shifts than with points of principle, despite Thatcher's hurried assurances to the contrary. For Unionists, British sovereignty was derogated by the agreement and a foreign power given 'illegal' joint authority over a part of the UK, an act of treachery all the more poignant since it was made by Mrs Thatcher, long thought a tinder-dry Unionist who had previously rejected all notion of joint authority over the province. Moreover, they believed British democracy had been betrayed since fundamental constitutional change had occurred without the consent of the people. Harold McCusker reflected the opinions of many when he confided to the Commons: 'I never knew what desolation felt like until I read this agreement last Friday afternoon. Does the Prime Minister realize that, when she carries the agreement through the House, she will have ensured that I shall carry to my grave with ignominy the sense of injustice that I have done to my constituents down the years – when, in their darkest hours, I exhorted them to put their trust in this British House of Commons, which one day would honour its fundamental obligation to them to treat them as equal citizens? Is not the reality of this agreement that they will now be Irish-British hybrids?'[17]

As with the previous Unionist struggles of 1912–1914 and 1973–1974, so the agreement was seen as the work of those familiar 'bogies' of Ulster Unionist paranoia: Irish imperialism and British treachery. Paisley and Molyneaux, leader of the Ulster Unionist Party, now joined forces to reconjure these ancient threats and past struggles into contemporary dangers. A week after the agreement was signed they led a huge rally in Belfast, of between 150,000 and 200,000 people, in a replay of the Solemn League and Covenant meeting of September 1912. Paisley, as he had in 1981 with his Carson trail speeches against the Anglo-Irish process, tried to squeeze himself into 'Sir Edward's' shoes with defiant rhetoric and typically thunderous and theatrical gestures, though, ironically, one of his more famous declarations that Thatcher was ready 'to wade knee deep in the blood of loyalists for this document of treachery and deceit'[18] was more of an echo of that die-hard Republican, Eamon de Valera, than his die-hard Unionist hero. While Paisley wrestled with the ghosts of conflicts past, Unionist resistance elsewhere took more practical forms. All 15 Ulster Unionist MPs resigned their seats and fought by-elections to advertise the depth of their unhappiness. Contact with British ministers ceased and leaders refused to negotiate a political solution until the agreement was abandoned. At a local level, Unionist councillors 'downed' pens, withdrew from local government and refused to collect the rates. Unionist martyrdom would now arise from mounting piles of rubbish on the streets. Self-inflicted pain seemed to be in vogue during the early 1980s, on both sides of the community divide.

> **While Paisley wrestled with the ghosts of conflicts past, Unionist resistance elsewhere took more practical forms**

Ominously, Molyneaux warned that 'this agreement will bring not peace but a sword'. His prediction proved horribly correct as loyalist violence spiralled to levels not seen since the mid-1970s. Maryfield, the home of the new Inter-Governmental secretariat, was besieged by loyalist demonstrators, as was the first meeting of the Anglo-Irish Conference. The 'day of action', a general strike for 3 March 1986, devolved into widespread rioting and attacks on the RUC, 47 of whom were injured. Across the region Ulster Clubs were formed to organize resistance but became ideal channels for loyalist paramilitary recruitment. Initially paramilitary activities took their traditional form of sectarian murder, house-burning and intimidation. But following several confrontations between police and loyalist demonstrators, they turned their rage against the RUC, already deeply suspect as 'agents' of a now traitorous regime. The once 'gallant' defenders against IRA violence were now shot at, ostracized in their own communities and petrol-bombed out of their homes, with some 50 forced to move by May 1986.[19] As violence increased, so it drew an equally bitter, sectarian response from the IRA. Events reached a low point in 1987–1988 with some of the worst atrocities of the entire Troubles. The bombing of a Remembrance Day service at Enniskillen in November 1987, which killed 11, was followed in March by Michael Stone's grenade attack on mourners at Milltown cemetery, killing three. Three days later two army corporals were murdered at another funeral, in full view of the world's press. All incidents of that 1987–1988 period were shocking and medieval in their barbarity.

With violence escalating, any chance that the Anglo-Irish Agreement would propel the two sides into a compromise looked doubtful. A power-sharing executive seemed remote if Ulster Unionists would not even talk to the British, let alone the SDLP. Violence had strengthened the political extremes at the expense of the middle ground. There seemed little to support Hume's assessment, made at the time of the Good Friday Agreement in 1998, that the Anglo-Irish Agreement was 'a document from which everything that has happened in the past few years stems'.[20] Yet one significant development did augur well for future attempts at a solution, namely an irreversible weakening of Unionism. For however impassioned their resistance or inconvenient their tactics, the agreement remained impervious to their efforts. There was, after all, no imposed political settlement for them to capsize. And being a framework for co-operation between two governments, the institutions were beyond the reach of Unionists. Herein lay the reason why their outrage and resistance could work in 1912–1914 and in 1973–1974 but not in 1985–1986, namely that the structures and changes introduced were immune to Unionist pressure and impossible for them to collapse or destroy. To declare they would never negotiate with ministers until the agreement was scrapped was tantamount to saying they would never negotiate and their future was one of isolation.

Betrayed by their friends, Unionists looked to their enemies for aid. They hoped for a Labour resurgence in the 1987 general election, sufficient to return a hung Parliament and so provide them with a bargaining power capable of destroying the Treaty. But once again Labour let them down by ensuring Thatcher returned with a majority of over 100. Ironically, Unionists also invested their faith in Haughey's return as Taoiseach in 1987. As a redoubtable old Republican he had voted against the Anglo-Irish Agreement in the Dáil ratification

> By blustering 'never, never, never' at an anti-agreement rally early in 1986, Unionist leaders simply displayed their own powerlessness

debate of 1985 and might have been expected to bring a certain irredentist feel back into Anglo-Irish relations sufficient to wreck things. But Haughey trod the unlikely course of moderation and chose to continue what FitzGerald had begun. Unable, then, to destroy the agreement and without hope of others doing it for them, the choice for Unionists was surrender or self-imposed ostracism, humiliation or impotence. The Unionist veto, be it the threat of armed resistance as in 1912–1914, the threat of mass resignation as in 1922 or the general strike in 1974, was finally nullified. The Republican idea that Unionists from this moment on had a veto over political developments, more that is than any other constitutional party, flew in the face of the considerable rebalancing of power and influence that the agreement of 1985 effected. So by blustering 'never, never, never' at an anti-agreement rally early in 1986, Unionist leaders simply displayed their own powerlessness. The supreme irony of it all was that this humbling occurred at the hands of Mrs Thatcher. Thatcher's infamous 'iron will', so recently deployed against the hunger strikers and initially such a comfort to Unionists after the pale greenness of Wilson and Callaghan, was now used to face down her 'own people'. In humbling historically truculent communities Thatcher had made strange bedfellows of the Ulster Unionists who, like Scargill and the National Union of Mineworkers, similarly felt the wrath of the Iron Lady. Paisley spoke for many in the Unionist community (and not a few elsewhere) when he implored the almighty to 'deal with the Prime Minister of our country ... O God in wrath take vengeance upon this wicked, treacherous, lying woman'.[21]

Yet it is too easy to blame Thatcher for Unionist woes. To a large extent their difficulties were self-inflicted. Until 1985 Unionists were 'unwilling to seriously evolve',[22] either tactically or ideologically. Their stance had been a monotonous incantation of majority-rule devolution, which meant their domination of any executive. Many were even quietly happy with the status quo, if for no other reason than Dublin had no influence over them. The Anglo-Irish Agreement shattered these assumptions by injecting an Irish flavour into the status quo while formally abandoning any possible return to majority-based devolved government. Unionists were therefore forced to confront the limitations of their tactical conservatism and to ponder what now was the best way to preserve the union. Some, particularly those in the middle ranks of the Ulster Unionist Party, frustrated by the self-defeating policy of isolationism, pushed for greater tactical flexibility and opening up of a dialogue with the British and Irish governments. Similarly, those at the sharp end of the loyalist struggle, the paramilitaries, showed a surprising degree of constructive thinking. In 1987 the UDA and its new political wing, the UDP, published *Common Sense*, which offered Catholics a substantial role in the governance of a 'secure' Northern Irish state along the lines of a proportional power-sharing executive. From elsewhere in the Unionist movement came calls for closer integration with the United Kingdom. And yet others looked in the opposite direction towards full independence, or UDI. Some were simply happy to ratchet up the levels of militancy, a course that for Peter Robinson deputy leader of the DUP involved an invasion of the Republic one hot summer night in 1986.

By 1987–1988 the combination of intellectual ferment and tactical sterility began to impact upon the Unionist leadership. In September 1987 John Taylor asked fellow Unionists to accept the challenge of devolution and open contacts with Dublin. Two weeks later Molyneaux and Paisley suspended their boycott of British ministers to meet Tom King, the Secretary of State, for exploratory 'talks about talks', and by May 1988 Molyneaux was expressing a public willingness for his party to exchange 'position' papers with Haughey. After two years of simple negativism Unionists were at last moving forwards to engage with the world around them, making contact with Dublin and exploring, however grudgingly, some type of constructive relationship with constitutional Nationalism. It was a tentative process, showing a greater focus towards present realities, but all the time under the cover of a determined, unbending outrage. A decade after Faulkner, Unionists were finally moving back to embrace the Faulknerite agenda from which a political settlement might grow.

CONFRONTING GHOSTS: REPUBLICANS AND REPUBLICANISM, 1984–1988

Just as the Anglo-Irish Agreement posed difficulties for Unionists, so it presented Republicans with some awkward choices. The earlier dramatic successes of the Republican movement, with the election of Gerry Adams and rapid political advance of Sinn Fein, began to plateau by 1985–1986. Part of the problem lay in their co-ordination of the military with the political, or the Total Strategy. This had made for a good slogan, 'the Armalite and the ballot box',[23] and offered a drop of reality into an otherwise sterile faith in armed struggle, but it suffered from discrepancies and had revealed as many contradictions as it had made progress across a broad front. For example, Sinn Fein's politics were about making the present state more bearable for some of its most downtrodden victims. Republican violence was about making the northern state unbearable. Sinn Fein politics necessarily involved working within the existing structures of power. Republican violence involved trying to collapse

those structures. Sinn Fein's activists looked to local and com-
munity-related questions. Republican violence had its eye on
the national question. And Sinn Fein strove to win political support whereas IRA activity ignored it: theirs was a struggle on
behalf of the Irish people, not *by* them. A political/military fault-
line was opening up within Republicanism, just as it had in
1921–1922 and in 1969–1970.

The fault-line grew increasingly bitter. One source of friction
was resources. Disagreements in April 1985 over the allocation
of funds for publicity and politics (as opposed to guns) led to the
expulsion of four IRA volunteers in April 1985, including Ivor
Bell, one of those who had met Whitelaw in 1972. More significantly, the destruction of property and economic interests, or
poorly targeted military actions, or the inevitable and unavoidable number of mistakes, were beginning to weaken Sinn Fein's
political presence within Nationalist communities. 'Could Sinn
Fein credibly campaign on a range of economic and social
issues, such as housing, jobs, health, while PIRA helped destroy
them?'[24] Civilian casualties also hit Sinn Fein's political position. The Harrods bomb of December 1983, in which six people
died, cut party support back into its working-class heartlands
and dried up tentative links with the British Left. That same
month the kidnapping of Don Tidey, a British industrialist, that
resulted in the death of an Irish soldier, seriously weakened Sinn
Fein's hopes of extending its message south of the border. Both
episodes suggested 'it was impossible to fight an antiseptic,
voter-friendly war'.[25] The 'Armalite and the ballot box' was
becoming the Armalite undermining the ballot box, or more
accurately limiting the party to its base of around 11 per cent of
voters in Northern Ireland. 'You cannot ride two horses at the
same time,' the one-time President of Sinn Fein, Ruairi
O'Bradaigh, had warned in 1986.[26] Politics and the 'armed struggle' were not always compatible. And for O'Bradaigh the former
inevitably corrupted the latter and thus had to be subordinated
to it.

For Adams and McGuinness logic flowed in the opposite direction. The armed struggle increasingly needed to be subordinated
to the political struggle (though not removed from it) if Sinn

Fein's local support was ever to break out of its core or if violence was not to become self-serving, its own *raison d'etre*. What they feared was 'that the fight for Irish freedom had become an end in itself to us. Instead of a means, it became an end'.[27] For all the rhetoric of war, militarism and undying commitment to the armed struggle, many younger Sinn Fein leaders regarded it as a double-edged sword – a sword that was now cutting into Republican fingers, as seen in Sinn

66 The armed struggle increasingly needed to be subordinated to the political struggle 99

Fein's faltering political advance. Back in the 1983 general election the party had won 13.4 per cent of the vote. This incredible result was interpreted as a springboard to supplant the SDLP, with its 'measly' 17.9 per cent. As it turned out, the springboard looked more like a high water mark. The 1984 European elections saw Sinn Fein lose 11,000 votes while the SDLP's share of the vote leapt back up to 22.1 per cent. The 1985 district elections compounded this downturn by returning just 59 Sinn Feiners compared with the SDLP's 101 seats. And if anyone thought these were electoral 'blips', the 1987 general election saw the balance of votes again swing strongly against Sinn Fein, which won just 11.4 per cent and came a long way behind the SDLP with 21 per cent of the vote. Republican advance had stuttered, wobbled and then stabilized into 'permanent second fiddle to the SDLP'.[28] It was all a far cry from Adams' claim that Sinn Fein would become 'the majority Nationalist party' in the north[29] or that the SDLP was a 'galloping irrelevance'.[30]

Indeed, if any party was going to be a 'galloping irrelevance' the Anglo-Irish Agreement made sure it would be Sinn Fein. The popularity of the agreement within Nationalist communities gave constitutional Nationalism a welcome boost and threatened to cut the electoral ground from under the Republican movement: an opinion poll even found 22 per cent of Sinn Fein supporters favoured the agreement, while a further 10 per cent 'were strongly supportive'.[31] This placed Republicans in a deep tactical fix. They could not accept the agreement without abandoning much of their ideology: the illegitimacy of the Northern Irish state, the unlawful occupation of the north by Britain and the Unionist 'veto' over a united Irish Republic. Yet the agreement was appreciated by all Nationalists, not least because it gave a 'hit (against) the Unionists, a kick in the balls', an appreciation Sinn Fein could not lightly ignore. Moreover, the agreement was couched in a new language, expressing a sense of impartiality, even 'conditionality', towards the union that amongst more moderate Republicans 'didn't go unrecorded'.[32] The alternative to accepting the agreement was to escalate the armed struggle, a course now as likely to endanger their position as strengthen it. As with the Unionists so Sinn Fein appeared to be in a difficult tactical situation, powerless to alter events and in danger of political marginalization and irrelevance. To salvage something from this dilemma Adams tried a neat piece of fancy footwork. While rejecting the agreement he claimed credit for forcing its concessions from the British and suggested Britain would only ever be moved by Republican pressure. He had a point. But claiming responsibility for reforms that stabilized and arguably strengthened British rule in the north seemed an odd riposte for a die-hard Republican and raised concerns amongst supporters as to what his own ideological position really was.

In light of its stalling political advance in the north, its growing political/military incompatibilities within the Total Strategy and the tactical quandaries exacerbated by the Anglo-Irish Agreement, Sinn Fein sought new directions and options. The most significant new direction, though more by symbolism than practical effect, was the decision to drop the party's historic policy of abstention, the very issue that had originally split the IRA into Officials and Provisionals back in 1970. The decision taken at the Ard Fheis of 1986 represented a victory for Adams and the northern leaders over the southern old guard, enabling Sinn Fein to now contest elections to the Dáil and take up seats if it won. The decision, though historic, was not surprising. The Ard Fheis of 1983 had already sanctioned candidates for the European election, a change that had brought about O'Bradaigh's replacement as President of Sinn Fein by Adams. Sinn Fein aspired to a 32-county Socialist republic, so building up support in all 32 counties was a logical step. And since it was increasingly frustrated in the north, opening a new electoral front in the south seemed the only alternative to stagnation. Sinn Fein also hoped to reap what it mistakenly believed to be a simmering outrage in the south at FitzGerald's 'copper-fastening' of partition in the Anglo-Irish Agreement, and reflected in Fianna Fail's rejection of it and a strengthening of its political support. Yet there was also a sense within the new, younger leadership that they enjoyed and relished politics. They had not forgotten the taste of success in 1983 and once savoured it was hard to put down, what O'Bradaigh characterized as the essential corrupting influence of all political activity.

The question of whether Republicans *should* involve themselves in the south and in what were still seen as British-constructed institutions, originating in the 1921 Treaty, was brushed aside by the onward march of new Republican pragmatism. The fact that this question lay at the heart of all major schisms within the Republican movement throughout the twentieth century (1922, 1926, 1948, 1969) should have engendered a degree of caution. And rightfully so, for the IRA only narrowly avoided splitting.[33]

> There was also a sense within the new, younger leadership that they enjoyed and relished politics

O'Bradaigh, the self-appointed guardian of the faith, in true Moses-style, led the most devout into the political wilderness, which they called Republican Sinn Fein. He left railing against the betrayal of the 1916 'martyrs' and the Republican oath made by the first and only 'legitimate' Dáil of 1919. More presciently he forecast that involvement in Leinster House, where the Dáil sat, was the thin end of the wedge and would inevitably lead to Sinn Fein's eventual involvement in a reconstituted Northern Ireland Executive. Removing abstention meant all other evils became not just possible but probable, and that included accepting partition and the principle of Unionist consent to any all-Irish Republic. It was, after all, the road travelled by the Official IRA following the split in 1970, which by the mid-1970s had evolved into the Workers Party. O'Bradaigh was half-right in his analysis. For while Sinn Fein would eventually sit alongside Unionists in a new Northern Irish Executive, its involvement in politics south of the border has not (so far) materialized. At the elections to the Dáil of 1987, Sinn Fein won no seats and an embarrassing 1.7 per cent of the vote. Two years later even that fell to 1.2 per cent. Shelving abstention, the cornerstone of Sinn Fein policy since its inception under Griffith and a massive ideological step in 1986, had brought little obvious or immediate political advantage.[34]

What it did do, however, was highlight various contradictions of the most glaring kind. It was clear, for example, that Sinn Fein, which regarded partition and the Northern Ireland state as illegitimate, could only win a meaningful share of the popular vote on the island of Ireland *within* that same 'illegitimate' Northern Irish state. As one expert has put it, 'espousing national ideals while in practice relying on a *community* to realize those ideals'.[35] This was the same flaw embedded in late nineteenth-century Irish Unionism, which lay claim to all Ireland for the union but could only win Parliamentary seats in the north-east part of it. For Sinn Fein, partition was both an ideological evil and a political life-belt. Moreover, entering elections in the south with a determination to take up the seats won was explicit recognition of the Dail's legitimate constitutional authority and its claim to speak for the Irish people. Here was a fundamental reversal of a 60-year assertion that that same legitimacy had actually been lodged with the Army Council of the IRA. In other words, Sinn Fein's entry into the Dáil elections of 1987 represented more than just an embarrassing non-event. It underscored what in reality had always been the case: that the Republican movement had no authority to speak for or act on behalf of the Irish people. Where now would the 'right' to plant bombs and murder people come from? According to whose authority were they acting? Sinn Fein had given up its ability to glide over democratic accountability. From now on it would have to listen to the people. Within these ideological shifts lay the seeds to the IRA cessation of 1994.

The split of 1986 worked to recast Republicanism in a more basic way. O'Bradaigh's exit from the movement shifted the epicentre of the Republican movement away from Dublin and towards the north, and power into the hands of the younger northern brigade centred around Adams and McGuinness. Republicanism became a more 'northern' experience, infected by the concerns, problems and political realities of its Nationalist community. The movement began to 'go native', attuning itself to the sharper, sectarian and more violent atmosphere of the north. It evolved into a community political force, at the expense of its older and more idealistic aspirations.[36] These developments persuaded some that the time had come for narrowing sights and focusing upon what might be achievable in the six counties rather than unachievable in all 32 of them. In this respect the move to drop abstention was a signal to the movement of wider, more far-reaching change, a desire to engage with mainstream politics and for Sinn Fein to step out of the shadow of the IRA. Also a need to modernize an increasingly self-defeating, out-of-date ideology, by injecting community concerns into the stuffy recesses of the Republican movement. Above all else to go 'slightly constitutional' to ensure long-term survival and involvement in any future moves towards a settlement.[37]

Going 'slightly constitutional' came at a price. To keep the hard-liners on board they were promised massive shipments of arms from Libya and, logically, an intensification of the armed struggle. Intensification, however, proved difficult against an enhanced British and Irish military response, following agreement to co-operate more closely on security. During the period 1986–1989, the security forces were able to make substantial inroads into IRA activity. The fatal ambush at Loughgall in May 1987 claimed the lives of eight IRA volunteers of the East Tyrone brigade, and was followed nine months later by a similar ambush of three leading IRA personnel in Gibraltar. The high human attrition rate was matched in terms of resources when in November 1987 the Gardai seized 150 tons of arms and ammunition on board the *Eksund*, en route from Libya to the north. Security arrangements were beginning to bite, a conclusion that reinforced a growing perception that military victory over the British could not be achieved. The logic of military stalemate was a cessation of the armed struggle. The problem, however, was that armed struggle remained the core belief of the

Provisionals and the wider Republican movement, the corner-stone of both its identity and purpose. Silencing or even removing it was to rip out the heart of the movement. Republicans were willing to go 'slightly constitutional' but not completely. So the problems and contradictions would have to deepen still further, and more blood be spilt needlessly, before this particular nettle could be grasped.

And deepen it did. On 8 November 1987 a bomb exploded at the Remembrance Day service in Enniskillen, killing 11 people. The public backlash was heartfelt and intense. Adams urged the IRA 'to be careful and careful again ... It's when the IRA, as in Enniskillen, omits to take this into account that tragedies take place'.[38] More directly, McGuinness saw the action as 'a total and absolute disaster. I felt absolutely gutted by it'.[39] Six months later popular outrage was 'treated' to another brutal and very public spectacle of two army corporals being dragged from their car by a baying nationalist mob, only to be executed by 'murderous thugs' of the IRA.[40] The political reaction spoke for itself. At the 1987 British general election Sinn Fein support fell while that of the SDLP leapt. At the 1989 district elections its support again fell, as did its seats on local councils, from 59 to 43. Sinn Fein was increasingly marooned on ever-decreasing islands of support in West Belfast and the Bogside. So by the end of 1987 the situation for Sinn Fein looked pretty dire. Military stalemate, electoral oblivion in the south and political marginalization in the north convinced Adams that a new direction was required. That new direction took the form of tentative conversations with John Hume, to explore some sort of pan-Nationalist co-operation.[41]

> At the 1987 British general election Sinn Fein support fell while that of the SDLP leapt

So the period 1984 to 1988 witnessed some profound shifts and reassessments. Little of this was done in public, but it is clear that behind the scenes pockets of leaders were beginning to scrutinize their tactics, revisit 'first' principles and re-examine fixed positions to see whether a changing world had not rendered them obsolete. Of most significance in this transition, first to a peace process and then a peace agreement, were developments within the Republican movement and within Unionism. Both movements edged away from their marginalized status into positions from where some involvement in political discussions and negotiation was possible. The ice was beginning to break, even if all could not yet sail their boats on the pond.

NOTES

1 R. Needham, *Battling for Peace* (Blackstaff Press, 1999) p 34.

2 M. Dewar, *The British Army in Northern Ireland* (Arms and Armour, 1985) p 175.

3 P. Taylor, *Brits: The War Against the IRA* (Bloomsbury, 2000) p 32.

4 For a broader analysis of this theme, see M. Smith, *Fighting for Ireland: Military Strategy of the Irish Republican Movement* (Routledge, 1995) pp 169–94.

5 M. Thatcher, *The Downing Street Years* (HarperCollins, 1993) p 385.

6 Ibid, p 394.

7 Bew, Patterson and Teague, *Between War and Peace* (Lawrence and Wishart, 1997) p 63.

8 G. FitzGerald, "Origins and rationale of the 1985 agreement", in D. Keogh and M. Haltzel (eds) *Northern Ireland and the Politics of Reconciliation* (CUP, 1993) p 201.

9 Anglo-Irish Agreement, 15 November 1985, article 1, section c.

10 B. O'Leary and J. McGarry, *The Politics of Antagonism: Understanding Northern Ireland* (Athlone Press, 1993) p 224.

11 P. O'Malley, *The Uncivil Wars* (Blackstaff, 1983) p 18.

12 Anglo-Irish Agreement, 15 November 1985, article 2, section b.

13 Ibid.

14 G. FitzGerald, op. cit., p 196.

15 Bew *et al*, op. cit., p 72.

16 O'Leary and McGarry, op. cit., p 234.

17 Bew and Gillespie, *Northern Ireland: A Chronology of the Troubles, 1968–1999* (Gill & Macmillan, 1999) p 193.

18 D. McKittrick and R. McVea, *Making Sense of the Troubles* (Blackstaff Press, 2000) p 165.

19 P. Taylor, *Loyalists* (Bloomsbury, 1999) p 182.

20 M. McGovan, 'Unity in diversity? The SDLP and the Peace Process', in C. Gilligan and J. Tonge (eds) *Peace or War: Understanding the Peace Process in Northern Ireland* (Ashgate, 1998) p 55.

21 Bew and Gillespie, op. cit., p 191.

22 T. Hennessey, *The Northern Ireland Peace Process* (Gill & Macmillan, 2000) p 48.

23 Danny Morrison speaking in 1981 made the now famous comment: 'Who here really believes we can win the war through the ballot box? But will anyone here object, if with a ballot paper in this hand and an armalite in this hand, we take power in Ireland?' M. Smith, *Fighting for Ireland: Military Strategy of the Irish Republican Movement* (Routledge, 1995) p 155.

24 Smith, op. cit., p 177.

25 Ibid, p 177.

26 Ibid, p 171.

27 Ibid, p 72.

28 B. O'Brien, *The Long War: The IRA and Sinn Fein* (Syracuse UP, 1993) p 198.

29 Ibid, p 127.

30 Jim McAllister delivering the Republican address at the annual Bodenstown commemoration in 1984, in Hennessey, op. cit., p 35.

31 Smith, op. cit., p 190.

32 D. McKittrick and R. McVea, op. cit., p 168.

33 Taylor, *Provos: The IRA and Sinn Fein* (Bloomsbury, 1997) pp 290–1.

34 M. Laffan, *The Resurrection of Ireland: The Sinn Fein Party, 1916–1923* (CUP, 1999) pp 18–19.

35 M. Ryan, 'From the centre to the margins: the slow death of Irish Republicanism', in Gilligan and Tonge, op. cit.

36 Ryan, in Gilligan and Tonge, op. cit.

37 O'Brien, op. cit., pp 118–32.

38 Smith, op. cit., pp 176–8.

39 D. McKittrick and E. Mallie, *Endgame in Ireland* (Hodder & Stoughton, 2001) p 63.

40 O'Brien, op. cit., p 165.

41 G. Murray, *John Hume and the SDLP: Impact and Survival in Northern Ireland* (Irish Academic Press, 1996) pp 161–75.

7

IN FROM THE COLD: THE ORIGINS OF THE PEACE PROCESS, 1988–1993

'The gate into the field has been opened but there is a lot of hard ploughing in front of us.'

I. Paisley, House of Commons, 26 March 1991

'There is a world of difference between agreeing to talk ... and talking to agree.'

S. Mallon, House of Commons, 26 March 1991

THE IDEA THAT THE ANGLO-IRISH AGREEMENT would operate like a slow-working incendiary upon the deadlock of Northern Irish politics gave way by 1988 to the realization that it might not explode at all. Three years after its signing the political landscape looked barren. Violence increased from 58 deaths in 1985 to 106 in 1987 and 105 the following year. Anglo-Irish relations frosted up with the collapse of FitzGerald's government in February 1987 and the return of Haughey. They cooled further in the wake of the rejection of the Birmingham six appeal in January 1988 and the allegations of a 'shoot to kill' policy within the RUC. The SDLP though strengthened by the agreement was demoralized by the lack of movement towards political negotiations. Unionists continued to sulk in their self-imposed exile, while privately scratching around for ways to extricate themselves. The IRA though under pressure could still murder eight soldiers on a bus at Ballygawley, with its alter ego Sinn Fein still 'fully' committed to the armed struggle. However, beneath the well-scripted public shows of defiance and implaca-

> **Everyone seemed to be talking to someone**

bility, signs of movement and discourse began to appear. Hesitant and secretive at first, these 'signs' grew into a rage of 'talking'. Lines of communications were established, soundings taken, briefings given, *'ballons d'essai'* floated, overtures offered and dialogue set in motion between and within the various groups and parties. Everyone seemed to be talking to someone. And even if they weren't actually talking they were communicating through signs, symbols, intimations, codes, gestures, body language, throwaway words, semiotics, untraceable leaks and 'off-the-cuff' remarks. Sinn Fein conversed with its bitter Nationalist rival the SDLP. Ulster Unionists mumbled to their 'traitorous' British allies and their long-term enemies in Dublin. Paramilitaries spoke to other paramilitaries, prisoners on one side of the wire to those on the other. The governments of Britain and Ireland discoursed through the Inter-Governmental Conference. And the British government began 'a practice of ... semiphor(ing)'[1] with Sinn Fein while, unbeknown to the other parties, her intelligence services reopened their highly secret 'back channel' to the IRA. The result of these various communications was a transformation of the political situation in Northern Ireland, laying the basis for the first substantive inter-party talks since Sunningdale and the Downing Street Declaration of 1993.

HUME–ADAMS TALKS, 1988

Perhaps the most significant conversations occurred between John Hume and Gerry Adams from January to September 1988. By this stage the Republican movement was already in a state of flux following the removal of abstention in 1986. On top of this sat a growing awareness of military stalemate and the impossibility of forcing a British withdrawal, tapering political support as the result of public relations disasters such as the Enniskillen bomb, and the collapse of Sinn Fein's electoral assault on the south. If Sinn Fein's political momentum was not to go completely 'belly-up' then a 'sense of realism'[2] had to replace blind faith and jaded dogma. The modernizers around Adams sought a new direction by looking to other Nationalist parties for 'a joint comprehensive strategy',[3] a pan-Nationalist front of Sinn Fein alongside the SDLP, the Dublin government, political parties in the south and Irish-American interests. The coalition would become a practical vehicle for engineering a British withdrawal and asserting Irish self-determination. Sinn Fein would play the part of stage manager, bringing unity to all the disparate elements of the production and reminding the cast that they were performing a tale of national unification.

From 1986–1987 Adams made contact with southern Fianna Fail politicians and to Haughey himself via Martin Mansergh, Haughey's advisor, where hints and winks were given towards the idea of some sort of pan-Nationalist coalition but only if the armed struggle was dropped. Adams also sent out 'feelers' to John Hume through a trusted intermediary Father Reid. Hume was initially sceptical. With the Anglo-Irish Agreement fresh in everyone's minds, the chance of constructing a system of governance with moderate Unionists was not beyond the realms of possibility, though any hint of contact with Sinn Fein would destroy that chance, something Hume was not alone in scenting might be Adams' real intention. The agreement also aimed at marginalizing Sinn Fein and with it the organization's justification for physical force. There was no point, then, Hume throwing a life-belt to someone he had always wanted to drown. So Hume decided to 'run' with the agreement.

By late 1987 he was less sure. Continued Unionist intransigence suggested the agreement had halted progress towards an internal solution in Northern Ireland. Nor had it done much to manoeuvre Sinn Fein from the path of violence. While its performance in the 1987 general election, though down on 1983, did confirm it as a permanent political presence in the region that would have to somehow be accommodated in any future settlement. These developments left Hume more receptive to overtures from Adams. He was encouraged further by a new emphasis and language emerging from within the Republican movement. In May 1987 Sinn Fein published a manifesto, *A Scenario for Peace*. Amongst the rehash of traditional Republican thinking lurked a small passage committing Sinn Fein to 'seek to create conditions which will lead to a permanent cessation of hostilities (and) an end to our long war'.[4] Seven months later Adams smuggled into an interview that he 'would be prepared to consider an alternative, unarmed struggle to attain Irish independence. If someone would outline such a course I would not only be prepared to listen but I would be prepared to work in that direction ... there's no military solution, none whatsoever. Military solutions by either of the two main protagonists only mean more tragedies. There can only be a political solution'.[5] Hume spotted these almost throwaway remarks as material he could work with and develop. If the Anglo-Irish Agreement could not entice Sinn Fein away from the armed struggle, maybe he could.

The timing of their meetings could not have been worse. In the wake of the Enniskillen atrocity, followed in quick succession by the 'death' of three IRA volunteers in Gibraltar, the Milltown cemetery murders and the brutal killing of two army corporals, community tensions were high and political sensibilities razor-sharp: though it may be that such a backdrop left both men more not less eager to talk. The talks, lasting much of 1988, were largely exploratory, searching for some common ground between them. Unfortunately they revealed more differences than points of agreement. Sinn Fein, for example, claimed Britain's 'occupation' of Ireland was based upon deep vested interests and amounted to a 'colonial' oppression of her people. The SDLP argued such oppression was a reaction to IRA violence, not a precursor to it, while the Anglo-Irish Agreement indicated Britain was more of a 'neutral' power rather than a colonial one. Similarly, where Sinn Fein believed 'real' peace could be accomplished only by a British withdrawal, the SDLP argued such a withdrawal without political agreement and community reconciliation would simply unleash civil war. On the question of self-determination (a more velvety way of referring to a united Ireland) Sinn Fein and the SDLP could agree that the

Irish people had an inalienable right to it. However, Sinn Fein denied Unionists the right to frustrate this, arguing partition was illegal and the will of the majority across all of Ireland had to prevail. The SDLP, on the other hand, saw the reality of the situation was that one million Unionists could not be forced into a united Ireland. They had a 'natural' veto which could be removed only by persuasion and consent. Moreover, armed struggle, far from being a valid tactic against an 'occupying' force, undermined any hope of persuading Unionists and further hardened the British presence. In any case Republican claims to be waging war against an occupying power were increasingly hard to sustain when their violence fell disproportionately upon the Unionist community. Armed struggle was not only rendering a solution more remote but was taking on the 'feel' of a sectarian rather than a colonial conflict.

Hume and Adams ended their meetings in September 1988. The two leaders offered some oblique statements of common purpose. Both, for example, believed the Irish people had a right to self-determination. Both supported the idea of a conference of all parties in Ireland to achieve that objective. And both hoped Britain would become a 'persuader' for Irish unity. But Sinn Fein and the SDLP could not yet go beyond this. New soft, woolly 'Humeite' Nationalism was still unable to accommodate old-style Republicanism. Yet some sort of Rubicon had been crossed. Dialogue between the two men would continue in secret over the next four years, laying the basis to their more substantive talks in 1993 and leading to a better understanding of each other's ideas and position. Contact had brought insight and clarity – enough to convince Hume he might be able to ease the Republican leadership towards abandoning the armed struggle. To achieve this an inclusive dialogue across and within all Nationalist parties was required as a bridge over which Republicans might move into mainstream political activity. If electoral marginalization gave

> **❝Republican claims to be waging war against an occupying power were increasingly hard to sustain when their violence fell disproportionately upon the Unionist community❞**

Sinn Fein the 'push', then a broad-based political process could be the 'pull' towards ending the armed struggle. Interestingly, talk of a pan-Nationalist alliance had shifted Hume's focus from a purely internal, six-county framework to an all-Ireland basis. This created some tensions within the SDLP from those whose horizons stretched little beyond a devolved internal government. But enhancing the all-Irish element within the SDLP's ambitions sat more comfortably with Hume and others' basic ideological concerns. It also, at a practical level, offered a strong mechanism for encouraging and influencing Britain to move in a more pro-unity direction.

For Sinn Fein, despite tough posturing and even tougher rhetoric, the meetings signalled some quite dramatic changes. The act of meeting and even discussing ideas of a pan-Nationalist coalition was in effect a repudiation of the notion of *Sinn Fein*, 'ourselves alone'. It evidently could not do it alone and its survival now depended on others. An acknowledgement then, albeit implicitly, that it was not the Praetorian Guard of a soon to be realized republic but a small northern community-based party, unable to expand beyond its core support of approximately 10–11 per cent of the Northern Irish population. Though claiming lineage back to the executed leaders of the Easter Rising, it was keen to navigate the road of pragmatic readjustment rather than court a principled, vainglorious demise: under Adams the Republican sacrificial ideal waned considerably. Here, then, were the 'embryonic stages'[6] by which Sinn Fein would enter constitutional politics by 1994. Of course, to more intuitive Republicans came the realization that for any type of pan-Nationalist front to coalesce, Sinn Fein would have to shed more than just the potency of its name. Even the most blinkered Republican could see there was little chance of co-operation with other Nationalist parties, especially the SDLP, until Republicans dumped the armed struggle and much of its irredentist ideological baggage. Adams faced a tough, perhaps impossible, task weaning the Republican movement off its pure milk of republicanism. 'It was quite obvious to me that Adams and the others were people who were on a hook and wanted to get off the hook.'[7]

TALKING ABOUT TALKING: BROOKE AND THE UNIONISTS, 1989–1991

Adams and Sinn Fein were not the only ones struggling to get off a hook. Since 1985 Unionists had been in a state of 'self-inflicted stagnation',[8] having followed the enlightened course of sending themselves to Coventry in protest at the Anglo-Irish Agreement. Here they wallowed for much of 1985–1987, exiled and alone, believing simple negativism was enough to remove the agreement. It was of course an unsustainable position, sorely exposed by the refusal of the British and Irish governments to budge. What made the situation politically dangerous rather than just inconvenient or embarrassing to the leadership was mounting pressure from within Unionism to open up a dialogue with the government. A good example of this was *An End to Drift*, a joint-party paper urging their leaders to re-involve themselves in the political process. Molyneaux and Paisley found, however, that like so many unsustainable positions it was easier to get in than to get out. What they needed were face-saving measures, something to convince their supporters of consistency, even victory, when the reality pointed towards a reversal of position. One temporary face-saving measure presented itself in 1987 when under the cover of a suspension of normal business King made tentative overtures towards the Unionist leadership. More hopeful were the contacts made in the course of 1988 between Brian Mawhinney, Tom King's number two, and various 'second-tier' Unionist leaders such as Peter Robinson of the DUP and Frank Millar of the UUP. This rather flexible interpretation of 'never talking to ministers until the agreement goes', though achieving little, did at least set a precedent and signal a willingness to talk. Relations between the government and the Unionist leadership were beginning to defrost. They were warm enough for the new Secretary of State from July 1989, Peter Brooke, to believe he could lead Unionists out of the wilderness and in time into meaningful inter-party negotiations. Brooke was all set to play Hume to Molyneaux's Adams.

> **❝Brooke was all set to play Hume to Molyneaux's Adams❞**

Brooke brought several advantages to this enterprise. One was that he was not Tom King, the man closely, if wrongly, associated by Unionists with the Anglo-Irish Agreement. Much more complicit than King had been Thatcher, who in 1990 was also removed from the scene, as were several highly influential pro-Ulster Tories (John Biggs-Davison died in 1988, while Ian Gow was murdered by the IRA in 1990). Another benefit for Brooke was that by 1989 Unionists were eager to be involved and chastened by their experience of the previous three years. If Unionists were not quite ready to 'bite the negotiating bullet',[9] they were undoubtedly keen to chew on it a little. On the other side, the SDLP and Alliance had been waiting since 1985 for such a development. Brooke also established a close working relationship with Gerry Collins, the Irish Foreign Minister. And Brooke had all the right personal qualities, nicely summed up as 'a fecund mix of doggedness and patience'.[10] To these we might add an impressive intellectual grasp of the situation, a calm approach to negotiating, an ability to inspire trust and a usefully ambiguous speaking style, all of which he hid behind a disarmingly bumbling and light-weight façade.[11] An amiable bloodhound had replaced a prickly 'Tomcat'.[12] These characteristics became clearer over the summer and autumn of 1989 as he took soundings from the various Unionist leaders to establish points of agreement. These formed the basis of his announcement in January 1990 of an initiative to promote inter-party talks in the near future. Flagging up his willingness to facilitate talks did not automatically mean all would start talking. Brooke had done little more than check the wicket and see whether the rain had passed. He had not coaxed the players onto the pitch, and the batting side remained resolutely locked in their changing room. A basic dilemma still confronted Brooke, that 'any Unionist capacity for dialogue continually foundered on the rock of their absolute refusal to engage under the auspices of the abhorrent Agreement'.[13] Yet London and Dublin absolutely refused to scrap the agreement and its secretariat just to accommodate Unionists. This chasm would have to be bridged if inter-party talks were ever to commence.

Brooke and Collins revealed themselves as inventive and flexible political engineers. Although neither would contemplate scrapping the agreement, both realized they could work its 'grey areas'. One such 'grey area' was for both governments to indicate a willingness to replace the agreement if negotiations were successful. This had already been hinted at in the Anglo-Irish Agreement and was more a statement of the obvious than a radical shift. Yet being spelt out was important reassurance for Unionists. Another 'grey area' lay in the definition of key words. Unionists had declared that 'suspension' of the Inter-Governmental Conference meant a complete shutdown. Brooke, in response to moderate tones from Peter Robinson, now gave suspension a more temporary flavour. If the Inter-Governmental Conference and its secretariat were arraigned for a long summer recess, as he and Collins agreed in April 1990, this might prove just the 'window of opportunity' to kickstart talks. Brooke had won these concessions from Collins in return for greater involvement of Dublin in the negotiations.

Unfortunately, while Unionists accepted the notion of a brief suspension, they would not agree to greater involvement by Dublin. The early 'splutterings' of life during the autumn of 1989 were dead by May 1990. Some progress had been made, however. All sides had agreed the talks should proceed along three fronts that addressed different aspects of the problem (originally Hume's idea), what Brooke described as relations 'within Northern Ireland, within the island of Ireland and between the peoples of these islands'.[14] This translated into strand one dealing with the internal government of Northern Ireland, strand two with relations between Belfast and Dublin, and strand three relations between Britain and the Republic of Ireland. A structure for negotiations now lay before the parties. They could all agree on what to talk about, but the question of who would talk and when they would do it now blocked progress.

Brooke's long summer recess for the IGC came and went. Behind the scenes, however, he and Collins edged slowly towards another compromise. Months of private bargaining resulted in Dublin agreeing its involvement would come in strand two and would start after strand one talks had commenced. The timing of strand two lay with Brooke, who had privately agreed with

Collins no more than a five-week delay. Unionists again dug in their heels, but under considerable pressure, including from the Prime Minister John Major and some dark warnings from Brooke that 'the moment for decision has come',[15] they swung behind the compromise. On 26 March 1991, after 15 months of grinding and tortuous negotiation with Molyneaux and Paisley, Brooke could announce to the House of Commons the commencement of inter-party talks. They were to begin on 30 April and end on 16 July, utilizing an 11-week 'gap' when the IGC was not in session. These were the first formal inter-party discussions since the Sunningdale talks 18 years previously. And though no one actually expected a settlement to emerge, all could appreciate that a vital precedent was being set and a longer political process begun. Just for good measure and to put pressure on the IRA, the loyalist paramilitaries, organized as the Combined Loyalist Military Command (CLMC), began a cease-fire for the duration of the talks.

> ❝ But no sooner had the talks begun than they stopped again. At issue now was the venue for strand two ❞

But no sooner had the talks begun than they stopped again. At issue now was the venue for strand two. Unionists, hypersensitive to symbolism, wanted all negotiations to be held in London. The Irish government and the SDLP felt, not unreasonably, that Dublin was the only place to negotiate possible changes to the Irish constitution. The dispute rumbled on for four weeks before Brooke and Collins finally reached agreement on a 'moveable feast' plan: the talks would open in London, continue in Belfast and then finish in Dublin. But as they reached agreement on this, so dispute flared up over who would chair strand two talks. Unionists rejected Brooke and Collins' choice of Lord Carrington, given his association with the imposition of direct rule back in 1972 and his well-publicized low opinion of Unionist politicians.[16] A compromise was found in Sir Ninian Stephen, a former Australian governor-general, though several weeks had been lost in the process. It was not, then, until 17 June, after seven weeks of painful waiting and bilateral meetings, that inter-party talks finally opened. Again some progress was made. At the plenary meetings, opening statements were delivered and interrogated by each party, views exchanged and positions understood. But it was all too little too late. Because of procedural haggling, the original 11-week 'negotiating gap' had shrunk to just four, and four weeks to end four centuries of conflict was never going to fit. Brooke realized this. So instead of focusing on the talks in hand, he turned his mind to the talks to come. 'We had got to conduct them (talks) so that if we were not able to reach conclusions, we would leave the conversations in such a way that they could be returned to'.[17] Ending the talks in a manner conducive to a resumption of contact in the future.

Unfortunately, ending the talks generated dispute. Having done all they could to frustrate discussions, Unionists were now unwilling to see them terminated simply because the IGC was scheduled to return on 16 July. They pressed instead for a further suspension of the IGC and raised the political stakes by publicly claiming both governments were 'trying to pull the plug'[18] on negotiations. One might be forgiven for thinking Unionists were intent on squeezing the timetable to prevent movement onto strand two or angling for a permanent suspension of the IGC, what they desired in the first place. Yet neither London nor Dublin was prepared to move on this. And in any case the talks looked poised to collapse on other issues. Press reporting, fuelled by 'briefings' and 'leaks', injected a bitter, suspicious tone into the talks and were a distraction from the main event. Additionally, John Hume seemed to lose interest, showing greater concern for talking about general problems than specific changes, and expressing a desire to move onto strand two rather than work constructively on strand one. This was not surprising for he had long argued that progress would come only by linking the issues across the three strands. With mounting stalemate and growing disillusion, 'we just started lecturing each other on history and our own interpretations of it, all that stuff. That isn't the right atmosphere in which to make progress'.[19] With *enpasse* all but complete, Brooke ended (or rather adjourned) the talks early on 3 July. Little measurable progress was made towards a settlement. Arguments and delay had typified proceedings from day one. And the end came in a welter of acrimony and bickering. To call these 'opening salvoes' would be an injustice to British naval gunnery. However, their importance lay not in what they did but in what they were. The act of meeting and talking was groundbreaking enough, a compass bearing from which all subsequent negotiations could pick up and orientate themselves.

'Picking up' the talks proved as tricky as starting them. Though both governments and all the political parties pledged themselves to try again, obstacles littered the path back. The re-opening of the Inter-Governmental Conference angered Unionists and raised again the whole question of finding a suitable tactical suspension. More debilitating was the speculation over the forthcoming Westminster general election that seemed to freeze the political landscape and sharpen intra-community rivalry. Parties scuttled away from the middle ground, back to the safety of their community 'fox holes', from where they speculated upon various post-election scenarios. The SDLP, for example, saw little point in re-opening talks with the chance (albeit a slim one) of a Labour victory and their commitment to Irish unity through consent. Similarly, Unionists saw no need to hurry back, predicting a substantial reduction in the Tory vote, leaving Major if not actually at the mercy of a 'hung' Parliament then eager to have the cushion of Ulster Unionist MPs around him. Molyneaux foresaw a brighter future ahead of Unionism. So Northern Irish politics went into cold storage until after the election, scheduled for early April. Ironically, given his immense efforts of the previous two-and-a-half years, Brooke himself became an obstacle to further talks. His 'immense faux pas',[20] when he was reluctantly encouraged into singing 'My Darling Clementine' on Irish television on the very night eight protestant workers were blown up by the IRA at Teebane, outraged Unionists. Brooke offered his resignation, which Major refused. Ministerial reshuffles were best done after, not before, an election.

'ONE TOFF FOR ANOTHER': THE MAYHEW
INITIATIVE, 1992

Brooke was replaced by Sir Patrick Mayhew in the Cabinet reshuffle of April 1992. Mayhew, the former attorney-general with experience of the tussles over extradition with Dublin, was a reassuring choice for Unionists but of little comfort to the Irish government or the SDLP. Yet once again a 'plummy' English patrician (and Mayhew spoke with a full 'fruit basket' of an accent) proved to be a most agile and pragmatic politician. Alongside David Andrews, the Irish Foreign Secretary, another 'gap' was engineered in the IGC and soothing words were applied to Unionists to entice them back. Agreement was reached to continue with the three-stranded approach to discussions and to follow Brooke's 'banking' principle that 'nothing is agreed until everything is agreed', designed to prevent parties cherry-picking what they liked at the expense of what they did not.[21] So by 29 April talks between the four constitutional parties resumed. The talking this time was more productive, moving beyond procedural wrangles to possible structures of governing and even onto the previously uncharted terrain of strands two and three. If Brooke broke ground, then Mayhew certainly planted seed.

In the opening skirmishes on strand one, the early pacesetter was the SDLP. It proposed a new *consultative* Northern Ireland Assembly and a six-person *executive* commission. Three of the commissioners would be elected, two appointed by each government and one a representative of the EU. These were radical ideas, reflecting what the SDLP had long desired, namely a government that mirrored both identities in Northern Ireland as well as the growing importance of the EU, what Bew called 'joint authority with a European flavour'.[22] Whatever the flavouring, Unionists and the Alliance Party condemned it as undemocratic, divorcing the operation of power from the people of Northern Ireland. The commission

> 66 Once again a 'plummy' English patrician (and Mayhew spoke with a full 'fruit basket' of an accent) proved to be a most agile and pragmatic politician 99

would be unrepresentative of the region and unchecked by their elected but purely consultative assembly. It would also give the south a direct say in the north, the same principle upon which Unionists continued to rail against the AIA. Ulster Unionists and the DUP countered with proposals for an 85-member assembly, with standing committees responsible for the various departments of government. The chairpersons for these committees would be elected according to the balance of parties in the assembly (the D'Hondt formula). There would be no executive body, power-sharing or otherwise, since the Protestant people had opposed it in 1974 and their own party manifestos at the 1992 election had precluded it *for the moment*. The plans, not surprisingly, were rejected by the SDLP as little more than dressed-up Unionist majoritarian rule. More substantially they failed to recognize the Irish identity of northern Nationalists by giving no role in the affairs of the north to the Dublin government. The most Unionists would contemplate was an external affairs committee, able to meet with representatives from the south on areas of common concern.

Confronted by deadlock between Unionist and Nationalist schemes, the British government speedily convened a small subcommittee of all four parties to bridge the two positions. Their compromise plan delivered on 10 June (and subsequently leaked to the press) consisted of the Unionist idea for an assembly and departmental committees but with a three-person elected panel to operate alongside them. The panel would have extensive powers to oversee, monitor and generally 'guard' the system but since elected from the region, contained no European or Irish representatives.[23] The compromise met with support from the Unionists and Alliance parties but with no clear Irish or European dimension to the proposals, the SDLP dug in its heels and withheld its approval. Again the British and Irish worked hard to forestall stalemate, this time by effecting the transition of negotiations onto strand two. Transition from one strand to another was imperative if any sort of momentum was to build up within the talks' process; indeed, failure to do so had broken the Brooke initiative. The step was especially difficult for Unionists. Their interest was limited to the governance of

Northern Ireland and few had a desire to open relations with the Republic on north-south contact. But unless they made the step there was no chance of an agreement with Nationalists on strand one. Realizing its importance, Mayhew tried warm words and reassurance to coax Unionists across this particular bridge. In a private letter to Molyneaux on 1 July 1992, he supported the 10 June compromise and rejected the SDLP's scheme. He also dangled that perennial carrot of a Northern Irish select committee, a well-used ploy whenever London wanted to 'encourage' Unionists in a particular direction.

❝ That sense of achievement evaporated almost immediately ❞

It was, then, with a very real sense of achievement and progress that on 6 July strand two talks opened at Lancaster House in London, with Ulster Unionists coming face to face with leaders of the Irish Republic to discuss north-south relations. That sense of achievement evaporated almost immediately. Three DUP members resigned even before the meeting took place, while the talks quickly marooned themselves on the thorny issue of articles 2 and 3 of the Irish constitution. These laid claim to the north and Unionists demanded their removal before any agreement or movement on north-south relations could be made. Dublin countered by arguing, unconvincingly,[24] that they represented no actual threat and were 'aspirational'[25] rather than assertive, a red herring rather than a red rag. Yet significantly, Dublin did not permanently rule out amendment or removal of the articles if full, equal recognition of the Irish identity and ambitions of northern Nationalists were gained. This, they argued, could be achieved through a north–south council of some substance, with designated executive functions sufficient to satisfy northern Nationalist demands for an 'Irish' dimension, perhaps even with the potential to be enhanced. Unionists saw little of value here. Instead they recommended a more limited body, along the lines of their external committee idea, with no executive powers, unless specifically given to it by a Northern Ireland Assembly and all within a wider grouping of regional governments of the 'British' archipelago. They envisaged a council of the British Isles, with east-west relations 'esteemed' as highly as north-south ones. The fact that few such regional governments existed in 1992, compared with the plethora by 1998, did not seem to dissuade Unionists.

As with strand one, so strand two revealed deep differences between each side. Nor did a summer recess and fresh start on 9 September look likely to narrow them, especially when Paisley and Robinson exited the talks just three days later in protest at what they 'richly' called Dublin's obduracy. With leaks to the press and acrimony rising between the parties, it was to nobody's surprise that all-party negotiations were formally ended on 10 November. What few could predict was that it would be another four years before all-party talks were con-vened again. Yet measurable progress had been made. Molyneaux and his Unionist team made the historic trek south, on 21 September, for three days of talks in Dublin Castle, once the home of British government across all Ireland and now the seat of government in the Republic. 'One (more) particular taboo had lost its relevance.'[26] Dublin had hinted, albeit in extremely muffled terms, that articles 2 and 3 could *possibly* be revised for movement towards an Irish dimension in strand two. The sub-committee's 'bridging' formula of 10 June was itself an act of unfamiliar compromise by representatives from all the constitutional parties, even if the SDLP leadership subsequently turned its nose up at the result. Furthermore, both the UUP and DUP had recognized that an 'executive' rather than committees was, long term, the preferred mechanism to govern Northern Ireland, though not one they could presently advocate. Moreover, in last-minute 'tactical' proposals, designed to throw blame for the collapse of talks onto the Nationalists and hoping to avert the reinstatement of the IGC, Ulster Unionists accepted the need for Nationalists to 'play a meaningful role' in the administration of Northern Ireland and for 'mutually beneficial co-operation' between the north and south along the lines of an Inter-Irish Relations Committee. Though hesitant and deeply ambiguous, this was Unionists recognizing the *possibility* of both a power-sharing executive and an Irish dimension at some future point. At the very least they had not permanently ruled these out, and in the world of Northern Irish political semiotics not permanently ruling something out *could* well mean ruling it in. Prospects, though 'bleak',[27] were not therefore without a few grains of promise. Indeed, for those with 20/20 vision and a passion for carrots, the pre-embryonic and watery outlines of possible areas of compromise were becoming visible.

ROASTING SNOW;[28] THE HUME–ADAMS INITIATIVE, 1989–1993

The watery outlines of political compromise were of little comfort to John Hume. He, like many others, saw the real problem as bringing a permanent end to the violence, and that required engagement with Sinn Fein. Accordingly he had never held much faith in the talks and had shown uncharacteristic inflexibility towards the sub-committee's compromise formula. He also had been frustrated by the Unionist tactic of eleventh-hour compromise proposals designed to collapse the IGC rather than address the problem. So with the conclusion of talks in November 1992, Hume returned to his earlier initiative of easing Sinn Fein away from the gun and into democratic, mainstream politics. By 1992 the task looked a lot more promising. The general election of 1992 saw Sinn Fein lose out again to a strengthening SDLP performance, falling from 11.4 per cent of the vote to 10 per cent, with Joe Hendron taking Gerry Adams' West Belfast seat. This sense of growing political marginalization was reinforced during the multi-party talks of 1991 and 1992, as Sinn Fein was compelled to 'spectate' events from the outside. The prospect of political irrelevance filled Adams and McGuinness with alarm, like two ugly sisters facing 'spinsterhood'[29] through their failure to talk to anyone. Anxious to have a political input, Sinn Fein struggled to open a dialogue with anybody but particularly with Hume and Fianna Fail. To this end it softened and moderated its rhetoric to such an extent that by 1992 sources close to the Sinn Fein leadership felt 'the tonality, the type of speeches, the type of responses that were coming from republicanism were now a million light years from where they had been a year beforehand'.[30] In February 1991, for example, Adams admitted he was ready to take political risks and for 'give and take' in pursuit of peace. Seven months later he declared he was willing to engage in open dialogue and wanted to see violence end.[31] At one point he even came close to refuting Sinn Fein policy since the early 1980s, when he claimed the slogan by 'the Armalite and the ballot box' was 'outmoded'.

In re-opening contact with Adams (in fact since 1988 contact had never really been broken) Hume was impressed by Sinn Fein's 1992 election manifesto entitled *Towards a Lasting Peace*, which claimed: 'There is an onus on those who proclaim the armed struggle is counterproductive to advance a credible alternative. Such an alternative would be welcomed across the island but nowhere more than in the oppressed Nationalist areas of the Six counties which have borne the brunt of British rule since partition and particularly for over 20 years past. The development of such an alternative would be welcomed by Sinn Fein.' We might note the caveat of 'credible', but the message was clear: Sinn Fein was in the market for inclusion and compromise. In pursuing these objectives Hume was aided by the Irish and British governments. Through Haughey and from February 1992 the new Taoiseach Albert Reynolds, a constant and secret dialogue was maintained between Fianna Fail, Hume and Sinn Fein. Yet of more significance, initially at least, were the interventions of Peter Brooke. Brooke had already 'whetted interest'[32] amongst Nationalists and Republicans with a speech after his first 100 days in office in which he believed 'it was difficult to envisage a military defeat' of the IRA and that if the armed struggle was terminated 'the government ... would be imaginative in how it responded'.[33]

> **In February 1991, for example, Adams admitted he was ready to take political risks and for 'give and take' in pursuit of peace**

In the autumn of 1990 Hume asked Brooke to respond 'imaginatively' to the internal debate within Republicanism. Brooke took the opportunity of a scheduled speech to his constituency party on 9 November 1990 to reply, coincidentally the same day Mary Robinson was elected the Irish President and whilst British political eyes were firmly on the imminent departure of

Thatcher. To the bemusement of his blue-rinse octogenarian members, who had no doubt assembled to hear a few words of comfort before bedtime, they were treated to a head-on confrontation with the ruling principles and strategy of Irish Republicanism. He repeated what Wilson, Whitelaw and he himself had said before, and was carved into the Anglo-Irish Agreement, that Britain was not *against* a United Ireland, merely *for* the majority opinion of the moment, and majority opinion at present wanted Britain there. The British presence, therefore, turned neither upon vested economic or political interests, nor as some potent symbol of Britain's 'great power' status, but upon the existence of one million Unionists. This, in a now famous phrase, represented 'no selfish strategic or economic interests in Northern Ireland; our role is to help, enable and encourage. Britain's purpose ... is not to occupy, oppress or exploit but to ensure democratic debate and free democratic choice'. What gave the speech potency was the new international context in which it was delivered and received.[34] With revolutions in Eastern Europe, the collapse of the Soviet Union and the end of the Cold War, Northern Ireland was no longer a significant point for NATO on the Atlantic approaches but a marginal, economically dependent region on the periphery of Europe. A British declaration of no strategic interest in Northern Ireland had a more truthful ring to it. As for economic interest, even Republicans could see the region was a net importer of British state expenditure.

Hume picked up these arguments and weaved them into a document, *A Strategy for Peace and Justice in Ireland*, that formed the basis of his conversations with Adams during 1991. These conversations intensified after the collapse of the Mayhew talks in November 1992 and in the wake of another 'imaginative' speech, this time by Mayhew at Coleraine in December 1992. Hume pointed out that Brooke's (and Mayhew's) declaration of British neutrality on the Union represented a watershed by challenging the central Republican notion that Unionism in Northern Ireland was *sustained* by the British presence. On the contrary, Unionism *maintained* the British residence in the region. As such a British withdrawal was neither here nor there, for a Unionist presence and presumably resistance would remain whatever the British decided to do. Accepting that premise, a united Ireland could only, then, come about through the persuasion of Unionists to join it, whether Britain withdrew or ended partition or even, as Hume and Adams hoped, tried to persuade Unionists to enter into it. A united Ireland was an imagined community, not a 'geographic expression';[35] it was the people of Ireland, not the island of its people, ideas Hume had first expressed during the New Ireland Forum back in 1984. There was simply no other way to unite Ireland, unless by refusing them consent over such an arrangement Unionists were to be coerced into it, a course liable to provoke civil war, with 12,000 armed RUC men alongside the thousands of loyalist paramilitaries ready to fight. These were powerful, even irrefutable arguments deployed by Hume to weaken Adams' rigidity upon the question of a British withdrawal and over the question of Unionist consent – the pole stars of Republican thinking.

Yet even pole stars shift their orbit. On 21 June 1992 a statement by a leading Sinn Feiner, Jim Gibney, at the Wolfe Tone commemoration, appeared to show movement on the issue of British withdrawal. 'The British government's departure,' he declared, 'must be *preceded* by a sustained period of peace and will arise out of negotiations (involving) the different shades of Irish Nationalism and Irish Unionism.' This was a significant development remembering that as recently as 1989 'spokespersons' for the GHQ of the Northern Brigade of the IRA had declared: 'We can state confidently today that there will be no cease-fire until Britain declares its intention to withdraw.'[36] Movement on consent had to wait a little over a year, and even then was slightly oblique. On 24 April 1993, after many months' hard negotiating, Hume and Adams issued a joint statement: 'We are mindful that not all the people of Ireland share the view or agree on how to give meaningful expression to it (self-determination). Indeed, we do not disguise the different views held by our own parties ... we have told each other that we see the task of reaching agreement on a peaceful and democratic accord for all on this island as our primary challenge. We both recognize that such a new agreement is *only achievable and viable* if it can earn and enjoy the allegiance of the different traditions on this island, by accommodating diversity and providing for national reconciliation.' Five months later came a second statement that advanced a few more inches: 'Such a (peace) process would obviously also be designed to *ensure* that any new agreement that might emerge respects the diversity of our different traditions and *earns* their allegiance and agreement.' Within the two statements lay acceptance of the need for Unionist consent, albeit whispered through clenched teeth and without the moving of lips. Though incomplete, vague, and like any post-Christmas waistline much in need of firming up, in the context of where Republicans had stood a few years previously these were seismic shifts of immense importance.

> " Movement on consent had to wait a little over a year, and even then was slightly oblique "

As with Unionists at the end of 1992, so within Republicanism by 1993, once deeply held positions and unshakable principles were altering, and altering rapidly. But the real importance of these shifts lay in the collateral damage they inflicted. If Republican arguments for no consent and a British withdrawal were becoming obsolete, then the necessity for armed struggle was withering. The counterproductiveness of violence to achieve political ends was already evident from the late 1980s. If Adams was now accepting the need to persuade, to 'accommodate' and to 'reconcile' Unionists into a united Ireland, violence was positively harmful to the cause. So in the Hume–Adams statements of 1993 lay the seeds to the IRA's cease-fires of 1994 and 1997. Of course, Hume realized that to catch Republican fish he needed tasty bait. This came in the form of growing co-operation with the Irish government, now in the hands of an expert 'wheeler-dealer', Albert Reynolds. Reynolds lacked Haughey's reverence for the 'divinely ordained' Republican agenda, which perhaps made him more enthusiastic to cut a deal – any deal – to bring peace to Ireland. Along with Hume, Reynolds wooed and charmed the Republican leadership. He negotiated various compromise deals, largely through

Martin Mansergh, and offered to put them before the British government. He also supported the idea of a pan-Nationalist coalition that all Nationalist parties, in Ireland and the USA, might work within towards their shared goal of a united Ireland. Within such an alliance Sinn Fein could claim responsibility for 'greening up' Irish Nationalism after 70 years of dull olive. And they would find kudos, influence and common purpose in pursuit of Irish self-determination. Indeed, foregrounding the right of all Irish people to exercise their self-determination, even if they then allowed Unionists the right to exercise it in a different direction, was a useful sleight of words Hume believed could entice Sinn Fein away from the armed struggle. Here, then, were precisely the type of 'soft landings' Adams needed if he was to bring the Republican movement with him. But it was open to him only if the physical force was given up.

TURNING MR MAJOR'S STOMACH,[37] 1990–1993

The Hume–Adams dialogue represented the Nationalist 'reeling in' of Irish Republicanism. Unbeknown to both Hume and Reynolds, the British government had also been secretly fishing in their pool. Like Hume, the British realized that attractive bait was needed to catch Adams and McGuinness. Their problem was how actually to effect this when the government's stated position was to never talk to terrorists. In fact, this was less of a problem than might be imagined. Contacts between Republican and British government representatives were not unprecedented if necessarily secret. Whitelaw had, after all, met the IRA leadership in 1972, as had Wilson and Rees, when in opposition. Clandestine channels of communication were maintained through the 1970s, between British intelligence and the 'Contact', go-betweens of neutral status close to the Republican leadership. Along this 'bamboo pipe' the truce of 1975 was assembled.[38] Under Thatcher and the impact of the hunger strikes the connection was dropped; 'the pipe rusted up' according to Michael Oatley, the MI6 link to the Contact.[39] But with her resignation Brooke reconnected it. Now for the first time in over a decade the government had a channel into the heart of the Republican leadership, at just the moment when that same leadership was undergoing a significant tactical rethink. These moves were again testament to the political courage that Brooke was willing to show. In this he was aided by changes at the top. John Major arrived at Number 10 with none of the baggage of his predecessor, who had lost friends to IRA violence, who had engaged in a bitter, high-risk struggle against the hunger strikers and who had herself very nearly been blown up. So in January 1991 Oatley, through the Contact, met McGuinness and outlined that 'if the IRA wished to pursue a political course, given considerable change in political circumstances with the development of the European Union, there might be things the British government could do to help'.[40] He also informed the Contact of his imminent retirement and his hope that a new MI5 operative, 'Fred', could be installed to replace him. Down this reactivated chain 'Fred' sent extracts from forthcoming speeches as well as more sensitive information, notably concerning the multi-party talks of 1991. The government was clearly trying to bring Sinn Fein into the loop, pursuing a covert policy of inclusion alongside its public commitment to finding a political settlement between the constitutional parties.

Information was not the only thing travelling down pipes from 1990 onwards. On 7 February 1991 the IRA mortared Downing Street, within a few yards of a key Cabinet committee then in session inside Number 10. A week later Victoria train station was bombed, and most spectacularly and expensively, the Baltic Exchange in London was destroyed on 10 April 1992, at a cost of three innocent civilians' lives and more than £800 million of damage. Long before 11 September 2001 the IRA had shown how terrorists might cripple the central business districts of a major city. While the IRA engaged in 'spectaculars' on the mainland, the monotonous thud of murder in Northern Ireland escalated to a higher pitch during the autumn and winter of 1991-1992. Seven Protestant workers were murdered at Teebane on 17 January, an act matched in

> "The government was clearly trying to bring Sinn Fein into the loop"

brutality only by the machine-gunning of five Catholics in a betting shop three weeks later. Significantly, despite (or because of) these atrocities both sides maintained contact. Indeed, the volume and quality of material passing along probably increased through 1992. Details of the 1992 talks, an advance copy of Mayhew's Coleraine speech of 16 December, Gerry Adams' positive reply six days later, and details of a three-day Christmas cease-fire all suggested both sides were keen for some type of fundamental change.

Quite how fundamental was brought home to the British on 22 February when John Deverell, MI5 head in Northern Ireland, delivered a message to John Major from Martin McGuinness via the Contact and 'Fred'. 'The conflict is over but we need your advice on how to bring it to an end. We wish to have an unannounced cease-fire in order to hold dialogue leading to peace. We cannot announce such a move, as it will lead to confusion for the Volunteers because the press will interpret it as surrender.'[41] The message raised as many questions as it provided answers. Was it genuine? Did it reflect a faction or majority opinion? Could the Republican movement actually be delivered? On top of these Ken Clarke, the Home Secretary, was quick to point out the significant and very high-risk political dangers of 'running' with this lead. Against this Major, Mayhew and their security advisers all saw the enormous potential benefits and so they decided to respond with a 'pretty substantive and pretty encouraging reply'.[42] On Friday 19 March they sent back to the IRA a message, via Fred and the Contact. The British response (though Republicans, as it was later to transpire not having sent the message of 22 February in the first place, regarded this as a British initiative and for some a sign of weakness) stated that a dialogue between the two sides was possible. The dialogue would be without strings or an agreed agenda or even a prior handing in of weapons, as long as whatever was agreed had the consent of the Northern Irish people. But dialogue could take place *only* if the violence was halted. The very next day the IRA gave its response by concealing two bombs in litter bins in Warrington and detonating them amongst busy shoppers. The bombs claimed the lives of two children, 12-year-old Tim Parry and three-year-old Jonathan Ball.

In the face of this pointless atrocity the government took the calculated, but still incredible, gamble to persist with communications and agreed to a meeting between Fred and McGuinness to further the process. According to notes taken by Sinn Fein after the meeting and substantiated elsewhere, Fred began with a survey of recent events and the difficulties both sides would encounter in this process. He assured McGuinness of the government's eagerness to engage Republicans in dialogue with no pre-set schemes or anything ruled out. He then offered an over-sanguinary prophecy of the future. 'Any settlement not involving all of the people north and south won't work. A north/south settlement that won't frighten Unionists. The final solution is union. It is going to happen anyway. The historical train Europe determines that. We are committed to Europe. Unionists will have to change. The island will be as one.'[43] But 'none of this can happen in an atmosphere and in a reality of violence. No British government will ever meet you while there are bombs going off in the street ... Now if there was to be a cease-fire, then that changes the whole atmosphere.'[44] For McGuinness and Gerry Kelly, his Belfast colleague, these words contained the seeds of what they had striven 20 years to achieve, and coming from a 'representative' of the British government. What they failed to see was that Fred was 'flying solo', dangling the possibility of a united Ireland in order to win a cease-fire.[45] And it worked. A message came back that a two-week cease-fire had been agreed by the IRA in which to open up a dialogue. Denis Bradley, one of those in the chain of contacts, believed that 'no matter what happens now, no matter what difficulties there are, there is going to be a major, major shift in this whole thing. I remember thinking, it's over ... I remember the change inside my stomach, the sensation of knowing that this is the beginning of the end, that things will never, ever be the same again.'[46]

In fact it was something of a false dawn. Having advanced quickly during a few extraordinary weeks in March and April 1993, the process then began to 'silt up'. Major and Mayhew 'reined in' the initiative against a backdrop of rising violence

that seemed if not actually designed to push the British backwards then to appease those Republican hardliners who stood
against a cease-fire. On 24 April a bomb at the NatWest tower
caused damage estimated at over £1,000 million. A month later,
on 20 May, the Grand Opera House in
Belfast was attacked, followed in the
next two days by bombs in Portadown
and Magherafelt. 'Well I mean,'
Mayhew reflected, 'one after another,
after another. A time comes ... when
I'm afraid every one said, "well that's it
– at least for the time being, that's it.".'[47] On 17 July Major effectively shut down the initiative by demanding of the Republican
leadership a more substantial period without violence.
Termination of the 'link' left both sides angry, with mutual
accusations of bad faith. The atmosphere soured further when
research showed the original message of 22 February had orig-
inated with the Contact, hoping to kickstart an engagement,
and then substantially embellished by Fred, before it was passed
on to Deverell. It was Chinese whispers Northern Ireland style.
Yet it reveals that the 'links' believed both sides were close
enough to risk a fertile untruth to advance the cause of peace.
And to a great extent their calculations proved correct. For
although events did not lead to a cease-fire or open up a dialogue, both sides had breached key tactical and ideological hur-
dles. If not actually negotiating, according to a strict legalistic
definition, the government and Sinn Fein were engaged with
each other in a formal, substantial and sustained manner. The
British had intimated to Sinn Fein that a place at the table was
waiting for it if it suspended the armed struggle. And in response
to a British request, the IRA had offered a two-week cease-fire. To
use a matrimonial metaphor, the bride and groom had finally
agreed to wed, though they still refused to talk and were unable
to agree on a ring, the church or where to hold the reception.

> **❝Termination of the 'link' left both sides angry, with mutual accusations of bad faith❞**

CHEWING THE BOLLOCKS AND TAKING SOME LUMPS:[48] THE ROAD TO THE DOWNING STREET DECLARATION, 1993

By the early autumn of 1993 the air was thick with joint statements, obliquely argued proposals, private assurances, tentative acknowledgements, heavy hints and meaningful extracts in otherwise orthodox speeches. What was needed was something to tie all the threads together, a declaration that said something to everyone and so allowed the 'process' to move forward. The roots to this lay once again with Hume. Through his conversations with Adams he came to realize that what above all else might convince the Republican movement to suspend their violence was a joint governmental statement, sufficiently inclusive and suitably supportive of Irish self-determination. During 1993, along with Adams and Reynolds, Hume worked to this end and by June, after several redrafts, a document was delivered to Major through Reynolds. As Reynolds had forewarned, the document met with little enthusiasm from Major, being far 'too green' for any British Prime Minister to accept, let alone the Unionists. Nor would any British government have relished the image of dancing to Hume's and Adams' tune, whether they liked what was in the document or not. In fact, the timing could not have been worse. From July the government was heavily in debt to the Unionists after they ensured its survival during a vote on the social chapter of the Maastricht treaty. Major could not, then, lightly ignore their intense anger with Hume following revelations about his secret meetings with Adams. In any case, the government was looking to relaunch multi-party talks rather than wean Republicans from violence, following a speech by Mayhew to the British Irish Association in September 1993. Under these circumstances Major could never have given the Hume–Adams document anything other than short shrift. So through the summer and early autumn the British chose to drag their feet rather than admit the initiative had capsized.

If, by late October, peace appeared a fragile plant, it was all but wiped out by a series of events that seemed to transport the region back into the Dark Ages. On 23 October an IRA bomb exploded in a Shankill fish shop, killing ten people, followed a week later by the slaughter of seven people at the Rising Sun pub in Greysteel by loyalist paramilitaries in retaliation for the Shankill bomb. The death toll for that October reached 27, the largest monthly 'bloodletting' since 1976. Yet ironically, events on the Shankhill and at Greysteel injected life back into an otherwise lifeless process. Both the British and the Irish governments realized the creation of peace rather than the creation of multi-party talks was perhaps the higher priority, though they also recognized that the Hume–Adams document could not form the basis of an agreement between them, not least because of the Unionist reaction. So they set about constructing their own joint statement. On 27 October Dick Spring, the Irish Foreign Minister, issued six guiding principles for establishing peace in Northern Ireland, followed two days later by a joint Anglo-Irish communiqué from Brussels. The communiqué rejected the Hume–Adams document and in its place endorsed the Spring principles. But in rejecting the document they were not rejecting the initiative of wooing Republicans away from violence; they were now simply combining this with sufficient comfort for Unionists, in order to gain their support. Major and Reynolds were 'broadening the canvass',[49] enlarging their agenda, in the hope of establishing a general framework that might nurture reconciliation and reassurance to both communities, and from which all sides might progress towards a political settlement. 'What began as an Irish peace initiative, addressing the fundamental concerns of Republicans, ended up ... addressing the fundamental concerns of Unionists in an even-handed way.'[50] At the Lord Mayor of London's banquet on 15 November Major indicated the direction he was moving in: 'If the IRA end violence for good, then – after a sufficient interval to ensure the permanence of their intent – Sinn Fein can enter the political arena as a democratic party and join the dialogue on the way ahead ... there can be no secret deals, no rewards for terrorism, no abandonment of the vital principle of majority consent.'[51]

Behind the scenes the British and Irish governments toiled hard and at times acrimoniously to compose their joint statement.

Both sides kept open channels with friends and foe alike – the Dublin government, for example, gaining valuable feedback from loyalist groups in the north through the offices of two Protestant churchmen, Dr Robin Eames, Archbishop of Armagh, and the Reverend Roy Magee, a Belfast minister; indeed, the former made a significant contribution to the drafting of paragraphs 6–8 of the eventual declaration. Major, meanwhile, aware of Thatcher's failure to talk to Unionists before the Anglo-Irish Agreement of 1985, kept

66 Behind the scenes the British and Irish governments toiled hard and at times acrimoniously to compose their joint statement 99

Molyneaux firmly abreast of developments. Discussions between the two governments were intense, detailed and grinding. The position and appropriateness of individual words became the source of heated debate, while at one point the location of a comma in a sentence was enough to provoke fiery exchanges. Martin Mansergh, a leading adviser to Reynolds, talks of 'an extraordinary series of diplomatic crises behind the scenes'.[52] But then Anglo-Irish discussions had rarely been anything other than passionate. What made the situation worse, however, were leaks about secret British contacts with Sinn Fein going back to 1990, which the government had 'failed' to inform Dublin about. On the other side an Irish Foreign Affairs document on the future of Northern Ireland, with a distinctly 'green' hue, mysteriously found its way into the Irish press, enraging Unionists. Such developments at a moment of high drama should not occasion surprise. Both sides may have been auditioning for the role of 'peacemaker', but they were all still politicians. There is also a sense that the leaks, admissions of secret contacts and general media frenzy that surrounded both governments through late November and early December was simply the storm before the lull. And on 15 December 1993 that lull came. From the steps of Downing Street, Albert Reynolds and John Major issued their joint statement, otherwise known as the Downing Street Declaration, some 24 years after Harold Wilson had delivered the first such declaration as British troops were being deployed for the first time.

The declaration was an Anglo-Irish 'mission statement' that sought to appeal to the broadest cross-section of Northern Irish politics. As was so often the case in Northern Ireland, it was not a point of saying something new but of saying it at the right time. The actual details of the declaration were far from original and rooted in the various statements, initiatives and speeches of the previous five years. But in an atmosphere of intense expectation and profound hope, and after five years of significant ideological and tactical movement on all sides, the moment was just right. It was also a case of saying something to each side or rather wording the declaration so that it could be read differently by both sides. It was essential that the declaration contained those characteristics of every Anglo-Irish statement: ambiguity, vagueness and subliminal transmission. *Both* Nationalists and Unionists had to feel the same document offered them enough of what they wanted, without alarming the other. Thus plenty of textual mist was required through which messages were sent in code or wrapped in loaded words and meaningful phrases or signalled by the position of a comma or full stop.

The core of the document was positioned in section 4. 'The British government agree that it is for the people of the island of Ireland alone, by agreement between the two parts respectively, to exercise their right of self-determination on the basis of consent, freely and concurrently given, north and south, to bring about a united Ireland, if that is their wish.' It was, as Fergal Cochrane has called it, a classic case of 'giving with one hand and taking away with the other'.[53] The right to Irish self-determination was clearly recognized, as Britain had done before, but it was inextricably tied to the consent of both the north and the south in order to effect it. If that consent was freely given, Britain would aid the process of uniting Ireland, but not before or in disregard of the wishes of the majority. Alongside this, Dublin recognized that the consent of the Northern Irish people was needed for any process of uniting Ireland and should a political settlement between the constitutional parties of the region emerge in the future they would alter articles 2 and 3 of their constitution. What was missing from the declaration was almost as important as what was in it. There was no blueprint for the type of government Northern Ireland would have, nor on relations between the north and south, omissions designed to suggest to Nationalists that robust, even dynamic, all-Irish institutions were more than possible. Conversely, there was no commitment to a British withdrawal or timetable for that to occur, nor would Britain 'persuade' Unionists into a united Ireland omissions designed to mollify Unionism. All would get something from the declaration, but no one would get everything. Most importantly, however, Reynolds and Major (and Hume) believed there was enough rope here for Republicans to hang up their guns, without alienating Unionists.

The joint declaration of 15 December 1993 represented the summation of five years of significant readjustment and revision by all sides. All parties and governments had crossed some sort of bridge during these years, and it is somewhere in the period 1988–1993 that the origins of the peace process lie.

NOTES

1 G. Adams in D. McKittrick and E. Mallie, *Endgame in Ireland* (Hodder & Stoughton, 2001) p 76.

2 G. Murray, *John Hume and the SDLP: Impact and Survival in Northern Ireland* (Irish Academic Press, 1996) p 189.

3 Ibid, p 162.

4 Ibid, p 173.

5 T. Hennessey, *The Northern Ireland Peace Process* (Gill & Macmillan, 2000) pp 39–40.

6 Murray, op. cit., p 187.

7 Fianna Fail politician Dermot Ahern in McKittrick and Mallie, op. cit., p 108.

8 D. Bloomfield, *Political Dialogue in Northern Ireland: The Brooke Initiative, 1989–92* (St Martins Press, 1998) p 2.

9 Ibid, p 7.

10 D. Bloomfield, *Peacemaking Strategies in Northern Ireland: building complementarity in conflict management theory* (Macmillan, 1997) p 100.

11 An unfair and inaccurate Parliamentary nickname was 'babbling Brooke'.

12 Ian Paisley coined the label 'Tomcat King' to describe the Secretary of State, Tom King.

13 Bloomfield, *Political Dialogue in Northern Ireland: The Brooke Initiative, 1989–92* (St Martins Press, 1998) p 2.

14 Hansard, vol 188, 26 March 1991, col 765.

15 Hansard, vol 187, 14 March 1991, col 1082.

16 Carrington was Defence Secretary in 1972 and along with William Whitelaw was believed to be in favour of unity by consent. Bew, Patterson and Teague, *Between War and Peace* (Lawrence and Wishart, 1997) p 41. He had also written rather unflatteringly of Unionists in his Memoirs.

17 Bloomfield, *Political Dialogue,* p 102.

18 Ibid, p 109.

19 Ibid, p 137.

20 Ibid, p 159.

21 Ibid, p 184.

22 Bew *et al*, op. cit., p 76.

23 Hennessey, op. cit., pp 59–60.

24 The McGimpsey case in 1990 saw the Irish supreme court rule that articles 2 and 3 were 'a claim of legal right' and not merely 'aspirational'.

25 J. Coakley, 'The Belfast Agreement and the Republic of Ireland', in R. Wilford (ed) *Aspects of the Belfast Agreement* (OUP, 2001) pp 223–44.

26 Bew *et al*, op. cit., p 80.

27 Hennessey, op. cit., p 66.

28 In reply to those who had criticized his meetings with Adams, John Hume replied that he didn't 'give two handfuls of roasted snow' what such critics thought of his action.

29 This analogy is taken from a description by Lord Birkenhead of Sir Samuel Hoare, British Foreign Secretary in the mid-1930s. See J. Campbell, *F. E. Smith: First Lord Birkenhead* (Pimlico Press, 1986).

30 Interview with the 'link' in McKittrick and Mallie, op. cit., p 91.

31 D. McKittrick and R. McVea, *Making Sense of the Troubles* (Blackstaff Press, 2000) pp 278–83.

32 M. Mansergh, 'The background to the Irish Peace Process', in Cox *et al* (ed) *A Farewell to Arms: From Long War to Long Peace in Northern Ireland* (MUP, 2000) p 17.

33 Bloomfield, *Political Dialogue,* p 16.

34 A. Geulke, 'International dimensions of the Belfast Agreement', in D. Wilford, *Aspects of the Belfast Agreement* (OUP, 2001) pp 245–63.

35 This phrase was used by Lord Lansdowne, a southern Irish landowner, in 1913.

36 H. Patterson, *The Politics of Illusion: A Political History of the IRA* (Serif, 1997) p 217.

37 On 1 November 1993, just weeks before the secret contacts between the British government and Sinn Fein were revealed, John Major had declared

in the House of Commons: 'If the implications of his remarks is that we should sit down and talk with Mr Adams and the Provisional IRA, I can only say that that would turn my stomach and those of most honourable members; we will not do it.'

38 P. Taylor, *Brits: the War Against the IRA* (Bloomsbury, 2000) pp 169–70.

39 Ibid, p 315.

40 Ibid, pp 316–17.

41 Ibid, p 323.

42 McKittrick and Mallie, op. cit., p 79.

43 Patterson, op. cit., pp 244–5.

44 McKittrick and Mallie, op. cit., p 99.

45 Ibid, p 102.

46 Ibid, p 103.

47 Ibid, p 84.

48 After one particularly acrimonious meeting with John Major late in 1993, Albert Reynolds, in answer to a civil servant's enquiry into how things went, is alleged to have replied, 'well, he chewed the bollocks off me, but I took a few lumps out of him'. See McKittrick and Mallie, op. cit., p 135. Although the respective roles are reversed in McKittrick and McVea, op. cit., p 196.

49 'The Taoiseach agreed to create some public distance from Hume-Adams by agreeing that both he and the Prime Minister had a broader canvass to take into account.' Martin Mansergh in P. Bew and G. Gillespie, *The Northern Ireland Peace Process, 1993–1996* (Serif, 1996) p 24.

50 M. Mansergh, op. cit., p 19.

51 Ibid, p 26.

52 Ibid, p 18.

53 F. Cochrane, *Unionist Politics and the Politics of Unionism* (Cork UP, 1997) p 314.

8

'ONE STEP FORWARD, TWO STEPS BACK': THE PIECEMEAL PROCESS, 1994–1996

'It's not about 800 Orangemen marching down a road. It's about the survival of a culture, of an identity, of a way of life. It's about our ability to still hold onto parts of the country. The Ulster people have their backs to the wall. They're in retreat. They have been chased from quite a large area of the country and they feel that the citadel of Orangism, where Orangism was born 200 years ago, that is the place where they want to take their stand.'

Interview by P. Taylor of a loyalist at Drumcree, 1995[1]

WITH THE DOWNING STREET DECLARATION Reynolds and Major believed they had a formula capable of weaning Republicans from the path of violence while simultaneously reassuring Unionists that the 'pass had not been sold'. The document was a bridge across the once thought unbridgeable, a position statement they hoped would win acceptance from all the political parties. Yet for the first eight months it resembled all previous attempts to solve the Northern Irish Question, a foolishly optimistic calculation. And then, on 31 August, the Provisional IRA declared 'a complete cessation of military operations', followed just over a month later by a loyalist declaration to 'cease all operational hostilities'. These were profound and very public transformations of epic proportions. People dared to hope that after 25 years the gun was finally out of Northern Irish politics. David McKittrick reflected the views of many (as his top-class journalism always has) that 'Northern Ireland was moving, slowly and awkwardly but unmistakably towards peace'.[2] And yet the cease-fires raised as many problems as they solved. Was it really peace or just tactical readjustment? Was it a permanent cessation or a temporary one? Did paramilitaries have to hand in weapons before they joined any future talks or could they talk with them lodged comfortably under the table? Even if these and other difficulties surrounding the peace could be sorted out, the problem of actually constructing a settlement still lay before them. Few believed this would be a quick or painless journey, as the failure of the Brooke/Mayhew talks suggested. Many still believed it was a journey that simply could not be made.

Events for much of the period between the first cease-fire and the second in July 1997 seemed to bear this out. The decommissioning of weapons crept into political dialogue from the moment the declaration was launched to become a drag-anchor on progress. Republicans firmly refused to countenance 'arms before talks', while Unionists would not 'talk before arms', an impasse few could see a way out of. The British and Irish governments drifted apart, to such an extent that on occasions they were barely on speaking terms. Unionists swung between confidence and truculence, flexibility and refusal to yield. So when the IRA cease-fire collapsed in February 1996, another false dawn or missed opportunity was thought to have passed.

> **❝Few believed this would be a quick or painless journey, as the failure of the Brooke/Mayhew talks suggested❞**

CESSATIONS, CEASE-FIRES AND CLARIFICATION, 1994

A key aim of the Downing Street Declaration had been to draw Sinn Fein out of its 'pariah status' in the same way that the Anglo-Irish Agreement had tried to coerce Unionists away from political marginalization. But to win over Republicans from the gun they had to believe politics offered them a more lucrative course and both Reynolds and Major certainly thought the agreement had enough to do this. Britain again expressed its neutral status towards Northern Ireland, subject only to upholding the wishes of the majority. She also formally recognized the right of Irish people to national self-determination and signposted a clear constitutional path Republicans could take towards a united Ireland, again subject only to the majority opinion of the Northern Irish people. Britain also confirmed that Sinn Fein could enter future multi-party talks, after a three-month 'quarantine' and as long as it followed established democratic conventions. In expressing these commitments the British and Irish governments believed they were pushing at an open door, given the clear signals from the Republican leadership through 1992 and 1993, that on the questions of British withdrawal and Unionist consent they were moderating their stance. Having tactically adopted the language of the 'peace process' in the late 1980s, people now expected Republicans to deliver on it. They had become prisoners of their own linguistic artifice. More fundamentally, where were Republicans going to go if not for the declaration? Were they really willing to spend another 25 years in conflict when the differences between the Hume–Adams document and the declaration were semantic at best, and minimal at worst? And were they willing to surrender the political advances made since the early 1980s? To reject it would be a propaganda disaster, undercutting their carefully manicured image and hitting their support in Dublin and in Washington. Strangely, these were also the conclusions of those at the sharp end of the struggle, the many Republican prisoners on parole over the Christmas break, who pressed the leadership to respond positively to developments. Logic and self-preservation were on the side of cessation.

But logic had never been particularly important amongst the more determined Republicans, indeed it was a quality some held in suspicion when compared with loyalty, honour and resolve. So despite the optimism, no cessation or cease-fire materialized immediately. In retrospect this was hardly surprising. No previous IRA campaign had called off the armed struggle. The preferred route had always been to 'dump arms', as at the end of the civil war in May 1923, or again in 1962, so avoiding the stigma of surrender and leaving open the door for future military action. For many Republicans armed struggle was less of a tactical option than an article of faith, a measure of commitment and a symbol of an ancient and enduring struggle against England. Even with the politicization of the movement and new pragmatic command of Adams and McGuinness from the mid-1980s, the armed struggle remained a devotional rather than a functional commitment.[3] Ditching it was akin to the Church of England dropping the Eucharist. The difficulty of accomplishing this early in 1994 was apparent in the growth of hardline resistance within the IRA. Sinn Fein leaders struggled to convince sections of the IRA's ruling Army Council and the wider Republican movement that suspending armed struggle would be more rewarding than continuing it. Adams bought some time by launching a Peace Commission to explore the feelings of local Sinn Fein supporters. Both Adams and McGuinness worked hard to re-invent the declaration as the final act of disengagement by the British.[4] Adams also demanded that the British clarify aspects of the declaration, hoping that if he could inveigle them in negotiations *before* suspending the 'armed struggle', a cessation would look less like a surrender than a generous act from a position of strength. As with decommissioning, so questions of timing and orchestration were absolutely vital for providing Adams with the leverage to carry the Republican movement with him. Scrapping the armed struggle had to be represented as a selfless move rather than a compelled necessity.

Recognizing their difficulties, Albert Reynolds tried to bolster Adams by offering Republicans a taste of what politics would be like once violence was discarded. In January he rescinded a 13-year broadcast ban against Sinn Fein. He attacked Major and Mayhew's tough stance on the IRA decommissioning before entering talks. He was also extremely active in Washington, lobbying hard with President Clinton to allow Adams a visa. He even intimated that Sinn Fein in giving up the armed struggle did not have to agree with or support the declaration. Here was pan-Nationalism in action, bringing tangible rewards that Adams could deploy against more hardline Republicans.

Three developments in particular showed Republican doubters that politics could work. One was the British decision on 19 May to offer some clarification on the declaration, in the form of a 21-page 'summary', after months of refusal. For Sinn Fein this was the result of pressure by Dublin and Washington, the pan-Nationalist front flexing its muscles for the Republican cause. More significant was Reynolds' public support for a north-south body with real executive power. This had been the primary concern of Dublin and the SDLP during the 1991–1992 talks and was purposely left out of the declaration to provide Republicans with an incentive for their otherwise frustrated all-Irish ambitions. For Adams, an effective all-Ireland body was the equivalent of the Boundary Commission established in the Anglo-Irish Treaty of 1921, a device that would ensure Irish unity in the long term and without the need to coerce the north in, but which allowed a short-term compromise on the so-called Unionist veto. Unity was to come through the bureaucratic creep of a dynamic and expansionist all-Ireland council. With Reynolds' public sympathy, Adams saw this as a line capable of persuading Republicans to give up the gun.

However, the most important initiative, in which Reynolds played a leading role, was in arranging an American visa for Adams on 29 January 1994. In the past President Clinton had refused the request, taking advice from the State Department, the FBI, the US Attorney General and the Secretary of State Warren Christopher, all of whom recognized the potential harm an Adams visit could do. By late 1993 Clinton was beginning to listen to others, particularly those within the large Irish-American community, a community that had long held a burning sense of grievance for Ireland, born of several thousand miles of insulation from the realities of the conflict. Channelled through the group Americans for a New Irish Agenda, under Bruce Morrison and Liam O'Dowd, and with the support of John Hume, Edward Kennedy and his sister Jean, the US Ambassador to Dublin, they exerted powerful pro-Nationalist leverage in the

> "Unity was to come through the bureaucratic creep of a dynamic and expansionist all-Ireland council"

White House. Into this equation came Reynolds, with contacts to Tony Lake and Nancy Soderburg, Clinton's National Security advisers, who now joined the call for Adams to get a visa. After much agonizing Clinton finally agreed, calculating that such a move might well facilitate the cessation. And in this he was proved correct. For the visa gave Republicans a glimpse of the stage they might strut upon if they gave up the armed struggle. It also generated confidence that Irish America was a powerful and effective third arm in the pan-Nationalist coalition. Politics *was* working for Sinn Fein and had brought Adams massive and invaluable publicity within the world's strongest and wealthiest power. The fact that he had not renounced terrorism and was committed to a socialist republic was quietly, and perhaps necessarily, brushed under the carpet by Americans.

In total, then, the Sinn Fein leadership was given substantial recognition to enable it to guide the Republican movement towards a cessation of violence. And yet when the cease-fire came, on 31 August, it still took many by surprise. Much of this was due to the recent Sinn Fein Ard Fheis at Letterkenny that had seemingly rejected the declaration. Letterkenny was, however, a 'political' rejection, more about reassuring the wider movement that their goal remained an all-Irish Republic. It was also part of the choreography of cessation that meant surrender could not look like surrender or be seen as dictated by the British or Irish governments. Mayhew even provided some help by denying that giving up the armed struggle represented surrender. In other words change had to be veiled under an image of continuity, as Anthony McIntyre has suggested: 'Republicans have in fact accepted the declaration under the very guise of having rejected it.'[5] The most significant guise under which the Republican movement effected its cessation was an IRA document released in the summer of 1994 entitled Tactical Use of the Armed Struggle (TUAS). TUAS argued that the armed struggle was a 'tactical' option, not a Republican goal. It was important, then, to separate ends from means, viable programmes from stale mantras, and objectives from methods. In the circumstances of 1994 those objectives were now best advanced by the unique confluence of interests that Republicans had never had before, a confluence that included an active pan-Nationalist front, a proactive government in Dublin, a sympathetic White House and a strengthening Irish-American presence. Given these conditions, Republicanism was 'tactically' better served by shelving the armed struggle. Physical force, though necessary (so it was argued) in the circumstances of the 1970s and 1980s, was now redundant.

And so on 31 August 1994 the IRA Army Council announced 'a complete cessation of military operations'. Cessation was clearly something more than just a cease-fire, yet less than permanent. But was the war over? The IRA did not (perhaps could not) elaborate on this, preferring instead to say: 'An opportunity to secure a just and lasting settlement has been created. We are therefore entering into a new situation in a spirit of determination and confidence, determined that the injustices which created this conflict will be removed and confident in the strength and justice of our struggle to achieve this.' Laudable words greeted by most with relief and joy, but by some with a sense of foreboding – 'the cease-fire has come and the British have not gone'.

'THE UNION IS SAFE – HA HA HA', 1993–1995[6]

A period of change, especially if it is rapid and unexpected, almost by definition will generate unease within the Unionist community. The very concept of change grates against a Unionist ideology that valorizes tradition, continuity and the past. For such a community change looks suspiciously like surrender, and progress like defeat. And from late 1993 political change was progressing at a fast pace, at times astonishingly quick and rarely according to predictable outcomes. In this new world Unionists were ill at ease. This nagging sense of alarm intensified throughout the summer and autumn of 1993 as rumours of back channels to the IRA, secret deals and clandestine promises leaked out. Despite the increasingly fervid atmosphere Molyneaux remained reasonably confident with his and the Unionist position. He had long prided himself on having a solid understanding with his friend, 'honest' John Major, and could not foresee him about to sell Unionists down the river, if for no other reason than he was heavily reliant upon Ulster Unionist support in the House of Commons. And although the Downing Street Declaration did cause a momentary intake of breath amongst the Ulster Unionist leadership, on reflection it was greeted with a resigned acceptance and passionless support. 'The document isn't as bad as I had feared,' John Taylor is alleged to have said, hardly a glowing endorsement but not a rejection.[7]

Beyond the 'Olympian' ranks of the Ulster Unionist leadership, a majority of Unionists, including Paisley and the DUP as well as a large number of grassroots Ulster Unionists, reacted to the Downing Street Declaration with hostility and profound suspicion. For these sections it seemed little more than a concoction of all-Ireland phrases, cross-border bodies, and 'Irish' rights to self-determination. It was an Anglo-Irish equivalent of the Nazi-Soviet Pact of 1939, with Unionists cast as defenceless Poles. Lost from their reading of the document were the subtle but numerous reassurances of majority consent. As such it was less a framework for peace than preparation for a 'sell-out', and by association those who gave it guarded support were guilty of treachery. Paisley lost no time in branding Molyneaux, his one-time colleague and partner during the Ulster Says No campaign of 1985–1987, as Judas Iscariot. With the European elections in June, Paisley was never one to miss the opportunity of a 'low blow' to his Unionist rivals if it could garner votes for his party. Less dramatically, but more significant, criticism of Molyneaux's stance grew within his party, exacerbated through 1994 by what

> **Less dramatically, but more significant, criticism of Molyneaux's stance grew within his party**

Unionists saw as an endless series of reversals and retreats. For example, the granting of a visa to Adams and the subsequent media circus that surrounded his visit filled them with alarm, as did Dublin's continued refusal to promise repeal of articles 2 and 3, a rigidity compounded by Britain's easy willingness to cave in over the clarification issue. Ulster suffered a double-whammy of having tough enemies but weak friends. Taken together it was all evidence of the slow, irresistible decline of Unionism in the face of an effective pan-Nationalist coalition. Molyneaux tried to shore up his position. He toughened his public stance by launching a *Blueprint for Stability*. The document called for a Northern Irish Assembly and an Irish dimension to evolve *only* by mutual consent between the north and south, and rejected all-party talks on the basis of the three-strand structure, as operated in the Brooke and Mayhew initiatives. This represented a hardening of Unionist opinion and a broadside across the government's bow that the type of 'dynamic' north-south body envisaged by Reynolds, Hume and Adams would not be acceptable. Growing community apprehension and intra-Unionist rivalry were, as in 1986–1987, driving the Ulster Unionist leadership in a less flexible direction. Those Unionist advances of 1991–1992 seemed a long way in the past.

If Unionist anxiety grew as a result of the Downing Street Declaration, the announcement of the IRA cease-fire deepened it still further. For many Unionists the cease-fire confirmed their suspicions that London *must* have cut a deal with the IRA – why else would they lay down their guns? In a sense, however, this was an anxiety too far. For to argue that the IRA had been offered a deal was to explicitly deny the declaration had anything substantial to attract Republicans or to worry Unionists about. They couldn't have it both ways. Ironically, loyalist paramilitaries seemed more inclined to accept promises from both governments that no secret deal had been done. On receiving suitably reassuring words from Dublin and London, they announced their own cease-fire on 13 October, tying it firmly to the continuance of the Republican one and offering, unlike the Republican message, an apology 'to the loved ones of all innocent victims over the past 25 years'.[8] The loyalist cease-fire launched a raft of young, pragmatic and sophisticated leaders onto the political stage, in the form of David Ervine, Gary McMichael and Billy Hutchinson, mirror images of Adams and McGuinness. But at the time most people were just content that both sides in the war had now put away their guns, at least for the time being.

Despite (or perhaps because of) the creation of peace after 25 years of conflict, Unionist trepidation continued and turned to anger when six days after the IRA cessation Reynolds and Hume greeted Adams in Dublin in front of the world's press. While many commentators saw this as a useful and speedy constitutional induction, Unionists regarded it as an unholy '*ménage à trois*' over-hasty recognition of men whose hands still carried the warm bloodstains of their victims. And all the more dangerous when a month later Reynolds hosted the Forum for Peace and Reconciliation for all Irish parties, including Sinn Fein, to discuss a broad agenda of issues relating to Ireland. Pan-Nationalism was fully operational, on the march and poised to strike at the north. That strike, when it came, took the form of the *Frameworks for the Future* document, a joint London and Dublin discussion paper launched in February 1995 as a preliminary to opening full multi-party talks. The paper largely picked up from where the Mayhew talks of 1992 had left things. On strand one, for example, a new Northern Ireland Assembly was envisaged, with executive functions run by committees and overseen by an elected three-person body. However, strand two, dealing with the Irish dimension of north-south relations, was more 'developed' and for Unionists amounted to Dublin being given a substantial role in the north, a replay of the Council of Ireland of 1974 and the intergovernmental secretariat of the Anglo-Irish Agreement.

The document proposed a cross-border body with executive powers over many areas, established through consultation between London and Dublin, and so independent of the assemblies in the north and south. The body would be obliged to 'harmonize' policy across many areas that included social welfare, industrial development, education, economic policy and trade. Though forewarned by a leak in *The Times* three weeks before, Unionists from both liberal and hardline wings reacted with horror and outrage. The Irish dimension had not been tied to a Northern Ireland Assembly as Molyneaux had argued during the Mayhew talks and in *Blueprint for Stability*, but was subject to legislation from Dublin and London, and equipped with independent executive powers. This gave it the ability to grow and develop what Nationalists called a 'dynamic'. And all wrapped up in a nice, woolly phrase called harmonization. It was nothing short of unification by stealth and fully in line with the direction in which pan-Nationalism had been moving since early 1994. Worse still, Unionists interpreted paragraph 47 to mean that if they refused to co-operate in such a north-south body, strand one would be null and void and the affairs of Northern Ireland run under a revised Inter-Governmental Conference or 'joint authority' by London and Dublin. It was the Anglo-Irish Agreement via the back door. Paisley spoke for a majority in the Unionist community when he declared of the Frameworks document: 'This is a finely tuned one-way street, it only has one proposal and that is to go down the Dublin Road.'[9] Of course, the biggest casualty of the whole episode was Molyneaux, whose position in the aftermath of Frameworks looked fatally undermined. Placing your trust in 'honest' John Major now appeared not the way of a wise man but the path of a fool.

DAVID AND THE 'TREMBLERS';[10] 1995–1996

Two years of retreat, backsliding and gradual surrender could not go unchallenged in a culture steeped in images of resistance and defiance. Increasing numbers of Unionists believed a stand needed to be taken. The problem was *how* to make a stand when the threat to the union was of a drip-drip variety rather than a direct and visible danger, as in 1912 and 1974 or even 1985. Was a joint governmental discussion paper really an adequate menace and symbol to rally Unionists against? Another problem was *where* Unionists would make their stand. Should they mass along the line of partition, defending their hallowed border from barbarians to the south? Or should they picket the airports and ferry terminals against barbarians from across the Irish Sea or rather St George's Channel? In fact, it was less of a problem than it might have seemed for every summer Unionists, as they had done for several centuries, made a regular 'stand' against the Nationalist 'enemy within' by 'parading' the roads and lanes of Northern Ireland. It was, then, no real surprise that by the summer of 1995 those pent-up fears and frustrations of the previous two years were focused upon 'parading'. When all else seemed to be crumbling around them, their right to march across the hallowed earth of Ulster became a metaphor for their right to remain British.

The summer of 1995 was always going to be a stormy one with Unionist sensitivities running so high. It was also the first marching season since the IRA cease-fire and against a backdrop of a strong pan-Nationalist coalition carrying all before it. Nationalist communities for the first time felt empowered to challenge a tradition they had long held to be little more than celebrations of Protestant power and ascendancy. In challenging the tradition of parading, there was also perhaps the hint of provocation. Republicans had long ago realized that nothing strengthened the Nationalist cause in the south, in London and especially in America more than the sight of red-eyed Orangemen rampaging and rioting. Developments converged on a small church on the outskirts of Portadown where on 9 July the RUC decided to reroute an Orange march away from the Nationalist Garvaghy Road. The reaction was immediate and immense. In defence of the traditional route that Orangemen had marched for 200 years, thousands of loyalists descended on Drumcree. Here, beside the muddy slopes of a small hill, loyalists found 'their' stand, their own 'via Dolorossa', in a stretch of concrete perhaps only a mile long. The stand-off threw Northern Ireland into a week of turmoil, violence, sectarian rioting and bitter communal relations, on a scale not seen since the 1974 strike and the 1985–1987 campaigns. Faced by nearly 10,000 Orangemen, the RUC rescinded its decision the next day and allowed the march along its traditional path, to almost universal condemnation from outside the Unionist community.

> 66 Was a joint governmental discussion paper really an adequate menace and symbol to rally Unionists against? 99

Making his entry onto the political or rather publicity stage for the first time was a young hardline David Trimble, the local MP, who outside of his upper Bann constituency was still largely unknown to the world. Trimble played a key role during the events of Drumcree. He negotiated between the RUC and the

Orange order. He spoke to loyalist crowds in uncompromising terms of the righteousness of their cause while imploring good order. And most dramatically he walked the end of the sacred mile holding hands with Paisley, to the enormous cheers of hundreds of Orangemen. With Trimble and Paisley performing their 'Drumcree jig', it appeared moderate, non-sectarian, rational Unionism had been all but snuffed out during the summer of 1995 by a lurch towards supercharged, overheated visceral loyalism.

Such a lurch could only work against Molyneaux's position and standing. The Frameworks document was the fatal blow even though he staggered on for several months. In March he faced the ignominy of a leadership contest against a Queen's University student; more of a hobby-horse than a stalking horse. Yet that same hobby-horse won an embarrassing 15 per cent of the UUC vote. In June the once-safe Unionist seat of North Down fell in a by-election to Robert McCartney, of the break-away UK Unionist Party and a close ally of the DUP. As Molyneaux's brand of 'steady as she goes',[11] common-sense Unionism declined, so more emotive varieties of Unionism strengthened. By the summer Molyneaux's position was untenable and on 28 August 1995 he resigned. Of the front-runners to replace him stood the liberal Unionist Ken Maginnis and the 'wily' John Taylor. Coming up fast on the outside, however, was the hardline David Trimble, fresh from skipping hand in hand with Ian Paisley down the end of the Garvaghy Road. For many Unionists he was a leader prepared to get his hands dirty and stand up and be counted, while for others he was wayward and emotional. In a rare act of general agreement, London, Dublin, all the Nationalist parties and Washington regarded him as little more than a 'bigot in a bowler'. Yet on 8 September, after several elimination rounds, Trimble beat off Taylor by 466 votes to 333: hardline Unionism had found its champion and he was now sitting at the top of the Ulster Unionist Party. If the peace process had looked bleak in February, it looked positively thunderous by the autumn.

Looks, however, could be deceiving. For Trimble, to those who knew him, was no slimmed-down Paisley but a thinking person's Unionist, a modernizer and someone willing to compromise. Indeed, within days of his election as leader he met Proinsias De Rossa, leader of the Democratic Left Party and one-time leader of the Official IRA. He immediately opened contacts to Dublin and in Washington, keen to counterbalance the pan-Nationalist tide. In London he began to court Tony Blair and the Labour Party, a year later becoming the first Ulster Unionist leader to speak at a Labour Party conference. His antics with Paisley over the summer might be seen in a similar light or role as Adams' carrying the coffin of Thomas Begley, the IRA bomber killed in the explosion at the Shankill fish shop in October 1993 – reinforcing your credibility and community support in a phase of profound change. In terms of negotiating tactics it certainly did no harm to come to the conference table, if they could ever agree to get there, with a hardline reputation and an image of not giving an inch.

DECOMMISSIONING, 1995–1996

If Drumcree was one lightning rod for Unionists' sensitivities, another was the question of the decommissioning of weapons. For both Republicans and Unionists the issue of decommissioning touched deep historic nerves. Even the very word to describe the act provoked disagreement. Republicans rejected decommissioning with its undertones of surrender, preferring demilitarization. This, for Unionists, was equally unsatisfactory, given its flavour of British withdrawal and 'troops out'.[12] Whatever you called it, the question of arms lay at the heart of the problem of bringing the Troubles to an end. For Unionism, drenched as it is in motifs of treachery, perfidy and threat, actions that proved sincerity and trust were a vital concern. Giving up arms became their litmus test of sincerity, their scale to measure whether the cessation was 'permanent'; a measure not helped by Republicans' sturdy resistance to ever use the word 'permanent'. 'It is not in our vocabulary,' McGuinness is alleged

> **If Drumcree was one lightning rod for Unionists' sensitivities, another was the question of the decommissioning of weapons**

to have said. For Republicans, arms signified a centuries-old struggle against England and, more practically, had been essential to the protection of their communities from loyalist mobs in the period since 1969. To actually hand them over was partially to accept the struggle could not be won and more particularly to leave 'their' people exposed and defenceless. Thus each side craved security. Unfortunately for one this meant giving up arms, while for the other it meant hanging onto them. Decommissioning, then, was rather like attitudes to sex and love: women need the proof of love before sex, men need the proof of sex before love. Finding a way out of this double bind was the key to the peace process, something not achieved by the Good Friday Agreement in 1998, nor with the establishment of a new, devolved governance in Northern Ireland in 1999. Indeed, it would take the unimaginable atrocity of two jet airliners flying into the World Trade Center in New York to trigger real, actual, demonstrable (if still very limited) movement on this core predicament.

Given these thoughts it is remarkable how nothing specific was said about decommissioning before the IRA cease-fire of August 1994. Both governments clearly realized establishing a cessation was a big enough hurdle for Republicans to jump without adding an extra fence. The Downing Street Declaration, therefore, omitted any mention of giving up arms as a pre-condition to entering talks, though it clearly states in paragraph 9, 'the achievement of peace must involve a permanent end to the use of, and support for, paramilitary violence'. More surprisingly, once the IRA cease-fire was established, the issue still did not gain immediate centrality. In October Major publicly made a 'working assumption' that the cease-fire was permanent and agreed to hold preliminary talks with Sinn Fein before Christmas. What references there are to decommissioning tend to be vague, isolated comments rather than a sustained line of argument. Ironically, given Dublin's greater flexibility on the question later on, Dick Spring in a speech to the Dáil on the Downing Street Declaration assured his audience that 'we are talking about the handing up of arms and are insisting that it would not be simply a temporary cessation of violence'.[13] Along similar lines Mayhew told the Commons that 'if they hold onto arms, if you know they have got them, then quite patently they are not giving them up for good'.[14]

However, against a backdrop of deepening Unionist unease the issue of decommissioning moved from the margins to centre stage in the politics of the peace process. Many Unionists suspected the cessation was tactical, a pause to see whether politics could deliver but with fingers still firmly on the trigger. A refinement of 'the Armalite and the ballot box' line to a strategy of 'whether to hand in the Armalite and the ballot box'. After all, the Republican document TUAS stood for '*tactical use* of armed struggle', not 'total unarmed struggle'.[15] Others, if more sanguine on this point, certainly wanted proof beyond the word of Adams and McGuinness – proof that became all the more pressing in the absence of any reference to the war being over or the cessation being permanent, and following a speech by Adams in August 1995 in which he reminded his audience that the IRA had not gone away. Unionists needed clarification on these issues and that could come only by giving up arms. From the moment of the cessation Unionists foregrounded the issue in the media and in Parliament. They found a ready echo among sections of the Tory Right, who were already snapping hard at Major's heels over Europe. Major was forced to respond in kind, recognizing the disenchantment within the Unionist community and the dangers this posed for Molyneaux's leadership and by implication to the government's majority in the Commons. In December 1994 Major now spoke of 'huge progress' needed on the handing over of weapons before Sinn Fein could formally enter the talks process, a 'clarification' of rather than a departure from the Downing Street Declaration. He repeated the point to John Bruton, the new Taoiseach since late November, though Bruton warned of the dangers of a 'stand-off' developing over the issue. During the first 'public' face-to-face meeting between British officials and Sinn Fein representatives, on 9 December 1994, decommissioning was also pinpointed as the major stumbling block to progress. What, then, was beginning to emerge on the British and Unionist side by late 1994 was the concept of *prior* decommissioning, the idea that guns had to precede talks. This was enshrined by Mayhew in a speech made in Washington on 7 March 1995, where he outlined three principles for the decommissioning of weapons, the so-called 'Washington Three'. Mayhew's Washington Three criteria included the core proposal that prior decommissioning would need to have at least *started* before entry into talks was permissible. This was necessary as a confidence-building measure to the Unionists and as a form of decontamination, distinguishing between a politician's violent past and their statesmanlike future.

Unionists balked at his reference to starting the process (they wanted all guns in before any talks) but recognized the speech as a clear firming up of the government's position since 1993. Britain had formalized the link between talking and decommissioning. And given the timing of Mayhew's Washington Three, just two weeks after the Frameworks document, it was hard not to see it as 'bowing' to a hostile Unionist wind. Like Republicans, Unionists clearly regarded questions of orchestration and the sequencing of arrangements as highly symbolic and vitally important. So in this respect perhaps the linkage of guns to talks was unavoidable, with Unionist anxieties running so high and the obvious need to carry Ulster Unionists in any political process or future multi-party talks. After all, neither the British nor Irish governments could force Unionists into negotiations. However, the danger of linkage was that the success of the peace process now turned on the issue of guns and the attitude of Sinn Fein. British policy had made Adams *the* central player in events, the man who could break or deliver peace, so enhancing his position, influence and public image. It was the old British talent of creating Irish heroes through tough (though inherently reasonable) action. Against the British-Unionist line stood a weighty pan-Nationalist phalanx of Hume, Adams, Reynolds, now in opposition, a nervous John Bruton and his Foreign Secretary Dick Spring, having reinvented himself from a 'guns before talks' to a 'talks before

> 66 What, then, was beginning to emerge on the British and Unionist side by late 1994 was the concept of *prior* decommissioning 99

guns' man. All demanded an immediate start to inclusive multi-party talks, pointing to the absence of the precondition of 'prior' decommissioning in the declaration of 1993 and the very serious dangers of delay. More pragmatically (and a position shared by the USA), they realized the IRA simply would not give up arms before talks and perhaps not afterwards either. So while prior decommissioning might well conform to democratic conventions and hold the balance of logic and fairness on its side, it was just not going to happen! 'There is absolutely no question of any decommissioning at all, either through the back door or the front door.'[16] They had a choice, then, between a soiled progress and a principled deadlock. For the moment, all sides chose deadlock.

Behind the scenes the British and Irish governments acted with feverish energy to break the impasse, conscious that deadlock in Ireland often led back into conflict. A 'rage' of bi-lateral and multi-lateral meetings took place to break the stalemate. Loyalist paramilitary parties, the UDP and PUP, travelled to Dublin for talks, and even applied their own form of pressure when Gary McMichael declared in August 1995 that loyalists were ready to start decommissioning. David Trimble, within a few weeks of being elected leader of the Ulster Unionist Party, was to be found lunching with John Bruton in Dublin. He also held discussions with John Hume and President Clinton. More historic, first contact between a British minister and Sinn Fein was made early in May by Michael Ancram, and followed a few weeks later by a 30-minute conversation between Adams and Mayhew in Washington. After this, contact was incessant and sustained, but still barren of movement. Despite the mounting political problems within his own party, Major conferred regularly, if not always amicably, with Bruton. Indeed, the negotiations on how to break the logjam of decommissioning between the British and Irish governments were amongst the most intensive and difficult of the entire peace process.

Yet slowly a compromise began to emerge. The idea of an international decommissioning body to advise on how weapons might be put beyond use was first mentioned by Ken Maginnis, security spokesperson for the Ulster Unionist Party.[17] It was picked up by Mayhew who then 'dropped' it into his speech at the Conservative Party conference on 12 October. Though not terribly attracted by the idea, Bruton could see some mileage in it, especially if somehow connected to talks. By November these 'positions' had firmed up into a 'twin-track' strategy. The strategy was launched by a joint-government communiqué on 18 November 1995 which recommended that invitations be sent to all political parties, including Sinn Fein, to start inclusive negotiations that February. In the meantime an international commission would be established, chaired by Senator George Mitchell, alongside Harri Holkeri, the former Finnish Prime Minister, and General John de Chastelain, one-time Canadian Chief of Defence Staff. The body would submit an independent assessment of the whole decommissioning issue and look in particular at methods for advancing the actual process of handing weapons. This would be published in January, though an escape clause hidden at the back gave each side the option not to act on the report. In other words, twin-track sought to combine the various positions; all-party talks to take place *alongside* 'modalities' for decommissioning. It was not a solution but a quick political fix to stave off a 'meltdown' in the peace process.[18]

Just how quick a fix it was became evident in the New Year when the international commission published its findings. The Mitchell Report of 25 January 1997 recommended, to intense British embarrassment, that talks start as soon as possible *before* the decommissioning of arms, though 'some decommissioning would take place during the process of all-party negotiations'. Mayhew's *prior* decommissioning had been replaced by Mitchell's *parallel* decommissioning. To offset this disabling of 'Washington Three' and to offer Unionists a confidence-building alternative, Mitchell introduced six principles to which each party had to sign up before entry into the talks. Despite this Britain believed that as a means of entry, promising to be good lacked the certitude of handing over weapons. Herein lay the core problem: how to win over Unionists to a confidence-building scheme in which they had no confidence. The answer lay in a little-read and largely buried phrase of the report that suggested other confidence-building measures might include an 'elective process'. Major seized upon this and in a statement to the Commons both accepted the Mitchell Report and announced an election to a new Northern Ireland Forum, from where leaders would be drawn for entry into multi-party talks. The idea of an election was popular amongst Unionists; indeed, Trimble had already suggested it as a way out of the decommissioning stand-off. It also represented the type of decontaminating process, a sort of democratic sheep-dip, capable of legitimizing (even sanitizing) the negotiators. And it equipped leaders with a popular mandate for entering discussions, something Trimble was especially keen to have, so early in his leadership.

> Mayhew's *prior* decommissioning had been replaced by Mitchell's *parallel* decommissioning

Unfortunately the British advocacy of an election, though for some strategists an agile and creative action to keep Unionists on board, resulted on a nosedive for the peace process. Opinion from across the Nationalist spectrum attacked what was seen variously as yet another precondition in the way of Sinn Fein entering talks or yet another British capitulation to the Unionist veto or merely yet more British duplicity. Hume called the move 'playing politics with people's lives' while for Dick Spring it was Britain using 'divide and conquer' tactics. Nationalists stuck to their original 'twin-track' agreement for immediate multi-party talks to begin by the end of February, although Spring did try to blur the edges of this a little by calling them 'proximity talks', a method of negotiation where everyone turns up but doesn't engage in face-to-face talking. However all-party talks were being defined, one thing was clear: a cleavage the size of the Irish sea had opened up between London and Dublin. The peace process was in grave trouble.

CANARY WHARF, 1996

Just how grave became clear on 9 February 1996 when the IRA announced the end of its 18-month cease-fire by detonating a bomb at Canary Wharf in London, killing two people.

Republicans blamed the British for constantly stalling on the question of talks and for rejecting the Mitchell Report (which they had not) in favour of an election. There is perhaps something in all of this, but not much. The British had cut the Republican movement a lot of slack. The Frameworks document, for example, had been a clear signal of good intentions and areas to 'work' on, at the considerable expense of Unionist wrath. Moreover, in October 1995 the government introduced legislation for the remission of sentences for prisoners convicted of Troubles-related offences, which saw some 88 prisoners released by the end of the year, again at considerable cost to Unionist goodwill. Running through the Republican interpretation was the myopia that in bringing peace to Northern Ireland only one side mattered. There would be no process, let alone a peace, if only Nationalists turned up at discussions. Unionists had to be sitting at the table as well and the task of getting them there was slow, delicate and painful. But they had to be got there!

Nor should it be forgotten that this was all done at a time of growing political difficulty for John Major's government. To introduce extremely sensitive legislation when your Parliamentary majority had all but vanished was politically hazardous to say the least and shows great commitment by a Premier who is all too often criticized. It might well have been Ireland again sacrificed on the altar of British party politics; but that was the way it was, and what politician does not play party politics. Indeed, it is hard to see why the cease-fire was broken at all. The British government had after all accepted the report and its more gentle line on decommissioning. And the introduction of an election was a vital sop to Unionists, not a bar to Sinn Fein entering talks, nor a terribly onerous hurdle to jump for a movement so fulsome in its commitment to an inclusive peace process. On the other hand, perhaps the Mitchell Report was a missed opportunity by the British government. To have accepted it would certainly

> 66 with the return of the IRA to violence came the smug satisfaction that their stance on decommissioning now had the force of proof behind it 99

have caused problems with the Unionists but it would also have confronted Sinn Fein with the six Mitchell principles. Instead, by rejecting the report, it was let off confronting this particular hurdle.

Ironically, the end of the cease-fire actually aided the peace process. Decommissioning became an academic question once Sinn Fein was out of the equation. This helped break the logjam between the British and Irish governments, which now quickly agreed to move forward to elections and multi-party talks to begin in June, whether Sinn Fein was there or not. For Unionists, a debilitating blow was struck against the pan-Nationalist alliance, sufficient to calm nerves and quell visions of Irish unity coming by the back door. Moreover, with the return of the IRA to violence came the smug satisfaction that their stance on decommissioning now had the force of proof behind it. Importantly, from their smugness came a certain confidence, perhaps for the first time since 1992. Lack of confidence, born of a sense that events were conspiring against them, had played a significant part in the drift of Unionism towards extremism after 1993. With that impression halted, if not reversed, it was hoped an element of balance would return to the movement. Certainly Trimble was beginning to send signals that he was willing to move and to talk.

NOTES

1   P. Taylor, *Loyalists* (Bloomsbury, 1999) pp 239–40.

2   D. McKittrick, *The Nervous Peace* (Blackstaff, 1996) p 3.

3   M. Smith, *Fighting for Ireland: Military Strategy of the Irish Republican Movement* (Routledge, 1995) p 18.

4   H. Patterson, *The Politics of Illusion: A Political History of the IRA* (Serif, 1997) p 253.

5   Ibid, p 252.

6   This was daubed on a wall in East Belfast the day after the Frameworks document was released in February 1995, in H. McDonald, *Trimble* (Bloomsbury, 2000) p 144.

7   F. Cochrane, *Unionist Politics and the Politics of Unionism* (Cork UP, 1997) p 319.

8 P. Bew and G. Gillespie, *The Northern Ireland Peace Process, 1993–1996* (Serif, 1996) p 72.

9 Cochrane, op. cit., p 335.

10 A phrase used by Sammy Wilson of the DUP at a conference in 1995, in Cochrane, op. cit., p 349.

11 McDonald, op. cit., p 144.

12 C. McInnes, 'A farewell to arms: decommissioning and the peace protest', in Cox *et al*, *A Farewell to Arms; From Long War to Long Peace* (MUP, 2000) p 78.

13 Bew and Gillespie, op. cit., p 35.

14 Ibid.

15 The *Sunday Tribune* had interpreted TUAS as 'totally unarmed struggle' in an editorial of 23 April 1995, only to be put right later on. See Bew, op. cit., p 306.

16 The quote was given by a 'spokesperson' of the IRA as part of a statement to mark the first anniversary of the IRA cease-fire, in Bew and Gillespie, op. cit., p 311.

17 T. Hennessey, *The Northern Ireland Peace Process* (Gill & Macmillan, 2000) p 100.

18 Bew and Gillespie, op. cit., p 152.

9

THE FINAL FURLONG, 1996–1998

'You cannot be a spectator, you cannot be someone who deals purely with an idealized situation or a situation as you want it. You have to engage with it as it is. It is not always the way you like, and you can never be certain exactly how it is going to work out, but you have to engage.'

D. Trimble, speech to Young Unionists, 1998

PROCESS WITHOUT PEACE, 1996–1997

THE END OF THE IRA CEASE-FIRE ACTED LIKE A LAXATIVE on the political stalemate. At a stroke differences over decommissioning sank into the background as all tried to salvage momentum from the debris of Canary Wharf. With unfamiliar haste both governments issued a joint communiqué, committing all parties to an election to a Northern Ireland Peace Forum, scheduled for 30 May 1996, with multi-party discussions to start ten days later. Unionists had got their election, but only by accepting their Northern Irish Forum would be little more than an electoral hoop. Nationalists would have to swallow the idea of an election, but in return would have a fixed starting date for the talks and the Mitchell Report, with its ruling that decommissioning need only be 'addressed' once talks were under way, fully accepted by both governments. Politics were moving again, and how they moved! Determined to refute the IRA's charge of indecision, the 'peace process' burst into a flurry of bi- and multilateral discussions, proximity talks, position statements, consultation papers, procedural guidelines and possible rules for proceeding. Activity went from the meandering to the mercurial almost overnight, although in the absence of Sinn Fein it remained a moot point how long or far they could realistically continue. Just as any settlement required Unionists to be at the negotiating table, so it needed Republicans there as well.

However, it became clear this was not going to happen in the near future. Both London and Dublin refused Sinn Fein entry into talks until the renewal of an unconditional cease-fire by the IRA, a line made all the more necessary by a series of bombs in London through February and the murder of detective-Garda Jerry McCabe in the south. So for the next 17 months Sinn Fein was forced to sit outside the peace process looking in. It was a situation Adams, McGuinness and much of the Sinn Fein leadership disliked intensely but could do little about. Power in the Republican movement, and on the IRA Army Council, had shifted back to the hardliners, many of whom had not wanted a cease-fire in the first place. Adams, who had long chastised Major for political feebleness, found himself similarly sat in the passenger seat rather than driving the car. The lion had taken charge of the lion-tamer but at the worst time imaginable, for Republicans gave up politics at the very moment politics gave them their biggest ever poll. At the elections to the Northern Ireland Peace Forum on 30 May 1996, Sinn Fein won nearly 16 per cent of the vote, a mere 6 per cent short of the SDLP. The result made a mockery of the election as the reason for returning to armed struggle or not suspending it again thereafter, since here was a huge electoral mandate and enhanced political leverage. But it was leverage and a mandate the Army Council would not allow Sinn Fein leaders to exploit.

If the success of Sinn Fein worried the British and Irish governments, then the performance of the DUP pushed them into acute unease. The DUP vote at the May election leapt to 19 per cent, against an Ulster Unionist poll of 24 per cent, and a big increase on the 1992 general election where their respective share of the vote had been 13 per cent against 34.5 per cent. Even the one-man band of Robert McCartney's UK Unionist Party culled nearly 4 per cent of the vote. It was a clear message that the Unionist community was deeply nervous at the prospect of multi-party talks, despite the confidence engendered by an end to the IRA cease-fire and the collapse of pan-Nationalism.

> 66 If the success of Sinn Fein worried the British and Irish governments, then the performance of the DUP pushed them into acute unease 99

Many also felt that Trimble, the hardline 'son of Ulster' and recipient of the Orange Order's commemorative 'Siege of Drumcree' medal, was in practice much more pragmatic than they had realized or indeed liked. For Trimble the election result was a big setback. Eight months as leader had seen his party's share of the vote fall by 10 per cent and his personal standing weaken considerably. This drift to the 'political extremes' within both communities was a cause for much concern. Whereas the more moderate parties, the SDLP, the UUP and the Alliance, had together polled 63 per cent in 1992, that share had fallen to 54 per cent in 1996, while the more extreme parties, Sinn Fein and the DUP, had gone from 25 per cent to 38 per cent.[1] The centre ground, the only place where a political settlement could emerge, looked extremely fragile. To say the least this was ill-timed and unfortunate, coming at just the moment when Dublin and London were about to launch the first multi-party talks since 1992, and suggesting to legislators in London and Dublin that 'letting the people decide' often returned the 'wrong' answer. If reaching an agreed settlement had always been a slim prospect, by 1996 it looked positively anorexic.

It was, then, against a backdrop of renewed violence, communal polarization, and with one party sat on the outside trying to get in and another on the inside plotting to get out, that Major and Bruton opened the long-awaited multi-party talks at Stormont on 10 June. It was an historic moment, marking (though few could foresee it at the time) the start of Northern Ireland's movement away from 'organized political violence'.[2] However, in the circumstances of mid-1996 they nearly did not start at all. In a strange replay of the opening moves of the Brooke/Mayhew talks, dispute immediately broke out over who would chair the talks and what powers they would have. The governments had chosen Senator Mitchell to chair the plenary meetings, fresh from his controversial but eminently sensible navigation of the decommissioning issue, with de Chastelain and Holkeri to help in various supportive roles. This provoked the wrath of all the Unionist parties, although only the DUP and the UKUP decided to leave the talks when Mitchell was finally instated after two days of intense wrangling. Given the intensity of the opening arguments, it is hard not to draw the conclusion that Paisley and McCartney had only walked into the talks to find the best terms for walking out of them, and then only to walk back in a few days later, a sequence of manoeuvres even the Grand Old Duke of York might have winced at. 'It was, to say the least, an unpromising start,'[3] Mitchell noted in his memoirs. 'I was extremely uncomfortable and had a fleeting urge to get up and go home.'[4]

The next few months did little to dispossess him of this impulse – interminable speeches, long-winded recitations, scathing attacks on each other, repetitive statements of position and a debilitating lack of trust across and within the parties. The most serious threat to progress came, perhaps inevitably given the time of year, from a renewed stand-off at Drumcree. As if scripted, events played out as they had during the previous summer, with an initial ban of an Orange march along the Garvaghy Road reversed in the face of overwhelming protest. Loyalist violence triumphed once more to the discredit of the RUC and in the face of bitter hostility of local Nationalist residents. And as was so often the case, confrontation outside impacted on the talks inside. Paisley and McCartney, like the 'ham actors' they were, *again* exited (temporarily of course) stage right, while those left inside 'hurled insults and invective at each other'.[5] Mitchell, recognizing possible long-term damage, recommended a two-week suspension of the talks to allow passions to cool. In the meantime it was revealed that

Trimble had negotiated with Billy Wright, 'King Rat', the leader of the Portadown UVF, largely to bring some control over events. Though well intentioned, the meeting did little to generate goodwill across the political divide and dealt a blow to the party's line of 'arms before talks' – Trimble was evidently willing to talk to one sort of terrorist but not another. Such inconsistencies were rendered all the more sensitive with the upsurge of violence and the murder of a Catholic taxi driver by the Portadown UVF. The SDLP stormed out of the Northern Ireland Forum in protest, though thankfully not out of the talks. Major met representatives of the PUP and UDP in an effort to maintain the loyalist cease-fire. And Trimble was criticized on all sides, in Dublin, London and especially in Washington, where months of wooing influential politicians were undone. After early signs of pragmatism and even moderation, Trimble, it seemed, was wrapping himself in an orange flag.

If Mitchell thought the end of 'Drumcree II' would inject a new energy into the negotiations, he was soon disabused as the talks continued at their familiar glacial pace. Debate now centred upon procedure and the vital question of how decisions would be passed, provoking discussions that were 'long, often continuing late into the night . . . tedious and arcane'.[6] The mechanism finally chosen was 'sufficient consensus' where any decision not passed unanimously had to pass four tests before acceptance. It had to have the support of a majority of the representatives present at the talks whatever the party; a majority from both the Unionist and Nationalist representatives; a majority of the political parties represented, each party having one vote; and the agreement of both governments. The design was ingenious, aiming to ensure the broadest expanse of support while focusing power into the hands of the more moderate parties, the UUP and the SDLP, without whose consent nothing could be agreed. It also avoided the need for unanimous consent, a sure recipe for filibustering tactics and permanent deadlock. Yet sufficient consensus was a system labyrinthine in complexity and spoke volumes about the degree of mistrust each party and community had for the other. Of course, finding effective rules of procedure was one thing; actually voting them into existence was quite another. It was not until mid-August, the day before the summer recess, that agreement on the rules of procedure was finally reached. It had taken three months of painstakingly slow, tortuous and on many occasions deeply acrimonious discussion to simply agree *how* the talks would operate. It was progress, but of a sort that could scarcely be seen as moving forwards.

After the summer recess the talks reconvened on 9 September 1996. Summers rarely dissipate tension or inspire rest and relaxation in Northern Ireland, amidst the din of the landbeg and the pipes. So the talks began as they had ended, mired in bitter dispute. This time dispute was over alleged breaches of the Mitchell principles. The DUP, intensifying the intra-Unionist squabbling, accused the small loyalist parties, the PUP and the UDP, of breaking the principles in relation to death threats to Billy Wright,

> 66 It had taken three months of painstakingly slow, tortuous and on many occasions deeply acrimonious discussion to simply agree *how* the talks would operate 99

who demanded an end to loyalist involvement in the talks. The Alliance Party meanwhile accused all the Unionist parties of breaching the principles with their activities at the time of Drumcree. The indictments, if proven, would have led to their expulsion from the talks. Realizing the death blow this might have dealt the negotiations, both governments rejected the charges and the peace process survived – and indeed for a brief moment prospered, as steady progress was made on the question of the agenda, *what* they would talk about. By mid-October all the discussants had agreed to follow the three-stranded format of the 1991–1992 talks (strand one on internal arrangements within Northern Ireland, strand two on north/south relations, and strand three on Anglo-Irish relations). Also they agreed to follow the Brooke rule that 'nothing was agreed until everything was agreed'. But just as genuine movement was beginning, so the process hit that all too familiar buffer of decommissioning. During the autumn and winter of 1996 the Ulster Unionist Party leadership dug in its heals and refused to negotiate with Sinn Fein, when or if it re-entered the talks, until actual decommissioning had begun.

A hardening stance by Trimble was not unexpected. By the autumn of 1996 he found himself in the political straightjacket of all previous Ulster Unionist leaders, whereby any movement towards moderation and the centre necessitated a counter-move back to the extremes to shore up political support and party standing. It was as basic as Newton's law of gravitational pull. With many Unionists, including the DUP and the UKUP, holding decommissioning as the supreme test for entry into political talks, despite the Mitchell Report, Trimble had little real option but to harden his stance. However, his response was not just part of the ongoing intra-Unionist struggle with the DUP over leadership of the Unionist community, for by mid-1996 IRA activity was also on the increase. A massive bomb in Manchester injured nearly 200 people, followed in October by a bomb attack on Thiepval barracks in Lisburn that killed a soldier. In February 1997 another British soldier was killed in a sniper attack. Yet both of these incidents pale in comparison with the base inhumanity of the failed assassination attempt in December 1996 on Nigel Dodds, a DUP councillor, while visiting his son in the intensive care unit of the Royal Belfast Hospital for Sick Children. As with Tim Parry and Jonathan Ball, and in 1998 with the sectarian murder of the Quinn brothers, Richard, Mark and Jason, Northern Ireland's terrorists drew no age distinction in their murdering.

The result was that little consensus between Unionists and Nationalists could be found on the problem of decommissioning during the autumn and winter of 1996/1997. Continuing attacks merely fortified the Unionist emphasis upon decommissioning. It was also a stance that drew increasing support from John Major, under growing pressure from twitchy Tory diehards alarmed by anything that smacked of weakness towards terrorism. With so little room to manoeuvre Major was forced to rebuff an offer from John Hume in October to help reinstate a cease-fire in return for Sinn Fein's immediate entry into talks. So negotiations effectively ground to a halt. This time not even Mitchell's renowned powers of slow persuasion could find a compromise to this obstacle, though his nimble chairmanship did manage to defeat a DUP 'wrecking' motion on the issue, thus ensuring the talks survived even if they remained dead-locked. Disillusioned and frustrated he admitted by mid-February 1997 that 'there seemed to be no way to reconcile the conflicting positions of the participants. The debates had become repetitious, the parties dispirited.'[7] In any case the long shadow of a British general election was looming over events, forcing all to contemplate a possible change of government. Progress under such circumstances became hopeless, so the talks were adjourned until June.

As Senator Mitchell flew back to the States he reflected on his experiences thus far. 'Nine months had passed since the nego-tiations had begun and almost no progress had been made. There appeared to be no prospect of breaking the impasse that had tied things up since October. Even if somehow it could be broken, what conceivable basis could there be to hope for an agreement on substantive issues, given the long and difficult time spent on procedural matters? The longer the process went on, the harder it was to be optimistic.'[8] In such circumstances, many wondered whether Mitchell would bother to fly back at all.

NEW ACTORS, OLD PLAY: MAY–SEPTEMBER 1997

That Mitchell did return to reconvene the talks on 3 June owed much to the altered circumstances of the month before. The British general election of May 1997 swept the Tories out of gov-ernment and brought in Labour under the modernizing leader-ship of Tony Blair. In taking up the Northern Irish peace process Blair was armed with the kind of advantages that had always eluded Major. One was a massive Commons majority, sufficient to comfortably ignore pressure from Ulster Unionists or from a small knot of pro-Nationalist Labour backbench sympathizers. Blair also enjoyed closer relations with Clinton, a not inconsid-erable factor given the significant role the USA was now playing in Northern Irish affairs. In terms of policy, Labour entered gov-ernment extolling the virtues of de-centralizing power to Scotland and Wales, a quasi-federalist approach that would comfortably accommodate devolution in Northern Ireland. And after 18 years slumped on the opposition benches, his ministers entered office brimming with optimism, energy and a keen desire to advance on all fronts.

However, Labour's track record in Northern Ireland did not inspire trust. Republicans still remembered what they saw as Labour's skulduggery at the time of the 1975 truce, in particular what Republicans regarded as the treachery of the Secretary of State, Merlyn Rees. Nor did they have much affection for his successor, Roy Mason, someone, in their view, as hardline and unimaginative as any Tory Secretary of State. For Unionists, traditionally associated with the Tory Party, the prospect was even worse. Labour was deeply distrusted by all in the Unionist community. The party was regarded as soft on the union, if not actually hostile to it, and more inclined to a pro-Nationalist and pro-unity stance, as seen with the green hue to its manifesto policy statements of 1987 and 1992. Indeed, so worried was Molyneaux at the prospect of a Labour victory in 1992 that he threatened not to re-enter talks if Neil Kinnock became Prime Minister. Northern Ireland and Labour had a chequered past.

> 66 Blair also enjoyed closer relations with Clinton, a not inconsiderable factor given the significant role the USA was now playing in Northern Irish affairs 99

In light of his party's cool relations with Unionism, Blair was determined to offer them reassurance and showed in his own way that he was as much a Unionist as Margaret Thatcher had ever been. He recognized just how destabilizing to the whole peace process was their lack of confidence and anxiety for the future. To obviate this he gave strong support while still in opposition, to John Major's line of multi-party talks combined with substantial confidence-building measures, and especially the need for a decommissioning of weapons. In 1995 he was quick to establish good relations with Trimble, which according to Ken Maginnis proved to be far closer than with Major.[9] Trimble, scenting the direction of the electoral wind, was quick to reciprocate Blair's goodwill. In October 1996 he became the first leader of the Ulster Unionist Party to speak at a Labour Party conference. He was also the first leader of a Northern Irish party to congratulate Blair on his victory in May. Trimble's political courtship paid off, for in a remarkable speech in Belfast just a week after being elected, Blair offered Unionists the type of comfort that Major and indeed Thatcher never had. 'Those who wish to see a united Ireland without coercion can argue for it, not least in the talks. If they succeeded, we would certainly respect that. But none of us in this hall today, even the youngest, is likely to see Northern Ireland as anything but a part of the United Kingdom. That is the reality, because the consent principle is now almost universally accepted ... so fears of betrayal are simply misplaced. Unionists have nothing to fear from a new Labour government. A political settlement is not a slippery road to a united Ireland. The government will not be persuaders for unity.'[10]

Of course, Blair was equally clear that reassuring Unionists was not the same thing as becoming a prisoner to their demands. And Unionists, never ones to easily swallow 'flannel', even if of a rich Blairite mix, were well aware that a British Prime Minister was at his or her most dangerous when heaping praise and support on the Unionist cause. Blair's key impulse, after all, was to force the pace of a political process that was bogged down and stalling badly. And that meant somehow tackling the decommissioning problem and perhaps more importantly engineering a new cease-fire by the IRA and the entry of Sinn Fein into multi-party talks, the absence of which had hitherto given the talks all the relevance of a cup of coffee without caffeine. In pursuit of these he was helped by a general election in the Republic that brought to power Fianna Fail headed by Bertie Ahern, renowned as a realist and deal-maker. In 'Bertie' and 'Tony' the peace process now had two leaders eager to inject dynamism into the talks, less encumbered by political restraints, free of the tribulations surrounding the previous three years, with more resolve to grasp difficult problems and iconoclastic enough to think flexibly and fertilely on all issues.

Just how flexibly was evident three weeks after the resumption of multi-party talks at Stormont. On 24 June 1997 in a joint communiqué, both governments declared that talks would begin after a summer recess, on 15 September and end in May 1998, the first time a deadline had been imposed on the process. More significantly, and drawing upon the Mitchell Report, decommissioning by the IRA would *not* be a pre-condition to Sinn Fein's entry into multi-party talks, though a six-week 'purifying' period was required. Once the talks were up and running it was hoped decommissioning would begin, but there was no obligation to do so. Sinn Fein's only obligation was, as with all the other participants, to sign up to the six Mitchell principles. For Sinn Fein this was the 'great leap forward' it had wanted since 1994 and a return to what it saw as the spirit of the Downing Street Declaration. More importantly, the offer of entry into talks with no strings attached was great ammunition for Adams and McGuinness to persuade the IRA Army Council to restore the cessation, ammunition which had already been enhanced by Sinn Fein's historic performance in the May 1997 general election where it reaped 16 per cent of the vote and captured the seat of Mid-Ulster from the DUP. Sinn Fein was riding high, but without a cease-fire none of that could be turned into real political influence and leverage. And failure to do so would simply leave the party marginalized, as Blair indicated during his Belfast speech: 'The talks cannot wait for them but must and will move on.' In other words Sinn Fein had the choice of getting involved or sitting on the fence. On

> **For Sinn Fein this was the 'great leap forward' it had wanted since 1994 and a return to what it saw as the spirit of the Downing Street Declaration**

19 July 1997, without fanfare or fuss, it chose involvement with the announcement of another 'complete cessation of military operations' by the IRA. After a trial separation of 17 months, the various strands of Irish Nationalism were reunited on the steps of Government Buildings in Dublin six days later, when Ahern and Hume clasped the hand of Gerry Adams. Six weeks later, on 9 September, Sinn Fein sat at the negotiating table, committing itself to the Mitchell principles. The party had come a long way.

If the joint communiqué helped ease Sinn Fein's entry into the multi-party talks, it also very nearly forced Unionists out of them. Not even the warmest of warm words from Blair could disguise the acute reversal in positions. At a stroke Blair and

Ahern had snapped the link between arms and talks, and undermined the stance taken up by Unionists since late 1994. Now, instead of confronting Republicans with the problem of handing in weapons, Unionists were themselves confronted with the choice of sitting across the table from Adams and McGuinness or leaving the room. The onus and initiative were lifted from the shoulders of Sinn Fein and perched squarely upon those of the Unionist parties. Both Blair and Ahern realized it was a necessary but terribly high-risk stratagem, finely balanced between kick-starting substantive talks and not driving the Unionists out of them. Predictably, Paisley and McCartney declared they would walk out. For them Unionism was best defended from outside the castle and by, amongst other things, attacking their own side. Both governments had expected this and probably rejoiced at the development. Certainly Mitchell regarded their exit as a catalyst for progress, as he reflected in his memoirs that 'reaching agreement without their presence was extremely difficult; it would have been impossible with them in the room'.[11] The real gamble, of course, was whether Trimble and his Ulster Unionists would follow them out. Both premiers realized such a move would bring the entire process to a shuddering end, a situation not helped by the IRA's brutal murder of two RUC men just days before the communiqué. Tantalizingly, Trimble rejected the communiqué in a rancorous session of the talks on 22 July, but kept his own counsel for the moment as to whether he would stay or go. With the summer adjournment of the talks until 9 September he had time to ponder what course of action to follow.

It quickly became apparent that both courses appeared equally unattractive. To follow Paisley and McCartney out of the talks, when they left on 16 July, would be to acknowledge that their scepticism and hostility had been well founded all along and thus inflict a mortal blow to his standing in the party and in the wider Unionist community. His exit would unavoidably capsize negotiations and throw the blame for ending the peace process firmly at the Unionist door. In terms of tactics, a walkout by Trimble would play into the hands of the IRA. Sean O'Callaghan, one-time IRA man but now adviser to Trimble, warned that 'the whole Republican project is based on the assumption that the Unionists would all walk out together once Sinn Fein entered the negotiations',[12] hoping then an agreement would be hatched between the Nationalist parties and an exasperated British government. If Trimble doubted O'Callaghan's advice, then a massive bomb planted by the dissident Continuity IRA splinter group at Markethill on the very day talks were to begin in earnest seemed to corroborate his thoughts. But to stay in the talks, though ensuring the continuance of the peace process, presented as many problems. It would seriously strain the unity of his party and loyalty to him as leader. Many Ulster Unionists simply could not stomach Trimble sitting at the same table as Adams, let alone in advance of decommissioning. Already the mutterings of revolt were being heard from the two 'Willies', Willie Thompson, MP for West Tyrone, and Willie Ross, MP for East Londonderry. If staying in the talks was liable to fan revolt in his own party, that was nothing compared with the vitriolic broadside he expected from the DUP and UKUP. Staying in would all but guarantee Trimble a prominent position within Paisley's pantheon of traitors to the Unionist cause, in the company no doubt of O'Neill and Faulkner. So Trimble was damned if he did and damned if he didn't.

In the end he backed entry and on 17 September led the Unionist delegation back into Stormont; a week later they took up their seats at the same table as Sinn Fein. It was an historic moment; the last time leaders of Ulster Unionism and Sinn Fein had sat in the same room was during the Craig–Collins negotiations of 1922. There was no disguising the fact that entering the talks represented a significant shift in position, from *prior* decommissioning through to *parallel* and now simply to the *prospect* of some weapons being handed in as discussions progressed. Central to this shift was the support Trimble had from key Unionist leaders, John Taylor, Ken Maginnis, Reg Empey and more surprisingly the young *enragé*, Jeffrey Donaldson, as well as the backing of 82 per cent of the ruling Ulster Unionist executive. Yet Trimble's decision also revealed a firm grasp of tactics. It was clear that the lesser evil, though perhaps the more uncomfortable ride, lay in remaining at the table. To leave was to wallow in negativism, even defeatism, wrapped up as a principled stand, and Trimble had seen enough of hollow gestures to realize they invariably failed. Remembering the party's reaction to the Anglo-Irish Agreement of 1985, Trimble was determined that this time 'Unionism would not be marginalized'.[13]

Trimble bought himself significant goodwill in both London and Dublin, goodwill that would prove invaluable at later stages of the talks process. He might also have speculated that with the mechanism of sufficient consensus operating in the negotiations, which gave his party a veto but not Sinn Fein, Republicans were perhaps in a weaker position inside the talks than they were outside them. Being inside gave him the opportunity to confront Sinn Fein upon its programme and ideology, both of which, for Trimble, would not stand up to sustained, rational criticism. Yet above all else Trimble, like all those now around the table, genuinely wanted to bring the Troubles to an end and was willing to take risks to achieve that. So even though Unionists and Republicans were not actually talking to each other, preferring to communicate through the chairman, they were both engaged. It appeared that after 15 long months of skirmishing at the margins, the talks were finally moving into substantial, full-blown discussions.

66 It was clear that the lesser evil, though perhaps the more uncomfortable ride, lay in remaining at the table 99

DEAD RATS, MAD DOGS AND MIGHTY MO; OCTOBER 1997 TO FEBRUARY 1998

In the autumn of 1997 it had been agreed that when, and if, substantive talks ever began, the discussions would proceed upon the three-stranded basis of the Brooke and Mayhew talks. Strand one, dealing with the internal political settlement of Northern Ireland, would be chaired by Paul Murphy, the British Minister of State. Strand two, with a remit to establish equitable north/south relations between Northern Ireland and the Republic, was to be chaired by George Mitchell. Strand three, looking at relations between Britain and the Republic (the east/west axis), would be left to the two governments. It was also agreed that in light of difficulties encountered during previous talks, each strand would be discussed simultaneously rather than sequentially. To co-ordinate matters and provide an overview, regular plenary meetings of the discussants were to be instituted.

One feature of the entire process pierced this confusion of conference structuring and sequential discussions, namely that strand two was the principal area of dispute. It was widely assumed that if agreement could be established here, all the other pieces of the puzzle would fall into place. North/south relations were the key to unlock a political settlement. After all, it had been differences over north/south relations that had destroyed the Sunningdale agreement, as well as being the most contentious part of the 1991–1992 talks.

However, the opening of substantive discussions did not herald a new spirit of progress and compromise. Profound distrust remained the prevailing sentiment of the talks. Indeed, the first move, once all the participants (except the DUP) were sitting around the table, was an unsuccessful attempt by Trimble to have Sinn Fein expelled over the Markethill bomb attack. This set the tone for the next few months, a period typified by 'insult, invective and recrimination'.[14] Through October and November, as all parties presented position statements, debate grew so heated that Mitchell was forced to demand restraint and moderation of the delegates, though with little obvious effect. On top of these difficulties came, in quick succession, a flood of problems that stood to de-rail the process, such as leaks to the press, an insensitive speech from David Andrews, the Irish Foreign Secretary, that sent Unionists into violent convulsions, and a bitter argument over the location for strand two talks, something that most thought had already been settled. Mitchell's famed and hitherto limitless patience was close to snapping. 'Rarely in my life have I felt as frustrated and angry as I did ... We had been meeting for a year and a half. For hundreds and hundreds of hours I had listened to the same arguments, over and over again. Very little had been accomplished ... Yet here the delegates were furiously debating what had or had not been agreed to in an earlier meeting about whether we should or should not move the whole process to London and Dublin, and who said what to which newspaper. I bit my lip, squirmed in my seat, and worked hard not to let my anger show.'[15]

Mitchell, with British and Irish backing, suggested several ways of moving things forward. One was to reduce party representations at certain plenary meetings to just two leaders, so making for a more informal and less unwieldy venue. Another was to impose a deadline to apply pressure and focus minds on the task of actually settling something. He reminded the parties that the joint communiqué of June 1997 had already set the deadline of May 1998, though he was already contemplating imposing a tighter one. More immediately he shifted the setting of the negotiations into a variety of bi- and multi-lateral meetings between the parties or between the chairman and the individual leaders. Mitchell found these types of intimate exchanges more productive for honing arguments, elucidating demands, defining meanings, winnowing down unsustainable reasoning, challenging and embellishing different positions, suggesting alternatives and options, and drawing out points of agreement and disagreement. For here was the fundamental work of any negotiating process: clarifying the issues, spotting priorities and establishing linkage between the different arguments – work that Mitchell, after his years as leader of the American Senate, excelled at. Unfortunately the quarrels he was trying to bridge were more deep-rooted than even he was used to. As a consequence a vital ingredient still escaped his wily efforts: a willingness by all parties to yield ground and bargain. Despite 18 months of negotiations they were still operating the politics of the megaphone rather than the politics of rapprochement. Without this the talks would get nowhere.

If relations were increasingly strained inside the talks, they were hardly aided by pressures outside, pressures that made acts of rapprochement seemingly impossible. This was true for all sides but especially for Adams, McGuinness and the Sinn Fein leadership during the autumn and winter of 1997. Opposition to their peace strategy emerged within the Republican movement as early as the first cease-fire, and developed sufficient strength and backing to force a return to violence in February 1996. Though a new cease-fire was subsequently engineered 15 months later, the demand from hardliners to abandon peace did not desist. That pressure intensified considerably with Sinn Fein's entry into the multi-party talks in September and its decision to abide by the Mitchell principles. The latter move, representing an unequivocal rejection of the armed struggle, drew a particularly sharp reaction from sections in the IRA. In an interview with *An Phoblacht* in September 1997, an IRA 'spokesman' went as far as to disclaim Sinn Fein's right to sign up to the Mitchell principles on behalf of the IRA. At the same time dissident Republican groups, the INLA and the Continuity IRA, recognizing the emergence of a highly placed and deeply disgruntled minority within the Provisionals, expanded their activities. The British and Irish governments responded to this growing unease by trying to bolster the Sinn Fein leadership. In October, Blair met Adams in Belfast, the first meeting between a British Prime Minister and Sinn Fein since Lloyd George entertained Arthur Griffith and Michael Collins, a parallel Adams would not have enjoyed, particularly as the latter was shot dead by dissident Republicans within a year of the meeting.

> 66 Despite 18 months of negotiations they were still operating the politics of the megaphone rather than the politics of rapprochement 99

Tensions within the Republican movement came to a head in October 1997 at a meeting of the IRA's Extraordinary Army Convention at Falcarragh in Donegal, at which an attempted coup by hardline 'Real' IRA members tried to dump Adams and McGuinness and overturn the peace strategy. The move backfired and Adams and McGuinness were able to preserve their peace strategy, and indeed save the entire peace process – though only just and at the cost of splitting the Provisionals, with a small but experienced and hardened section, styling themselves as the 'Real' IRA, leaving the organization to move into a loose alliance with the Continuity IRA. Even amongst the majority who stayed loyal to the Adams–McGuinness line, dissatisfaction gently smouldered away and often led to sporadic violence. This became apparent in February 1998 after the IRA murdered Brendan Campbell and Robert Dougan, leading to Sinn Fein's temporary expulsion from the talks. Dissident Republicans and dissatisfaction within the movement were ominous and probably unavoidable developments that threatened the very continuity of the peace process. They were also a major restriction to Sinn Fein's room for manoeuvre. For like the Ulster Unionist Party, Sinn Fein would have to keep one eye on the enemy over its shoulder as well as one eye on the enemy across the table. This was especially the case from December with the emergence of the 32 County Sovereignty Committee, fronted by Bobby Sands' sister, Bernadette Sands-McKevitt, which in terms of linkage was for the Real IRA what Sinn Fein was to the IRA. It was 1970 all over again, except the Provisionals were now the party determined to work within the political system and not seek to destroy it.

While Adams and McGuinness struggled to preserve their hold over Republicans, British and Unionist politicians laboured hard to keep loyalist groups wedded to the peace. Already disturbing signs of a hardening stance against the peace process were emerging within loyalism, with the formation of the Loyalist Volunteer Force (LVF) under Billy Wright, the former UVF commander. This became all the more alarming with rising levels of Republican violence, clearly calculated to stir loyalist paramilitaries into retaliation and to breach their cease-fire. It was a cold and cynical ploy, born of a realization that the only way to advance their cause was to spread fear and violence. But it very nearly paid off. Two days after Christmas the INLA managed to shoot dead Billy Wright, while he sat waiting in a prison van *inside* the Maze. The LVF launched a wave of bloody vengeance against the Catholic community, unaware or indifferent to the fact that this played into Republican hands. The loyalist cease-fire teetered on the edge of collapse, as elements within both the UDA and UFF pushed their leaders to unleash a violent backlash. This situation was worrying enough, but it became potentially catastrophic when loyalist prisoners voted against their participation in the peace talks, in the words of Johnny Adair one-time leader of the UFF and proud holder of the sobriquet

Mad Dog, 'Shove the dove'. This immediately jeopardized the cease-fire and the continued involvement of the UDP and the PUP. Without their support, Trimble's ability to work the voting structure based upon 'sufficient consensus', and more generally his claim to speak for the majority of Unionists, were invalidated. For a second time within a few weeks the very survival of the peace process was thrown into serious doubt by developments outside.

It quickly became clear that something dramatic was needed to calm loyalist anger and to put the discussions back on track. That something came in the larger-than-life form of Mo Mowlam, the forceful and outspoken British Secretary of State for Northern Ireland. Against civil service advice and with clear risks to her political position as well as physical safety, she entered the Maze prison to discuss the crisis with 130 men of violence. The gesture as much as the words of reassurance helped the loyalist leadership draw back from the brink, as a relieved Gary McMichael of the UDP recounted: 'It wasn't what she said, it was the fact that she was there.'[16] The leaders restated their commitment to the loyalist cease-fire and support for the peace process, thus allowing the UDP and the PUP to re-enter the talks. Mowlam's daring, perhaps reckless, act had saved the peace process. The irony was that within a few weeks a proven breach of the Mitchell principles saw the UDP, as with Sinn Fein, temporarily expelled.

❝ It quickly became clear that something dramatic was needed to calm loyalist anger and to put the discussions back on track ❞

But if Mowlam had kept the talks alive, she could do little about the paroxysm of violence, from both dissident Republicans and dissident loyalists, that continued to engulf the province through January and February 1998. The lowest point in this tit-for-tat cycle of violence came with the LVF murder of Phillip Allen, a Protestant, and his closest friend, Damien Trainor, a Catholic, as they sat talking in a bar in Poyntzpass. It was doubly tragic, a needless murder of innocents as well as a blow against cross-community relations, an attack on the present but also a strike against the future of Northern Ireland. When Seamus

Mallon and David Trimble together visited the parents of both victims, they sent their own alternative and more powerful message of what the future of the province should be.

HOME STRAIGHT, JANUARY–APRIL 1998

The surging violence of early 1998 reflected growing unease within both communities at what the immediate future might hold in store for them. Yet rather than undermine the talks, as had happened in the past, developments outside served to intensify the efforts of those searching for a political settlement. 'It reminded us,' Trimble would write, 'of what it was we were trying to replace.'[17] Mitchell, still frustrated by the slow progress, sought to channel this new determination into more concrete advance. He recommended both governments 'take stock' of where the talks were and where each of the parties stood by compiling a draft agreement that embraced all the various issues and strands. Only when this was in front of them, Mitchell believed, would the parties actually knuckle down to the necessary rough horse-trading. Over Christmas and the New Year, the British and Irish governments haggled away behind the scenes to finally produce on 11 January a paper entitled 'Propositions on Heads of Agreement'. The next day Mitchell presented this to the parties as the basis for more concerted discussions over the next few months. The document was necessarily light on detail, purposely vague in many areas and little more than an outline, indeed with only two pages it could scarcely be otherwise. But it did set out for the first time an embryonic settlement.

The agreement embraced the principle of consent for constitutional change, a Northern Irish Assembly, a North/South Council, plus 'suitable bodies' to deal with proscribed cross-border issues, a British-Irish Inter-Governmental Council to transact east-west relations, 'balanced' change in the Irish and British constitutions, and a variety of safeguards and protections for all people in Northern Ireland. Little of this was new or unexpected, forming the basis of all discussions on Northern Ireland since Brooke had launched them back in 1991. What was contentious was not so much the three institutions but how much power each should have and the balance of importance and influence between them. For many the balance of the Heads of Agreement was tipped in a Unionist direction. The Northern Irish Assembly would be a strong, viable body with executive functions. No mention was made of a power-sharing executive, long a bone of contention for Unionists. And, importantly for them, the North/South Council was to be a consultative body, accountable to the northern and southern Parliaments and lacking any 'dynamic' or free-standing role. For Trimble the paper was a significant triumph, the result of months of painstaking pressure upon both Blair and Ahern. It eased the epicentre of the talks away from the overly green Frameworks document of 1995 and towards a more Unionist-friendly stance. Of course, a cynic might argue it was payment for staying in the talks back in September. Or, more likely, a stick to beat off the increasingly vociferous attacks from Unionists within his own party, spearheaded by the 'gang of four' Unionist MPs who were demanding he leave the talks.[18]

> **The idea of consent for constitutional change still smacked of a Unionist veto**

Despite its Unionist lustre, the SDLP found much that it could welcome in the Heads of Agreement paper. But it was alarmed by its failure to mention a power-sharing executive and by the weak, non-executive definition it gave north/south arrangements. Yet it saw it for what it was, a draft to be worked on and not a finely polished settlement. Over the coming weeks the SDLP engaged robustly with Unionists, targeting its arguments primarily on these two areas. Sinn Fein, on the other hand, regarded the Heads of Agreement as 'Unionist sabotage'[19] and a cowardly retreat from the Frameworks Document of 1995. The party had strong misgivings about pretty much everything. The idea of consent for constitutional change still smacked of a Unionist veto. Balanced constitutional modification in the Irish constitution, code for altering articles 2 and 3, implied Dublin was cutting the north adrift and ignoring its historic duty to unite Ireland. A powerful Northern Ireland Assembly filled Sinn Fein with dismay given it still found the very idea of it an abomination. While a purely consultative North/South Council with limp cross-border bodies undermined its core demand for a dynamic all-Irish body, capable of harmonizing governmental functions through the island of Ireland. Even the rights and safeguards seemed limited and weak. The paper exposed just how far Sinn Fein's position was from the other parties, including the SDLP, and how far it would have to travel to be part of an agreement. It also exposed its relative powerlessness. It had, after all, voted against the agreement, only to see it passed by sufficient consensus. Despite Adams' slick rhetoric about Sinn Fein pursuing the 'politics of peacemaking',[20] in the circumstances of early 1998 they bore greater resemblance to a politics of the periphery. Betrayed and isolated, Sinn Fein turned its ire against its 'weak-kneed' Nationalist 'colleagues' in the SDLP and Irish government, with all the venom of a family spat. It took the eye of an old negotiator, such as Mitchell, to recognize that it simply 'was too early for Sinn Fein to accept these things',[21] though he seems in no doubt that it would eventually accept. Where else could it go?

The British and Irish governments were certainly worried by Sinn Fein's reaction. To recover the situation Mowlam tried to offer reassurance and concessions elsewhere, particularly on the increasingly important issue of prisoners. 'We recognize prisoner issues are important to parties on both sides. They too need to be resolved.'[22] Both governments also issued a joint statement on 27 January muddying the waters on strand two by claiming the paper still adhered to the Frameworks document. This placated Sinn Fein a little but at the expense of incurring the wrath of Unionists who similarly felt angry and cheated. It was an object lesson in what both governments should have known already, that in this context to give with one hand is automatically to take from the other. Further proof of this maxim came when Ulster Unionist delight at the successful expulsion of Sinn Fein from the talks on 20 February quickly turned to anger when Mowlam re-admitted the party with almost indecent haste on 9 March. It was good practical politics with an eye fixed on the overall picture, but it permanently soured relations between Unionists and the Secretary of State. It also gave sustenance to Trimble's growing band of critics within his increasingly restless party. And as before, so Unionist unease settled upon the issue of decommissioning as the necessary confirmation of how much faith they could place in the British and Irish governments and how much trust in the Republican movement's commitment to peace. If Blair and Ahern thought they had successfully brushed the issue under the carpet, then nervous, brow-furrowed Unionists were dragging it out again, towards whose fears Trimble was forced to bend.

Yet beyond (or beneath) all the ill-natured quarrelling and barefaced 'politicking', progress was slowly being made. Mitchell, by the end of March, found himself hoping 'that maybe this was leading somewhere. When we left the meeting that evening I thought this is going well.'[23] Negotiations on strand three, never terribly contentious and conducted largely between the two governments, were close to agreement. Similarly, talks on the necessary changes to the British and Irish constitutions were far advanced, upon an eminently sensible basis of Britain repealing the Government of Ireland Act 1920 in return for a redrafting of articles 2 and 3 of the Irish constitution. The actual wording of the latter redraft was still a point of dispute, particularly as Ahern was linking it to the creation of a strong, executive North/South Council. Unionists could have Dublin formally recognizing Northern Ireland as long as they gave ground on north/south bodies. More surprisingly, discussions on strand one had come a long way. Agreement seemed close on the overall shape of the assembly, its mode and manner of operation, the nature and powers of the committees under it, the voting system and the safeguards for each community. Even Sinn Fein began to face up to the reality of a northern-based institution, though packaging its co-operation as a 'transitional' and tactical step towards a united Ireland. By the end of March, it was less a case of finding areas where all the parties agreed than finding where they disagreed. Unfortunately, where they disagreed was fundamental: should the assembly have a power-sharing executive to co-ordinate things (the SDLP line) or could that be done by the committee chairperson, the Ulster Unionist argument? Strand one talks had certainly travelled far but they still had a mountain to climb.

If strand one had some distance to go, discussions on strand two seemed to have barely begun their journey. Unionists would not budge from the vague Heads of Agreement definition of a consultative north/south body. On the other hand, Dublin, the SDLP and Sinn Fein were equally determined to have a more dynamic institution, with executive functions as prescribed by the Frameworks document of 1995. As everybody realized, if a deal was done here everything else would fall into place. It was the magic key to open up a settlement but it looked as far off now as it had back in 1996 or even 1992.

NOTES

1 S. Farren and R. F. Mulvihill, *Paths to a Settlement in Northern Ireland* (Colin Smythe, 2000) p 176.

2 G. Mitchell, *Making Peace* (Heinemann, 1999) p 187.

3 Ibid, p 53.

4 Ibid, p 50.

5 Ibid, p 61.

6 Ibid, p 57.

7 Ibid, p 96.

8 Ibid, p 98.

9 H. McDonald, *Trimble* (Bloomsbury, 2000) p 178.

10 T. Hennessey, *The Northern Ireland Peace Process* (Gill & Macmillan, 2000) p 104.

11 Mitchell, op. cit., p 110.

12 McDonald, op. cit., p 181.

13 D. McKittrick and E. Mallie, *Endgame in Ireland* (Hodder & Stoughton, 2001) p 215.

14 Mitchell, op. cit., p 126.

15 Ibid, p 126.

16 McKittrick and Mallie, op. cit., p 222.

17 Ibid, p 224.

18 The gang of four included William Ross, William Thompson, Roy Beggs and Clifford Forsythe. See McDonald, op. cit., p 192.

19 G. Adams, *An Irish Journal* (Brandon, 2001) p 43.

20 Ibid, p 44.

21 Mitchell, op. cit., p 133.

22 M. Von Tangen Page, 'A most difficult and unpalatable part – the release of politically motivated violent offenders', in M. Cox *et al*, *A Farewell to Arms: From Long War to Long Peace in Northern Ireland* (MUP, 2001) p 99.

23 Ibid, p 138.

10

THE HAND OF HISTORY:[1] THE GOOD FRIDAY AGREEMENT 1998

'The prize is within reach. We may be about to witness the most exciting, and most hopeful moment in Irish history since the island was partitioned in 1921.'

Financial Times, 3 April 1998

' "Oh my God, what have Gerry and Martin agreed to?" was the reaction of one veteran supporter whose loyalty had survived all the bitter pills the peace process has required Republicans to swallow. These have included: the deletion of articles 2 and 3 of the Irish constitution; the return of a Northern Assembly; Sinn Fein abandoning its traditional policy of abstentionism; reliance on British government-appointed commissions ... and the implicit recognition of the principle of Unionist consent on the constitutional question.'

D. Morrison, *Guardian*, 13 July 1999

'PLAYING HARDBALL': WEDNESDAY 1 TO MONDAY 6 APRIL 1998

ON 25 MARCH MITCHELL ANNOUNCED TO ALL PARTIES that he was imposing a deadline, Thursday 9 April, by which time an agreement had to be reached. To achieve this, the talks would remain in permanent, round-the-clock session, with delegates required to move into hotels nearby if need be. Both governments and parties were given until Friday 3rd to submit their final comments, which would then be drafted into a 'comprehensive accord'[2] for distribution later that same evening. Saturday and Sunday would involve further negotiations upon that 'accord' between Mitchell and leaders, with the results assimilated into a redraft for circulation on Monday 6th. That left three days for any final mediation, last-minute hitches and polishing up. A month after signing the agreement, a referendum would ratify it and a month after that, elections would take place for the new assembly. To say the least it was an optimistic timetable, but probably unavoidably so. For if the talks had kept to their original timetable of May, the election would have fallen in mid-summer when community tensions were at their highest. Mitchell also realized that despite the progress made, the talks remained a long way from an actual settlement. Parties were still manoeuvring for position and their leaders shadow-boxing. All seemed fixed in a mind-set that they had more to lose from compromising than to gain by agreeing, and somehow that had to be reversed. Pointing a loaded pistol at the talks and saying 'we shall agree by the 9th or go no further' was perhaps the 'dramatic something' the discussions needed.

In this Mitchell showed himself to be a good amateur psychologist. A deadline injected a sense of urgency and seriousness into the process: if they were brought to realize the Promised Land was but a week away it might encourage some to finally make the journey. It also raised the level of media and public expectation, making failure to agree, let alone being blamed for that failure, a difficult prospect to handle politically. And a deadline drew delegates' attention to the fact that they had now been negotiating for nearly two years and invested too much time, effort, personal credibility and party prestige for it all to flop. Moreover, a demanding timetable and continuous meetings would place the leaders under intense

> **Parties were still manoeuvring for position and their leaders shadow-boxing**

pressure and into a state of deep exhaustion. These were not unwelcome qualities in a negotiating setting, where they could help to blunt resistance, weaken public facades, reveal individual personalities, generate a sense of common struggle, even common purpose, humanize each other and generally encourage communication. If fresh and fully rested leaders wouldn't agree, Mitchell had few qualms about trying it when they were fatigued. The stage was well and truly set for one last heave.

The initial signs were promising as the conference went into overdrive from 30 March. Strand three proceeded well enough and was on track for Friday's deadline. Strand one made deep inroads, firming up areas of tentative agreement and fleshing out others in talks that Seamus Mallon described as 'intense, detailed and real'.[3] Sinn Fein in particular made considerable movement, arguing that although it opposed a Northern Assembly, '*if* such a body came into existence' it wanted 'a detailed position on the safeguards', safeguards that included 'the Irish language, prisoners, policing and the equality agenda'.[4] In other words, for accepting a Northern Irish Assembly, Sinn Fein wanted prisoner releases and community protections. It was a big and brave step, though realizing the SDLP and Unionists were able to contrive a deal on the basis of sufficient consensus, a sceptic might say their 'movement' smacked of salvaging something from nothing or even just saving face. There was, then, much to support the statement of John Alderdice, leader of the Alliance Party, that in strand one 'we are three-quarters of the way there'.[5] And even that last quarter, of whether there should be a power-sharing executive or not, though stubborn and resilient was showing signs of yielding. Both smaller Unionist parties, the UDP and PUP, were more or less satisfied with power-sharing plus some safeguards. Indeed, even with Ulster Unionists, who were inching towards the scheme, the objection was less ideological than tactical, in waiting upon the outcome of strand two before jumping. Or rather linking the two strands together, as a Unionist spokesperson let slip: 'If we move towards their position on strand one then they will have to move to our position on strand two.'[6] An exchange Mitchell was also convinced of after a late-night meeting with the SDLP and Ulster Unionists. By Friday, 3 April the skeleton of a possible deal was beginning to cast its shadow over the talks.

So all eyes turned towards strand two negotiations, then being conducted by Blair and Ahern well away from the Belfast 'bear pit' in the relative sanctuary of Downing Street. Here progress was slow, with press reports suggesting 'stormy waters' between the two premiers.[7] If there were storms it was hardly surprising. Ahern recognized that without a viable North/South Council, with executive functions, Sinn Fein would not buy into the agreement. Blair similarly understood that if a north/south body were given those functions, Unionists would not sign up to it. In their respective positions, the SDLP and Sinn Fein looked to the Frameworks document of 1995 for guidance, while the Unionists looked to less detailed but more recent Heads of Agreement. It was quite simply unbridgeable unless one side gave way. Yet giving ground flew in the face of communities that for three centuries had been weaned on a diet of 'not an inch' and 'no surrender'. These 'large disagreements'[8] between Blair and Ahern explain why, when both premiers spoke to Mitchell on Friday evening, they could report no agreement and needed more time, at least until Sunday afternoon, if not Monday morning.

66 The talks moved into the uncharted territory of improvised negotiation 99

Mitchell's carefully choreographed script was, in the space of a telephone call, thrown out of the window. The talks moved into the uncharted territory of improvised negotiation. With little real alternative, Mitchell agreed to the new timescale, and spent much of Saturday and Sunday twiddling his thumbs awaiting their plans for strand two. He also agreed to take the blame for the delay, recognizing that with the world's press looking on, now was not the time to reveal a significant divergence of opinion between the British and Irish governments. So Mitchell duly played the 'patsy' for public consumption, while away from the cameras Blair and Ahern 'slugged it out' in a desperate attempt to narrow their differences. Just how wide those differences were was made all too evident to Mitchell and his team late on Sunday when government officials finally delivered a draft agreement on strand two. It arrived with all the effect of a piece of smoking Semtex. Examining its terms for a North/South Council, Mitchell 'knew immediately that Trimble would never, could never accept this'.[9] A key Unionist demand had been that any such council and its powers had to originate from the Northern Assembly, and thus its authority lay with the 'people' of Northern Ireland. The plan just delivered was for both governments to constitute the council as well as prescribe what areas it would deal with. In other words, authority would reside with the British and Irish governments. Blair and Ahern had clearly moved away from the Heads of Agreement paper back towards the more Nationalist-friendly Frameworks document. To make matters worse, Mitchell was instructed to change nothing in their plan and merely absorb it into the draft settlement as it stood, regardless of their serious misgivings about it. This was worrying because it looked like closing the door on any further renegotiation, something he predicted would be absolutely vital if Unionists were not to storm out of the talks on this issue.

To add insult to injury the prescribed 'areas' or annexes were not attached to the plan, since the prime ministers still could not reach agreement. Without the annexes the strand two plan was incomplete and so progress on strand one was delayed and Monday's deadline for a full draft agreement looked unlikely. Alarmed by differences between Blair and Ahern and troubled by the expected Unionist reaction, Mitchell spent much of Monday waiting for the annexes to turn up. His optimism deserted him and he perhaps even allowed himself a private sympathy with John Taylor's forecast at the start of April that the talks had between a '4 per cent and a 7 per cent chance of success'.[10] The earlier shadow of a skeleton settlement had turned out to be dark storm clouds massing in the sky above.

'OVER-EGGING THE PUDDING'; TUESDAY, 7 TO THURSDAY, 9 APRIL[11]

If Mitchell was uneasy as he waited for the annexes, their arrival at almost midnight filled him with profound alarm. Instead of just a handful, the annexes included more than 60 areas to be covered by cross-border bodies. As instructed he incorporated them into the unamended strand two proposals the governments had forced him to swallow and then assembled the party leaders in the small hours of now Tuesday morning for a short meeting. Here he delivered the draft proposals with all the wariness of a man lighting the fuse of a stick of dynamite. The Unionist explosion on Tuesday morning was loud enough to be heard in Dublin and Downing Street. 'I'm away,' John Taylor told waiting reporters as he left Stormont, and 'I wouldn't touch it with a 40 ft barge pole.' David Adams of the UDP told Nationalists to 'plug into planet reality' if they thought Unionists were going to accept this, while Trimble, already feeling the hot breath on his neck of those who stood against the talks, stormed into Mitchell's office to bluntly explain 'it is a bad paper. A very bad paper.'[12] It was Sunningdale all over again, where, for Unionists, over-ambitious plans from the Irish government on north/south relations had helped collapse the attempt at peace. To avoid a Sunningdale mark two, the talks now devolved into a flurry of meetings and exchanges in a desperate attempt to find a way through. Recognizing the danger, Blair flew to Belfast that evening where he immediately immersed himself in the 'hot-house' atmosphere of Stormont, shuttling between meetings and trying to mollify Unionist anxieties, though it quickly became apparent to both Blair and Mitchell that only a willingness to renegotiate strand two by London and Dublin could now prevent the collapse of the talks.

With Blair keen, the question of renegotiation resided with Ahern. Unfortunately his room for manoeuvre on this was extremely cramped, relying as it did upon his ability to carry the SDLP and Sinn Fein with him on any agreement. To re-open negotiations on strand two would bring down upon his shoulders the wrath of Nationalist Ireland. 'There is no room for slippage,' a Sinn Fein spokesperson exclaimed, 'and no room for this document to be unpicked.'[13] The problem was, as Mitchell saw only too well, that unless it was 'unpicked' the entire peace process would unravel then and there. Earlier in the day Mitchell had stressed to the Irish Foreign Minister, David

Andrews, that the Unionist stance was more than just usual histrionics, and implored him to talk to Ahern. The Taoiseach during much of Tuesday had been in Dublin attending a church service for his mother who had died a few days before. Hearing of the far from unexpected Unionist reaction, Ahern's initial response was to stand firm and not re-open the strand two can of worms. But after two hours of reflection, he altered his stance and agreed to come to Belfast the next day to renegotiate. It was an immense change of heart and absolutely central to the eventual success of the peace negotiations – 'a big decision by a big man' Mitchell recorded, a sentiment shared by many in the Unionist camp and not least Trimble.

Of course, big decisions aren't always the best or the right ones, and for Sinn Fein this was a step backwards. Re-opening strand two did not, then, presuppose agreement, but it did at least offer the chance for it. To not renegotiate stood no chance of agreement. It was perhaps this basic calculation, that renegotiating offered a glimmer of hope, that weighed most with Ahern on that Tuesday evening – helped of course by a fair dose of blunt talking, even threats, from Blair and some last-minute creative thinking from Reg Empey on the Unionist side.[14] Whatever had produced the Irish shift, the fact that they did allowed the talks to step back from the brink.

> 66 Having looked death in the eye, all were now more amenable and pliable as a consequence 99

Returning from the brink turned out to be just the dose of reality the leaders needed to 'go that extra mile', long the missing ingredient since the start of the talks back in 1996. Having looked death in the eye, all were now more amenable and pliable as a consequence, what Mao Tse Tung might have called the sobering effect of peering down the barrel of a gun. Indeed, it might well be, as a student of the Machiavellian arts of political manoeuvre would claim, that taking the talks to the 'brink' had been Blair and Ahern's original intention when they forwarded their draft plans late on Monday. Pushing the nuclear button to see what fell out. And what fell out during Wednesday and Thursday was the clear outline of a settlement. Ahern's decision to re-open discussions on strand two was accompanied by a fairly sudden 'cave-in' to Unionist demands. During intense talks the proposals for strand two edged back towards the Unionist position of the Heads of Agreement paper. Trimble, aware that for this to stick with Nationalists Ahern needed something in return, now allowed strand one to ease towards the Nationalist position on a power-sharing government. It was a classically executed quid pro quo – a swing of the pendulum in one area was reciprocated by a reverse swing in another. It was the kind of deal hinted at by Unionists back on 3 April and by Mitchell on the 4th. But it took the cold dread of failure to actually achieve it.

Much detail still needed to be filled in. During Thursday and into the early hours of Friday, Mitchell's 'D-Day', the negotiations proceeded with an unaccustomed speed and verve. The main difficulties, understandably, were reeling in the Nationalists to the altered position. The SDLP continued to push hard to restrengthen strand two but were generally mollified by the Unionist shift on strand one. Sinn Fein, on the other hand, fumed and scratched at what it saw as the Unionist veto in action. The party tabled some 72 issues of concern that Ahern was forced to wade through. But for all its fulminations, its heart now lay in smaller battles where victory could be won, namely on the issues of prisoner releases, policing, de-militarization and safeguards to ensure an equality of treatment for all people in Northern Ireland. Both governments were flexible and creative on all of these, recognizing that if they could 'purchase' Sinn Fein's overall agreement on these issues it was a price well worth paying. Most problematic and sensitive of all of these was the question of prisoner release. Sinn Fein and the loyalist parties sought a quick-release programme, which translated into a time-span of two years, whereas the British government felt compelled for rather obvious political reasons to make a stand on three. Unionists sought to slow it up even further by linking it to that old chestnut of decommissioning. 'Arms before talks' had now become 'arms before prisoners', though having shifted so far on strand two, and secured what looked like Sinn Fein's overall agreement, neither Ahern nor Blair was keen to move very far in this direction.

Come Friday morning when the final draft agreement was presented to all the leaders for ratification, the remaining sticking points were Unionist concerns over prisoner release and the closely related issue of the entry of Sinn Fein into any new Northern Irish government before decommissioning. The severity of these sticking points was not appreciated at first, until the scale of the revolt within Trimble's Unionist delegation became clear. David Campbell, Peter Weir, David Brewster and most damagingly Jeffrey Donaldson all walked out of the conference, motivated as much by personal history and conviction as they were by pre-election manoeuvring and expectations of rejection within the Unionist community. Whatever their motives it was a very damaging blow to Trimble, forcing him to put a hold on signing until some sort of reassurance was given, if not the actual linkage all Unionists craved for. The hold-up sent the talks into spasms of incredulity and deep anxiety. Could the ship really capsize when all thought it was safely in the harbour and about to secure its bow line? The usually quiet and emollient John Alderdice was almost moved to blows with Donaldson, so frustrated was he by eleventh-hour Unionist tactics. Temperatures rose all round Stormont, as tempers flared and exhaustion threatened to end the negotiations not in smiling agreement but in a brawl. Reports even began to seep out of delegates fainting under the pressure.

Blair moved now to offer the Unionists reassurance. It was too late to alter the agreement, it was after all the afternoon of Friday the 10th. But he would provide an addendum in the form of a letter offering his personal guarantee to Unionists on the question of decommissioning in the future. This was substantially short of what Trimble had hoped for but was the best he was going to get in the circumstances, and faced with the alternative of collapsing the entire negotiations, he accepted the guarantee and consented to sign the agreement.

BEATI PACIFIC[15]

At five o'clock on Friday, 10 April, almost exactly 22 months after the talks had begun, all the main political parties of

Northern Ireland, except the DUP, signed a settlement outlining the future political structures for the region. These structures followed the three-stranded basis of the talks themselves. Thus on strand one a Northern Irish Assembly was created composed of 108 members, elected by proportional representation, with a 12-strong power-sharing executive, to provide the overall direction of business in the region. On strand two a consultative North/South Council was established, answerable to the Northern Assembly and the Dail, with cross-border co-operation in at least six areas. In strand three an Inter-Governmental Conference would replace the one set up in 1985 and loathed by Unionists, as well as a British-Irish Council of all the Isles. Articles 2 and 3 of the Irish constitution would be amended and the Government of Ireland Act of 1920 repealed. A whole raft of safeguards, rights and protections for the individual were built into the agreement. A vague commitment to decommissioning was inserted (so vague it had warranted the Blair letter) to be monitored by the Independent Commission for Decommissioning, as well as a commission on police reform, a commitment to de-militarization and an accelerated prisoner release scheme to be completed after two years.

The Good Friday Agreement of 1998 put in place a new political structure for Northern Ireland based upon a consensus of both communities. It introduced a constitutional system within which all people and groups in the province could feel they had ownership of. It was inclusive rather than exclusive, and it recognized the region's many different and conflicting identities rather than championing just one. And although the political violence had ended back at the time of the various paramilitary cease-fires, the Good Friday Agreement helped to copper-fasten the end of politically motivated violence by locking representatives of those groups into the political structure. It was a turning point in the history of the region every bit as much as 1801, 1920 or 1921 had been.

> A whole raft of safeguards, rights and protections for the individual were built into the agreement

NOTES

1 Tony Blair on arriving in Belfast on 7 April 1998 told waiting reporters: 'A day like today is not a day for sound bites, we can leave those at home, but I feel the hand of history upon our shoulder with respect to this, I really do.'

2 G. Mitchell, *Making Peace* (Heinemann, 1999) p 145.

3 *The Irish News,* 2 April 1998.

4 G. Adams, *An Irish Journal* (Brandon, 2001) p 55.

5 *The Irish News*, 3 April 1998.

6 Ibid.

7 Ibid, 2 April 1998.

8 *Financial Times*, 3 April 1998.

9 Mitchell, op. cit., p 159.

10 H. McDonald, *Trimble* (Bloomsbury, 2000) p 201.

11 Trimble, in an interview with the BBC on the strand two proposals, said: 'The pudding had been over-egged, quite considerably. The minute we saw that we said, we've got a problem.'

12 Mitchell, op. cit., p 168.

13 Sinn Fein statement in T. Hennessey, *The Northern Ireland Peace Process* (Gill & Macmillan, 2000) p 166.

14 Hennessey, op. cit., pp 166–7.

15 Blessed are the peacemakers.

11

LOOSE ENDS AND NEW BEGINNINGS, 1998–2001

'Let the dog sleep, and let's do politics, and the better politics get, the sleepier the dog is.'

Gerry Adams

RESISTING CLOSURE

AFTER THE GOOD FRIDAY AGREEMENT AN OBSERVER of the political scene in Northern Ireland might have been forgiven for thinking it was business as usual in the region. Finding what had actually altered after April 1998 was not always a clear, straightforward task. Communal conflict and tension had not gone away and continues to surface at or along many of the points of friction. The murder of the Quinn brothers just three months after the agreement and more recent events in the Ardoyne area of Belfast surrounding the Holy Cross school reveal that questions of community defence, sectarianism and territoriality still dominate the urban politics of Northern Ireland. Leaders may sit around tables agreeing to historic bargains on behalf of their community, but on the streets and at the many hundreds of communal interfaces throughout the province the process of finding a stable, settled and permanent peace will be a slow, agonizing and painful development – something that the plethora of groups dedicated to reconciliation, integration and communal bridge building realize only too well as they painstakingly seek to negotiate down each barrier and boundary separating the people of the province.

Yet communal conflict will not be eradicated by simply legislating a new, equal, fairer and consensual society into existence. Sources of symbolic injury and historic grievance will need to be addressed. For a divided society to develop trust and contact, communal skeletons (whether real or imagined) need to be dug up, re-examined and shown to the world. In South Africa this process was carried out by a Truth and Reconciliation Commission, where past crimes and injuries were given the oxygen of exposure to encourage a process of healing and closure. The 1998 agreement did not institute such a body but some initiatives have been made in this direction. A commission has been established on the victims of the conflict, while more high profile, and expensive, has been the creation of a new inquiry under Lord Saville into the events of Bloody Sunday – an inquiry which is now several years old, with no clear submission point in sight, and running at a cost of many millions of pounds of public money. It seems likely the inquiry will be able to offer a more rounded picture of that day's events and probably one much more critical of the role and performance of the Parachute Regiment that day than the version offered in the now universally discredited Widgery Report. Though whether prosecutions will flow from its findings, given the length of time and conflicting accounts, or whether truth and reconciliation will be advanced as a result of the process, seems less clear.

> 66 Sources of symbolic injury and historic grievance need to be addressed 99

Again to advance truth and reconciliation long-running Nationalist doubts about the RUC have been addressed by the Good Friday Agreement setting up an independent commission under Chris Patten to look into the future of policing in the province. The RUC has played a central role in the Troubles, regarded by Nationalists as a largely sectarian force and by

Unionists as the thin dark green line defending law and order in the most testing of conditions. For one side they are the upholder of state power, for the other the defenders of it. For one the RUC is a force it feels alien to and alienated from, while the other holds it close to its bosom.[1] Hence recruitment into the force from the Protestant community has been strong, while amongst Catholics one it was a mere 8 per cent in 1998. Reforming the service was therefore both necessary and absolutely certain to provoke division. If too much was altered, Unionist anxieties would be raised; if not enough change was recommended, Nationalist hostility would grow, while the inevitable delay and speculation of what lay ahead would simply generate unease and uncertainty in both communities. Patten's recommendations were finally published in September 1999 and legislated upon almost in their entirety, and did indeed generate hostility particularly from the Unionist community. Yet by 2001 progress towards their full implementation had been made and although Sinn Fein has yet to take up its posts on the new ruling body, the Police Board, which is selected according to the same d'Hondt principle as the new Northern Ireland Assembly, it seems inconceivable that in time it will not. After all, it had once said it would never sit in a power-sharing executive.

Moreover, Sinn Fein realizes, as do all the political parties, that communal conflict is unlikely to recede until the general level of violence in the province is reduced. Paramilitary groups on a cease-fire for politically motivated violence have not gone away nor have they refrained from violence in maintaining their hold over communities or protecting their economic interests. Beatings, pipe-bombs, woundings, threats, murder and intimidation continue to plague Northern Ireland and provide paramilitary groups with a role and activity, though probably at a level of violence no more or less than London, Dublin or Manchester, let alone New York and Los Angeles. Of potentially more 'political' danger are those rogue paramilitary groups which had not signed up to the agreement. On the loyalist side this included the LVF (initially) and the Red Hand Defenders, as well as other smaller groups and individuals, while on the

Republican side the INLA, the RIRA, the 32 County Sovereignty Committee and the CIRA all opposed the agreement. Indeed, it was the latter who were to shatter the post-agreement euphoria with a bomb placed in the centre of Omagh on a busy Saturday, killing 28 people. Ironically the bomb, rather than inspiring party recrimination and the raising of the political (and communal) drawbridges, actually produced a sense of common purpose and resolve, tangible proof of the world the vast majority of people in Northern Ireland wanted to leave behind. The tone and the symbolism of Unionist and Nationalist standing together in joint condemnation was reminiscent of the tragedy of Poyntzpass just over a year before. So men of violence retain their power to kill and maim after the Good Friday Agreement, though they are less certain it can produce their desired ends of political instability and communal retrenchment.

In any case political instability was not removed from the scene in Northern Ireland by the Good Friday Agreement. For no sooner was the ink dry on the agreement than problems over decommissioning resurfaced to divide and hinder forward political movement. As the wheels of the new devolutionary structure began to move, with assembly elections in June, the appointment of Trimble and Mallon as First Minister and Deputy respectively in July and the first meeting of the assembly in September, the Unionist stance of 'no guns, no government' grew ever more prominent. Yet without the power-sharing executive, the north-south institutions could not be formed, regardless of the details having been all but agreed between Trimble and Mallon and the Irish government. On the other side were Sinn Fein which argued the agreement prescribed it a place in the power-sharing executive which the Unionists were unable to frustrate; and when later Trimble tried to expel its representatives, a court of law found his action to be unconstitutional. Moreover, Sinn Fein, so it argued, was simply incapable of forcing the IRA to give up its arms and so it stood firm on ambiguous wording of the agreement that decommissioning was more of an aspiration to start decommissioning within two years rather than a definite commitment. Around this dichotomy politics in Northern Ireland veered from crisis to crisis in the aftermath of April 1998 until by the summer of 1999 they stopped altogether. Anglo-Irish rescue plans collapsed, divisions emerged between London and Dublin, the power-sharing executive had still not been established, and to cap it all Seamus Mallon resigned as Deputy First Minister. The only one happy at the chaos and the prospect of the Good Friday Agreement unravelling was Ian Paisley.

Of course, one option still lay open to all the participants, namely to send for George. George Mitchell arrived in September 1999 to conduct what was called a review of the Good Friday Agreement but which for many looked more like a post-mortem. In November he recommended a twin-track approach to the problem: all guns to be handed in by May 2000 in return for an inclusive power-sharing executive to get going at once. The review gave Trimble some currency to go to the UUC and recommend acceptance even if it meant giving up the 'no guns, no government' stance. In its place he advocated, and received, a narrow endorsement for a 'jump first' policy, designed to place extra pressure on the IRA to decommission having taken such a leap of faith, though as it quickly transpired his 'jump first' line had come at the cost of a pre-dated resignation letter to be sent if the IRA again failed to live up to its agreements. Once Trimble and the Unionist Party had agreed to jump, events moved rapidly. Three days later, on 30 November 1999, Peter Mandelson, the new Secretary of State for Northern Ireland, devolved powers agreed in the Good Friday Agreement to a power-sharing executive in Belfast, while the already agreed north-south institutional arrangements became operational. Nineteen months after signing, the terms and responsibilities of the agreement were finally introduced. The only question left in everyone's mind was whether the IRA would respond to the terms of Mitchell's review, evidence of which would appear early in the new year when the first review of the Independent International Decommissioning Commission under John de Chastelain was due to report.

> 66 The only one happy at the chaos and the prospect of the Good Friday Agreement unravelling was Ian Paisley 99

When it came at the end of January 2000 the report indicated what everybody had suspected: that little by way of progress towards decommissioning had been made. When the UUC convened an emergency meeting for 12 February to consider the report and no doubt consider Trimble's resignation letter, not only did his position as First Minister but the future of the entire power-sharing executive looked extremely vulnerable. To forestall this catastrophe Mandelson suspended the devolutionary process by placing it into cold storage. Like the British economy in the 1970s, the Good Friday Agreement had gone from start to stop to start and now to stop again. Stand-off had turned to stalemate as the institutions were 'parked'. Only this time the cycle of stop-go was restarted several weeks later by the IRA. On 6 May 2000 it issued a ground-breaking statement saying that it had renewed contact with the IIDC and had 'completely and verifiably put weapons beyond use' by concreting over an arms dump, a claim hesitantly backed up by John de Chastelain. Three weeks later, on 27 May, the UUC authorized Trimble to re-enter the power-sharing executive, followed on 29 May by Mandelson unfreezing the devolutionary institutions. Good Friday was once more up and running, even if the 'cat and mouse' game between Sinn Fein and Ulster Unionism would continue to run, and plague, the operation of constitutional government in Northern Ireland. But then nobody really believed taking the gun out of Northern Irish politics would be an easy or quick process.

REFLECTIONS

If the Good Friday Agreement was a turning point, then for many it turned the wrong way. Large sections of the Unionist community, including the DUP, the UKUP, the paramilitary LVF, the Orange Order and even sections of Trimble's own party, all interpreted the document as a route map leading to all-Irish unity. On the other side many dissident Republican groups, such as the Real IRA, the Continuity IRA, the 32 County Sovereignty Committee and the INLA, read it as a traitors' charter, with Republicans sitting in an assembly at Stormont, implicitly recognizing partition and abandoning the armed struggle before the British withdrawal. Criticism from such quarters was not unexpected and was not a danger as long as moderates at the centre were able to hold enough support from their respective communities to keep the extremes quiet. All the leaders knew, and none more so than Trimble, that generals who ran too far ahead of their army were liable to get shot down, perhaps quite literally so. As it turned out this did not occur. On 18 April 1998 Trimble won a 540 to 210 vote in the UUC in support of the Good Friday Agreement. On 10 May Adams won a resounding vote at the Sinn Fein Ard Fheis in favour of taking up seats won in a future Northern Ireland Assembly. And collectively the pro-settlement forces gained 71.1 per cent of the vote in a referendum on the agreement on 22 May, although slightly worryingly only a tiny majority of Unionists had voted in favour (calculated at 55/44 in favour). The same day a referendum in the Republic saw 94 per cent agree to changes to articles 2 and 3 of the Irish constitution. In light of these results it is arguable that too much focus both at the time and since has been placed upon the opposition to the agreement, artificially distorting (and belittling) what in actuality was and remains an enormous range and size of interests, groups and individuals in favour of it.

As with all turning points attention inevitably moves towards establishing when and why the turn was made. A good case could be made for establishing the roots to 1998 with the efforts of Brooke. It was he who drew the Unionists back from self-imposed ostracism, authorized contacts with Republican sources, engineered the first substantive multi-party talks since Sunningdale and sought to woo Sinn Fein into the political arena through his use of fertile language. The eventual Good Friday settlement owed much to Brooke, and indeed to Mayhew who, in 1992, progressed the talks to a point where agreement was perhaps for the first time a real possibility. Of course, what the Brooke and Mayhew initiatives lacked was the inclusion of Sinn Fein and the fact that it was eventually an integral part of the agreement suggest that the roots to 1998 might also lie in shifts within the Republican movement from armed struggle to political inclusion. Shifts there certainly were as a whole litany of once

sacrosanct Republican principles (no Unionist block to unification, no end to the armed struggle before British withdrawal,
no recognition of partition or sitting in a Northern Ireland
Assembly, let alone in a power-sharing executive) were quietly
shelved or reinvented. Whatever tacti-
cal, economic, strategic or structural
reasons lay behind these changes, what
cannot be ignored is the vital role
played by the leadership of Gerry
Adams and Martin McGuinness in
steering, coaxing and reassuring the movement towards politics.
No one should under-estimate the difficulties and dangers both
faced in furthering this project or the observation that unless they
had there would have been no agreement in 1998. Though perhaps as much credit should go to John Hume as it should to Gerry
Adams for moving the Republicans from war to peace. His willingness in 1988 and again in 1993 to engage with and persuade
those held in pariah status that there was a New World around
them was as politically and morally brave as it was influential.

> 66 Perhaps as much
> credit should go to John
> Hume as it should to
> Gerry Adams 99

If we are locating the origins of the Good Friday Agreement in
the spread of new realism amongst various leaders, few confronted reality in a more head-on way than David Trimble, who
arrived at the leadership of the Ulster Unionist Party in 1995. In
the task of moving a deeply sceptical and anxious community
towards a settlement, he showed a remarkable ability to present
a sustainable and constructive vision of the future for Unionism
and to weld onto it the loyalty of a significant proportion of the
Unionist community – a vision that accepted many of the
things long thought unimaginable for Unionists to agree to: a
sharing of power with Nationalists and Republicans, an all-
Ireland dimension, reforms to the RUC, prisoner release
schemes and latitude on the issue of decommissioning. And all
done while the ghost of Faulkner (and indeed O'Neill before
him) sat on one shoulder and the hawk of Paisley sat on the
other. In resisting the easy route, towards negative and hardline
Unionism, Trimble led Unionism along a more inclusive, less
neurotic, and arguably more secure road, without which agreement would not have been possible.

However, the Good Friday Agreement was more than just the sum of a clutch of very able leaders. For even the most agile, perceptive and courageous leader operates in a specific cultural, economic and political context. In this all benefited from various developments over the 1990s. A general war weariness pervaded all groups and parties in 1998 that was less evident or powerful in 1973–1974. The inviolability of national boundaries and questions of sovereignty were more blurred in the 1990s than in the 1970s, the result of two decades of involvement in Europe and the shift towards 'post-modern' politics, where once entrenched, totalizing political creeds (such as Unionism and Nationalism) were rendered more fragile and old fashioned. All this meant that Northern Ireland's problems could be better accommodated or neutralized in the climate of the 1990s than at any previous time. Shifts in the international economy and in the economies of Britain and the Irish Republic altered the base upon which the Troubles had been sustained for so long. More specifically, the cease-fires of most leading paramilitary groups reduced the possibility of violence polarizing or destabilizing the movement towards an agreement. The Republic's willingness, from the early 1990s, to alter articles 2 and 3 of its constitution removed a deep and enduring obstacle to Unionists and provided Trimble with vital capital with which to sell the agreement to the Unionist community. Nor should the significant role of third parties, such as Bill Clinton, George Mitchell, Harri Holkeri and John de Chastelain, be ignored in mediating, managing and arbitrating the process of finding a settlement.

Establishing the when and the why of the Good Friday Agreement raises the associated question of what the 1998 agreement represents: what was it? Here, as in most analyses of the Troubles, or aspects of them, each side will offer a representation favourable to itself or its own interests. Thus for Unionists, though probably only a minority now share this view, as well as anti-agreement Republicans, it was a victory for Unionism, cementing the union for the future by locking into a constitutional arrangement both Nationalists and Republicans. Moreover, despite the fair amount of 'high pitch' Nationalist language that riddles the document, the hard reality is that

Northern Ireland is fully recognized by all parties, including the Republic, and will remain British for as long as the people of the region want it to. Nationalists and Republicans, and anti-agreement Unionists such as Ian Paisley, see it as a victory for Irish Nationalism, putting in place the constitutional infrastruc-ture upon which a united Ireland will emerge in the future and by consent, a fact underlined for the likes of Paisley by the almost total unanimity of support for the agreement from within the Catholic community.

The agreement might, on the other hand, be represented as a triumph of a process begun in 1973 with the creation of a power-sharing executive and an all-Irish dimension in the Sunningdale agreement. 1998 was the completion of a process begun 25 years earlier, and since it was undermined by Unionists, so 1998 can be represented as a failure for them. We might, however, go back further than 1973. For the Good Friday Agreement could also be seen as the achievement of the civil rights programme of the late 1960s when Catholics had cam-paigned not for an end to partition and a united Ireland but for an equality of esteem, fair treatment and an end to economic and political discrimination all *within* Northern Ireland. 1998 might represent, then, the final act in a civil rights narrative begun back in the 1960s but distorted by violence and political polarization for some 30 years. The legion of safeguards for people's rights and indeed the human rights agenda in the Good Friday Agreement lend weight to this particular discourse. Yet we might even go further back to the original intentions of the 1920 Partition Act where Britain's hope was for temporary separation between north and south and possible move-ment towards a united Ireland via the Council of Ireland, but only with the consent of both parts: an explicit rec-ognition that the north could not be forced into the south. The Act had also insisted upon various safeguards for the minority, proportional representation in local and national elections, and clauses upholding religious toleration and outlawing discrimi-

66 **The Good Friday Agreement could also be seen as the achievement of the civil rights programme of the late 1960s** 99

nation. What problems subsequently arose were the product of the British not policing the Act in the face of Unionist obstinacy and aggression. So perhaps 1998 represents a return to the priorities and intentions (but not the reality) of the 1920 Partition Act.

NOTE

1   Clive Walker, 'The Patten Report and Post-Sovereignty Policing in Northern Ireland', in R. Wilford (ed) *Aspects of the Belfast Agreement* (OUP, 2001).

ABBREVIATIONS, GLOSSARY AND PERSONALITIES

ABBREVIATIONS

CIRA   Continuity Irish Republican Army

CLMC   Combined Loyalist Military Command

DUP   Democratic Unionist Party

IIDC   Independent International Decommissioning Commission

INLA   Irish National Liberation Army

IRA   Irish Republican Army

LAW   Loyalist Association of Workers

LVF   Loyalist Volunteer Force

NICRA   Northern Ireland Civil Rights Association

OIRA   Official Irish Republican Army

PIRA   Provisional Irish Republican Army

PUP   Progressive Unionist Party

RIRA   Real Irish Republican Army

RUC   Royal Ulster Constabulary

SDLP   Social and Democratic Labour Party

TUAS   Tactical Use of Armed Struggle

UAC   Ulster Army Council

UCDC   Ulster Constitution Defence Committee

UDA	Ulster Defence Association
UDI	Unilateral Declaration of Independence
UDP	Ulster Democratic Party
UDR	Ulster Defence Regiment
UFF	Ulster Freedom Fighters
UKUP	United Kingdom Unionist Party
UPNI	Unionist Party of Northern Ireland
UPV	Ulster Protestant Volunteers
UUC	Ulster Unionist Council
UUP	Ulster Unionist Party
UUUC	United Ulster Unionist Council
UVF	Ulster Volunteer Force
UWC	Unionist Workers Council

GLOSSARY

All-Irish Dimension	A term used to refer to institutional links between the north and the south.
Ard Fheis	Annual conference of Sinn Fein.
Dail	The Irish Parliament.
d'Hondt principle	A formula of proportionality whereby the number of seats in the NI Assembly determined the make-up of the executive and other bodies where power was to be shared.
Fianna Fail	Traditional Republican political party in the Republic.
Fine Gael	Seen as a 'softer' Republican party in the south.

Gardaí	Police in the Irish Republic.
Mitchell principles	As part of the Mitchell Report of January 1996, George Mitchell included six principles to be affirmed by all parties involved in the multi-party talks. They included commitments to exclusively peaceful means of resolving political issues; total disarmament; disarmament must be verifiable by an independent commission; renouncing the use of violence and opposing efforts by others to resort to it; agreeing to abide by any agreement reached through the multi-party talks; urging punishment beatings and killings to stop.
Power-sharing	An executive system for dividing and sharing power and responsibility so as to avoid the dominance of government by one party or community.
No-go area	A method of providing communal security by ringing it with barricades and controlling entry. Used by both communities, though exploited most effectively by the IRA as a source of protection, resources, cover and manpower.
Sinn Fein	'Ourselves alone'.
Taoiseach	Irish Prime Minister.
Washington 3	A three-point plan for the decommissioning of arms while allowing Sinn Fein to enter all-party talks, delivered in a speech by Patrick Mayhew in Washington on 7 March 1995. The plan included an agreement to disarm, agreement on the method for disarming and an immediate start to be

made to disarmament as a confidence-building measure.

PERSONALITIES

Adams, Gerry	b. 1948, part of the Provisional delegation that met Whitelaw in 1972; alleged command of the Belfast brigade, imprisoned in the Maze prison 1973–1976; President of Sinn Fein 1983–; MP for West Belfast 1983–1992, 1997–; member of the NI Assembly, 1998–.
Ahern, Bertie	b. 1951; leader of Fianna Fail 1994–; Taoiseach June 1997.
Andrews, David	b. 1935; Fianna Fail; Minister of Foreign Affairs, 1992–1993 and 1997–.
Atkins, Humphrey	b. 1922; Secretary of State for Northern Ireland, 1979–1981; initiated the Constitutional Conference in 1980.
Blair, Tony	b. 1953; leader of the Labour Party, 1994–; British Prime Minister, 1997–.
Brooke, Peter	b. 1934; Conservative Secretary of State for Northern Ireland, 1989–1992; architect of the Brooke Initiative and arguably one of the most progressive, successful occupants of the office.
Bruton, John	b. 1947; leader of Fine Gael, 1990–; Taoiseach 1994–1997.
Callaghan, Jim	b. 1912; Home Secretary, 1967–1970; leader of the Labour Party,

	1976–1980, British Prime Minister, 1976–1979.
Chichester-Clark, James	b. 1928, d. 2002; Prime Minister of Northern Ireland, 1969–1971.
Clinton, Bill	b. 1946; Governor of Arkansas, 1983–1993; US President, 1993–2000.
Collins, Gerry	b. 1938; Fianna Fail; Minister of Foreign Affairs, 1982 and 1989–1992.
Durkham, Mark	b. 1960; political aide to John Hume; chairman of SDLP, 1990–1995; senior SDLP negotiator in peace talks 1996–1998; director of campaign in referendum; member of NI Assembly; Minister of Finance and Personnel in NI Executive, 1998–2001; Deputy First Minister, 2001–.
Faulkner, Brian	b. 1921, d. 1977; the last Prime Minister of Northern Ireland under the old Stormont system, 1971–1972; First Minister in the Power-Sharing Executive, 1973–1974; forced to resign as leader of the Ulster Unionist party in 1974; leader of the Unionist party of Northern Ireland, 1974–1977.
Fitt, Gerry	b. 1926; MP for West Belfast, 1966–1983; leader of the SDLP 1970–1979; Deputy Chief Executive of the power-sharing government of 1973–1974; independent socialist 1979–.
FitzGerald, Garret	b. 1926; minister responsible for NI, 1973–1977; leader of Fine Gael, 1977–1987; Taoiseach 1981–1982 and 1982–1987; launched New Irish Forum in 1983.

Goulding, Cathal	b. 1922, d. 1998; IRA Chief of Staff 1962–1970; took the IRA in a Marxist direction during the 1960s; at the split in 1970 became leader of the OIRA. Urged PIRA in early 1990s to take the 'political path' as OIRA had.
Haughey, Charles	b. 1954, leader of Fianna Fail, 1979–92; dismissed as Minister of Finance for alleged gun-running to the IRA in 1970; Taoiseach, 1979–81, 1982, 1987–92.
Hume, John	b. 1937; Vice-President of Derry Citizens Action Committee, deputy leader of the SDLP, 1973–1979, leader 1979–; MEP 1979–; MP for Foyle, 1983–; member of NI Assembly 1998–; engaged with Adams in conversations in 1988 and 1993; key role in the peace process, 1988–1998; campaigned with Trimble for a Yes vote in the May 1998 referendum; joint winner (with Trimble) of the Nobel prize for Peace, 1998.
King, Tom	b. 1933; Conservative Secretary of State for Northern Ireland, 1985–1989; Secretary of State for Defence, 1989–1992.
Lynch, Jack	b. 1917; leader of Fianna Fail 1966–1979; Taoiseach, 1966–1973 and 1977–1979.
MacStiofain, Sean	b. 1928, d. 2000; led Provisionals against Goulding in 1970 IRA split; Chief of Staff 1970–1972; led delegation that met Whitelaw in 1972; hunger strike for 57 days in 1973 but in coming off lost

	leadership of PIRA; left Sinn Fein in 1981; strong appeals for a PIRA cease-fire through the 1990s.
Maginnis, Ken	b. 1938; Unionist security spokesman; MP for Fermanagh-S.Tyrone, 1983–; contestant for the leadership in 1995; key member of the peace talks 1996–1998; member of the NI Assembly.
Major, John	b. 1943; leader of the Conservative Party, 1990–1997; British Prime Minister, 1990–1997.
Mallon, Seamus	b. 1936; chairman of the SDLP, 1973–1979; deputy leader of the SDLP, 1979–; MP for Mid-Armagh 1986–; leading role in the peace negotiations, 1989–1998; member of the NI Assembly; Deputy First Minister 1998–2001.
Maudling, Reg	b. 1917, d. 1979; Conservative Home Secretary, 1970–1972.
Mayhew, Patrick	b. 1929; Solicitor-General, 1983–1987; Attorney-General, 1987–1992; Secretary of State for Northern Ireland, 1992–1997; took up and continued initiatives opened up by Brooke with talks through 1992.
McCartney, Robert	b. 1936; leader of the UKUP; MP for North Down; critic of the peace process, 1996–1998; opponent of the Good Friday Agreement; member of the NI Assembly, 1998–.
McGuinness, Martin	b. 1950; leader of the PIRA in Derry and long alleged to have been the

	PIRA Chief of Staff; Vice-President of Sinn Fein 1983–; at the centre of meetings with British contacts and officials since 1990; MP for Mid-Ulster 1997–; member of NI Assembly 1998–.
McLaughlan, Mitchell	b. 1945; leading role in the peace negotiations, 1996–1998; chairperson of Sinn Fein, 1998–; member of the NI Assembly, 1998–.
Mitchell, George	b. 1933; US Senator for Maine 1980–1995; Senate Majority leader, 1988–1995; economic envoy to NI 1994–1995; chairman of the NI peace talks, 1996–1998; chairman of the review of the peace process, 1999.
Molyneaux, James	b. 1920; MP for S. Antrim, 1970–1983 and Lagan Valley, 1983–1997; leader of the Ulster Unionists in Parliament 1977–1979 and of the party as a whole, 1979–1995; co-leader of the 'Ulster Says No' campaign against the Anglo-Irish Agreement; resigned leader after the Frameworks document.
Morrison, Danny	b. 1953; external spokesman during hunger strikes, 1981; director of Sinn Fein publicity; leading proponent of political strategy.
Mowlam, Marjorie (Mo)	b. 1949; Secretary of State for Northern Ireland, 1997–1999; helped keep the loyalist cease-fire in place by visiting loyalists in the Maze jail.
O'Bradaigh, Rurai	b. 1932; President of Sinn Fein 1970–1983; defeated by Adams on ending abstention in 1986; set up

	Republican Sinn Fein; implacable opponent of the Belfast Agreement and against Republicans entering the NI Assembly or Dail.
O'Neill, Terence	b. 1914, d. 1990; Prime Minister of Northern Ireland, 1963–1969.
Paisley, Ian	b. 1926; founder of the Free Presbyterian Church, 1951; MP for North Antrim 1970–; leader of the DUP 1971–; MEP 1979–; co-leader of the 'Ulster Says No' campaign in 1986; critic and opponent of the peace process and the Good Friday Agreement, and campaigned for a No vote in the referendum; member of the NI Assembly.
Prior, Jim	b. 1927; Conservative Secretary of State for Northern Ireland, 1981–1984; responsible for rolling devolution.
Reynolds, Albert	b. 1932; leader of Fianna Fail 1992–1994; Taoiseach 1992–1994.
Robinson, Peter	b. 1948; general secretary of the party, 1975–1979; deputy leader of the DUP; MP for East Belfast 1979–; opponent of the peace process and the Good Friday Agreement; member of the NI Assembly; Minister for Regional Development in the NI Executive, 1998–.
Sands, Bobby	b. 1954, d. 1981. Republican Hunger Striker; O/C Republicans in H. Block; on hunger strike 1 March 1981 until his death on 5 May 1981; 9 April 1981 elected MP for Fermanagh and South Tyrone.

Spring, Dick	b. 1950; leader of the Irish Labour Party 1982–1997; deputy Taoiseach and Minister of Foreign Affairs, 1993–1997.
Taylor, John	b. 1937; Minister of Home Affairs in the Stormont government 1970–1972; Ulster Unionist MEP, 1979–1989; MP for Strangeford 1983–; runner-up in the leadership contest of 1995; leading member of talks team 1996–1998; member of the NI Assembly.
Thatcher, Margaret	b. 1925; leader of the Conservative Party, 1975–1990; Prime Minister, 1979–1990.
Trimble, David	b. 1944; deputy leader of the Vanguard; MP for Upper Bann, 1990–; leader of the Ulster Unionist Party, 1995–; led the Unionist delegation during the peace talks of 1996–1998; member of the NI Assembly; First Minister of the Northern Ireland Executive, 1998–.
Whitelaw, William	b. 1918, d. 1999; the first Secretary of State for Northern Ireland, 1972–1973, the architect of the Power-Sharing Executive and Sunningdale experiment; Conservative deputy leader, 1979–1988, Home Secretary, 1979–1984.
Wilson, Harold,	b. 1916, d. 1995; leader of the Labour Party, 1963–1976; British Prime Minister, 1964–1970 and 1974–1976.

SELECTED BIBLIOGRAPHY

Adams, G., *Towards a Lasting Peace* (Dublin, 1995).

Adams, G., *Before the Dawn: An Autobiography* (Dublin, 1996).

Adams, G., *An Irish Journal* (Dublin, 2001).

Arthur, P., *Special Relationships: Britain, Ireland and the Northern Ireland Problem* (Belfast, 2001).

Aughey, A., *Under Siege: Ulster Unionism and the Anglo-Irish Agreement* (Belfast, 1989).

Augusteijn, J., *From Public Defiance to Guerrilla Warfare: The Experience of Ordinary Volunteers in the Irish War of Independence, 1916–1921* (Dublin, 1996).

Bardon, J., *A History of Ulster* (Belfast, 1992).

Barton, B. and Roche, P., *The Northern Ireland Question: Perspectives and Policies* (London, 1991).

Beresford, D., *Ten Dead Men: The Story of the 1981 Irish Hunger Strike* (London, 1987).

Bew, P., *Ideology and the Irish Question, 1912–1916* (Oxford, 1994).

Bew, P., Patterson, H. and Teague, P., *Between War and Peace: The Political Future of Northern Ireland* (London, 1997).

Bew, P. and Gillespie, G., *Northern Ireland: A Chronology of the Troubles, 1968–1999* (Dublin, 1999).

Bew, P. and Gillespie, G., *The Northern Ireland Peace Process, 1993–1996* (London, 1996).

Bishop, P. and Mallie, E., *The Provisional IRA* (London, 1987).

Bloomfield, D., *Peacemaking Strategies in Northern Ireland: Building Complementarity in Conflict Management Theory* (London, 1997).

Bloomfield, D., *Political Dialogue in Northern Ireland: The Brooke Initiative, 1989–92* (London, 1998).

Bowman, J., *De Valera and the Ulster Question, 1917–1973* (Oxford, 1982).

Bowyer-Bell, J., *The Irish Troubles: A Generation of Violence, 1967–1992* (Dublin, 1993).

Boyce, D. G. (ed) *The Revolution in Ireland, 1879–1923* (London, 1988).

Boyce, D. G., *Nationalism in Ireland* (London, 1982).

Boyce, D. G., *The Irish Question and British Politics, 1868–1986* (London, 1988).

Boyce, D. G. and O'Day, A., *The Making of Modern Irish History* (London, 1996).

Boyce, D. G. and O'Day, A. (eds) *Defenders of the Union; A Survey of British and Irish Unionism since 1801* (London, 2001).

Boyle, K. and Hadden, T., *Ireland: A Positive Proposal* (London, 1985).

Bruce, S., *'God Save Ulster': The Religion and Politics of Paisleyism* (Oxford, 1986).

Bruce, S., *The Red Hand: Protestant Paramilitaries in Northern Ireland* (Oxford, 1992).

Bruce, S., *The Edge of Union: The Ulster Loyalist Political Vision* (Oxford, 1994).

Buckland, P., *The Factory of Grievances: Devolved Government in Northern Ireland, 1920–1939* (Dublin, 1979).

Callaghan, J., *A House Divided* (London, 1973).

Campbell, J., *Edward Heath: A Biography* (London, 1994).

Canning, P., *British Policy Towards Ireland, 1921–1941* (Oxford, 1985).

Catterall, P. (ed) *The Northern Ireland Question in British Politics* (London, 1996).

Cochrane, F., *Unionist Politics and the Politics of Unionism* (Cork, 1997).

Cohen, J. M., *Dictionary of Modern Quotations* (London, 1971).

Coogan, T. P., *The IRA* (London, 1970).

Coogan, T. P., *The Troubles: Ireland's Ordeal and the Search for Peace, 1966–1995* (London, 1995).

Cox et al. (ed) *A Farewell to Arms: From Long War to Long Peace in Northern Ireland* (Manchester, 2000).

Cunningham, M., *British Government Policy in Northern Ireland, 1969–2000* (Manchester, 2001).

Curtis, L., *Ireland and the Propaganda War* (London, 1998).

Dewar, M., *The British Army in Northern Ireland* (London, 1985).

Dixon, P., *Northern Ireland: The Politics of War and Peace* (London, 2001).

Donohue, L., *Counter-Terrorist Law and Emergency Powers in the UK* (Dublin, 2001).

Edwards, R. D., *The Faithful Tribe: An Intimate Portrait of the Loyal Institutions* (London, 2000).

Elliot, S. and Flackes, W. D., *Northern Ireland: A Political Directory, 1968–1999*, 5th Edition (Belfast, 1999).

English, R. and Walker, G. (eds) *Unionism in Modern Ireland: New Perspectives on Politics and Culture* (Dublin, 1996).

Farren, S. and Mulvihill, R. F., *Paths to a Settlement in Northern Ireland* (London, 2000).

Faulkner, B., *Memoirs of a Statesman* (London, 1978).

FitzGerald, G., *All in a Life* (Dublin, 1991).

Follis, B., *A State under Siege: The Establishment of Northern Ireland, 1920–1925* (Oxford, 1995).

Foster, R., *Modern Ireland, 1600–1972* (London, 1988).

Garvin, T., *1922: The Birth of Irish Democracy* (Dublin, 1996).

Geraghty, T., *The Irish War* (London, 2000).

Gilligan, M. and Tonge, J. (eds) *Peace or War: Understanding the Peace Process in Northern Ireland* (London, 1998).

Hamill, D., *Pig in the Middle: The Army in Northern Ireland, 1969–1984* (London, 1985).

Hart, P., *The IRA and its Enemies, 1916–1923* (Oxford, 1998).

Hennessey, T., *A History of Northern Ireland, 1920–1996* (London, 1997).

Hennessey, T., *The Northern Ireland Peace Process* (Gill & Macmillan, 2000).

Hopkinson, M., *Green Against Green: The Irish Civil War* (Dublin, 1988).

Hume, J., *Personal Views: Politics, Peace and Reconciliation in Ireland* (Dublin, 1996).

Ignatieff, M., *Blood and Belonging* (Vintage, 1994).

Jackson, A., *Ireland: 1798–1998* (Blackwell, 1999).

Kennedy-Pipe, C., *The Origins of the Present Troubles in Northern Ireland* (London, 1997).

Keogh, D. and Haltzel, M. (eds) *Northern Ireland and the Politics of Reconciliation* (CUP, 1993).

Laffan, M., *The Resurrection of Ireland: The Sinn Fein Party, 1916–1923* Cambridge, 1999).

Lawlor, S., *Britain and Ireland, 1914–1923* (Dublin, 1983).

Loughlin, J., *Ulster Unionism and British National Identity since 1885* (London, 1995).

Lyons, F. S. L., *Ireland Since the Famine* (London, 1973).

McDonald, H., *Trimble* (London, 2000).

Mansergh, N., *The Unresolved Question: The Anglo-Irish Settlement and its Undoing, 1912–1972* (New Haven, 1991).

McGarry, J. and O'Leary, B., *Explaining Northern Ireland* (Blackwell, 1995).

McKittrick, D. and McVea, D., *Making Sense of the Troubles* (Belfast, 2000).

McKittrick, D., *Nervous Peace* (Belfast, 1996).

McKittrick, D. and Mallie, E., *Endgame in Ireland* (London, 2001).

McKittrick, D., et al, *Lost Lives: The stories of the men, woman and children who died as a result of the Troubles* (Mainstream, 1999).

Miller, D. (ed) *Rethinking Northern Ireland* (London, 1998).

Mitchell, G., *Making Peace* (London, 1999).

Murray, G., *John Hume and the SDLP: Impact and Survival in Northern Ireland* (Dublin, 1996).

Needham, R., *Battling for Peace* (Belfast, 1999).

O'Brien, B., *The Long War: The IRA and Sinn Fein* (Syracuse, 1993).

O'Brien, C. C., *States of Ireland* (London, 1972).

O'Brien, C. C., *Ancestral Voices: Religion and Nationalism in Ireland* (Dublin, 1994).

O'Clery, C., *Ireland in Quotes* (Dublin, 1999).

O'Day, A., *Irish Home Rule, 1867–1921* (Manchester, 1998).

O'Dochartaigh, N., *From Civil Rights to Armalites: Derry and the Birth of the Irish Troubles* (Cork, 1997).

O'Leary, B. and McGarry, J., *The Future of Northern Ireland* (Oxford, 1990).

O'Leary, B. and McGarry, J., *The Politics of Antagonism: Understanding Northern Ireland* (Athlone Press, 1993).

O'Malley, P., *The Uncivil Wars: Ireland Today* (Belfast, 1983).

O'Malley, P., *Biting at the Grave: The Irish Hunger Strikes and the Politics of Despair* (Dublin, 1990).

Patterson, H., *The Politics of Illusion: A Political History of the IRA* (London, 1997).

Porter, N., *Rethinking Unionism* (Belfast, 1996).

Pringle, P. and Jacobson, P., *Those are Real Bullets Aren't They?* (London, 1999).

Prior, J., *A Balance of Power* (London, 1986).

Purdie, R., *Politics in the Streets: The Origins of the Civil Rights Movement in Northern Ireland* (Belfast, 1990).

Purdy, A., *Molyneaux: The Long View* (Belfast, 1989).

Rees, M., *Northern Ireland: A Personal Perspective* (London, 1985).

Rose, R., *Governing Without Consensus: An Irish Perspective* (London, 1971).

Rose, R., *Northern Ireland: A Time for Choice* (Macmillan, 1976).

Ruane, J. and Todd, J., *The Dynamics of Conflict in Northern Ireland* (Cambridge, 1996).

Ryder, C., *The RUC: A Force under Fire, 1922–2000* (London, 2000).

Sales, R., *Women Divided: Gender, Religion and Politics in Northern Ireland* (Routledge, 1997).

Smith, M. L. R., *Fighting for Ireland: The Military Strategy of the Irish Republican Movement* (London, 1995).

Stewart, A. T. Q., *The Narrow Ground* (Faber, 1977).

Taylor, P., *Beating the Terrorists* (London, 1980).

Taylor, P., *Provos: The IRA and Sinn Fein* (London, 1997).

Taylor, P., *Loyalists* (London, 1999).

Taylor, P., *Brits: The War Against the IRA* (London, 2000).

Thatcher, M., *The Downing Street Years* (London, 1993).

Toolis, K., *Rebel Hearts: Journeys within the IRA's Soul* (Picador, 1995).

Townshend, C., *The British Military Campaign in Ireland, 1919–1921* (Oxford, 1975).

Townshend, C., *Political Violence in Ireland* (Oxford, 1983).

Townshend, C., *Ireland: The Twentieth Century* (London, 1998).

Urban, M., *Big Boys' Rules* (London, 1992).

Walsh, D., *Bloody Sunday and the Rule of Law in Northern Ireland* (London, 2000).

Wells, R. A., *People Behind the Peace: Community and Reconciliation in Northern Ireland* (Michigan, 1999).

White, J., *John Hume: Statesman of the Troubles* (Belfast, 1994).

Whitelaw, W., *The Whitelaw Memoirs* (London, 1989).

Whittaker, D., *Conflict and Reconciliation in the Contemporary World* (Routledge, 1999).

Whyte, J., *Interpreting Northern Ireland* (Clarendon, 1990).

Wilford, R. (ed) *Aspects of the Belfast Agreement* (Oxford, 2001).

Wilson, H., *The Labour Government 1964–1970: A Personal Record* (London, 1974).

Winchester, S., *In Holy Terror: Reporting on the Ulster Troubles* (London, 1974).

INDEX